Beyond the Bottom Line

Putting Social Responsibility
to Work for Your Business
and the World

Joel Makower

and

Business for Social Responsibility

SIMON & SCHUSTER

New York London Toronto Sydney Tokyo Singapore

SIMON & SCHUSTER
Rockefeller Center
1230 Avenue of the Americas
New York, New York 10020

Designed by Irving Perkins Associates
Manufactured in the United States of America

1   3   5   7   9   10   8   6   4   2

Library of Congress Cataloging-in-Publication Data

Makower, Joel.
Beyond the bottom line : putting social responsibility to work for
your business and the world / Joel Makower and Business for Social
Responsibility.
p.   cm.
Includes index.
1. Social responsibility of business—United States.   2. Success
in business—United States.   3. Green movement—United States.
I. Business for Social Responsibility (Organization)   II. Title.
HD60.5.U5M327   1994
658.4'08—dc20   94-30058
                                                                CIP

ISBN: 0-671-88325-9

Contents

5
Forces for Change   87

6
The Greening of the Bottom Line   113

7
The Workable Workplace   167

Chapter One

Taking Care of Business

"The surest road to success in our ventures is to discover the authentic needs and yearnings of people and to do our best to serve them."

—JAMES W. ROUSE,
founder, The Rouse Company

Something strange and wonderful is taking place in business.

Slowly, but ever so surely, companies of all sizes and sectors are discovering that they function best when they merge their business interests with the interests of customers, employees, suppliers, neighbors, investors, and other groups affected, directly or indirectly, by their companies' operations. Some of these companies are led by forward-thinking leaders who have come to recognize that the dangers threatening society—the breakup of families, inadequate schools, unaffordable health care and housing, escalating crime, a deteriorating environment, inner-city turmoil, apathetic citizens, and all the rest—also threaten productivity and profits. The effects that some business leaders' corporate reputation and their workplace, environmental, and community policies can have on financial performance include: increased sales and stock prices, reduced turnover and retraining costs, increased efficiencies, and reduced waste and energy costs. Others have built their companies' operating principles around a business philosophy or moral vision that views employee well-being, environmental stewardship, or community welfare as central to success. These leaders are developing bottom-line strategies based on the belief that long-term profitable performance and corporate social responsibility are not only compatible but are inevitably linked.

Listen to Arnold Hiatt, retired chairman of Stride Rite Corporation, a leading footwear manufacturer long acknowledged as an innovator in the arena of socially responsible corporate programs. "You can't run a healthy company in an unhealthy society for long," he says.

Hiatt offers an example of how the new socially responsible strategy can link company policy to the bottom line: "The millions of Americans who live below the poverty line deprive us of a market equal to the combined populations of Holland, Belgium, Denmark, Norway, and Sweden. American businesses spend billions to develop new markets in these five countries of Northern Europe, while we could spend a portion of that money developing new markets here. If people aren't employed, they don't have purchasing power. If they don't have purchasing power, they don't buy products made by Stride Rite or Ford or General Motors or AT&T." By Hiatt's definition, an investment in socially responsible corporate behavior will yield dividends to a company's bottom line.

Welcome to the world of socially responsible business.

It wasn't very long ago that "caring capitalism" would have been a contradiction in terms. Companies weren't generally concerned with the lot of people's lives, even of their own employees. Companies were in business to produce goods and services and to make money for their owners; everything else was seen as a distraction at best, a threat to corporate survival at worst. Ideas such as workplace diversity, community involvement, employee empowerment, work-family balance, and environmental stewardship were dismissed by executives as amorphous, feel-good concepts with little or no relevance to the business at hand.

No longer. Today, a growing number of companies are finding that business success is inextricably linked to creating healthy and fulfilling workplaces that recognize the value and dignity of individual employees, promote cultural diversity, foster worker empowerment, and acknowledge family priorities through a variety of policies and practices. And they are finding that there are dividends to be reaped from investments in community outreach, environmental responsibility, child and elder care, adult literacy, employee training, urban revitalization, family-leave programs, diversity training, and other initiatives that improve people's lives, even for those not directly connected to their companies.

Arnold Hiatt is a testament to the fact that socially responsible business is not just about saving the world. It's also about helping business, creating the means for employees, customers, and others to look to your company with loyalty and pride. Hiatt, who established the first in-house day care center in American business, saw the facility as helping provide security to employees while providing benefits to the community around his company's plant. It was a classic win/win proposition, in which everyone—employees, communities, and the company—prospered.

Hiatt is one of the growing number of business leaders committed to socially responsible business practices. Like all collections of business leaders, it is a diverse group. Some reflect the well-worn stereotype: children of the sixties who have embraced a brand of capitalism that reflects their idealism and desire to "do good." Other socially responsible business leaders of that generation don't fit the stereotype, having gone from college and business school into the corporate world with the express goal of "making it." And there are plenty of adherents from earlier and later generations—like Hiatt, who, after more than four decades in the shoe business, is hardly a flower child. The adherents include political liberals, conservatives, and centrists. Some of these men and women are entrepreneurial success stories; others have worked their way up the ladders of the nation's largest corporations. A number of their companies are name-brand firms readily associated with socially responsible business practices; others purposefully keep their socially responsible activities far from the

---

We're all here in the world and we share the space. I'm in a position of enough power in a large corporation that I would like to be a good role model for how the world should operate. I could write checks to a point, but if I could be a role model for how employees can work, then I think it will be a benefit to the world one day. I hope it's contagious.

—PAUL FIREMAN,
CEO, Reebok International Ltd.

limelight or are small local firms that go quietly about their business, implementing progressive policies without seeking media fanfare.

There is no single definition of "socially responsible business" among these believers and practitioners. Indeed, there is considerable debate and controversy over what companies' roles and responsibilities should be—for example, whether they should take the lead in solving the world's problems or leave that to others, focusing exclusively on their own operations. It is a dynamic, healthy, and exciting debate, in which some of the leading lights of the business world are reexamining the means and motivations by which their companies—and all companies—operate in the larger society.

Whatever their means and motivations, all of these socially responsible leaders, consciously or unconsciously, have hit upon a very powerful notion: Embracing corporate responsibility is not only the right thing to do, it is key to companies' competitiveness and survival.

Exactly how and why is what this book is about. In the pages that follow, we will examine this still-emerging world of socially responsible business—the philosophies, policies, programs, and practices that bring social responsibility into the workplace in some of today's most successful large and small companies. We'll examine the academic and bottom-line rationale that makes social responsibility more than a "program of the month" or a few well-chosen anecdotes. We'll look at what's working, what's not, and how all of this can affect the bottom line. We'll examine strategies you can use to implement these policies at your company. We'll hear from some of the leading thinkers on the subject, and look into how some companies are confronting the challenges they view as critical for surviving and thriving in the coming decades.

WHAT IS A SOCIALLY RESPONSIBLE BUSINESS?

After interviewing more than a hundred companies, academics, and other experts, and reviewing hundreds of articles, academic theses, and other documents on the subject, we can safely say that there is no consensus on a definition of the term "socially responsible." Far from it. Indeed, many practitioners don't even use the term to describe the way they conduct business. If they refer to anything at all, it might be the Bible or the Golden Rule, New Age philosophies or age-old traditions, the growing body of research about "what works" or the undeniable bottom-line results they experience.

Some of the most ardent supporters of socially responsible business are motivated by how much better well-treated employees perform on the job in terms of productivity and innovation; they may have little recognition of any benefits that accrue from this in the form of, say, more stable families and communities. Or they may undertake an energy-efficiency measure to improve their bottom line, without consciously acknowledging the environmental benefits they could be generating in the process. Others' actions are motivated explicitly by their belief that business can and should be an agent for changing society or saving the world. Most business leaders' motivations lie somewhere in the middle.

Further complicating the issue is the question of how much a company must do in order to be deemed socially responsible. Is a single, innovative program enough? Can a company be socially responsible if it still faces serious problems in one or more parts of its operation? In other words: How good is good enough?

We believe that social responsibility is less programmatic than philosophic. It stems from a deeply held vision by company leaders that business can and should play a role beyond making money. It includes an understanding that what companies do and make has a variety of direct and indirect impacts on those both inside and outside the company, from customers and employees to communities and the natural environment. Therefore, a company's goals, missions, and policies must take into account this entire range of constituencies. So, having one or more commendable programs doesn't make a company socially responsible unless those programs are part of a larger vision. But a company can be socially responsible without having an all-star roster of programs and practices.

However labeled, whatever the rationale, the sensibility behind it is the same: Business as usual simply won't get us through the challenges facing today's companies and communities—local, national, or global. "As we move into the twenty-first century, it is increasingly clear that the key elements of social responsibility—especially how we support our workers, their lives, and communities—will be key elements in a company's productivity and competitiveness," says Michael R. Bonsignore, CEO of Honeywell.

Of course, a sensibility or rationale alone does not constitute social responsibility. Robert Dunn, vice president of corporate affairs at Levi Strauss & Company, the giant clothing manufacturer, and one of the most articulate spokespeople for the socially responsible business movement, sketches a portrait of what a socially responsible company looks like. "First, there has to be a charter of some sort for

people in the organization," says Dunn, who oversees social responsibility issues for a company with a nearly 150-year record of exemplary corporate behavior. "Second, there has to be some leadership
because it's meaningless without that. That leadership has to invest in
creating a culture which gives people permission to venture out
beyond where others are. There has to be a recognition that what
matters really is the long-term success of the enterprise and that
something like reputation is an asset. There have to be reward systems so that people are not measured only on the basis of gross profit
margin. And there have to be penalties or sanctions for people who
fail to honor the framework. It's all of this: values, leadership, a process for decision making, training, communication, recognition, and
rewards."

Dunn continues. "There is an obvious difference between window
dressing and serious commitment. The question is to what extent is
this charter language really meaningful? What kind of leadership has
been exercised and to what extent are managers given tools? For
example, what's the planning process like in the organization? The-
oretically, there may be a real commitment to consider the consequences of what they do in the communities and countries where
they do business. But when you look at the process they use to make
major decisions, is there some kind of impact analysis? If there isn't,
then it means nothing. It just looks good on an annual report or for
PR purposes. I think you have to judge a company by what it does,
not just by what it says or writes down as fancy documents."

Leadership. Cultural change. Long-term success. Values. Reputation as an asset. Dunn's descriptors are instructive, because they
describe a process more than a program. Under his definition, for
example, a company that enjoys outstanding relations with its employees and has a history of synergy with its communities, but whose
environmental record is less than sterling, could still be described as
socially responsible, but only if its leaders have created a new vision
and undertaken to change the company's culture and values—and
made an earnest attempt to clean up its problems. To do this effectively, a company might set up one or more environmental teams to
plan and implement operational changes, establish tangible goals for
improving the company's record, establish an independent advisory
panel as a vehicle for listening to the concerns of local residents and
environmental activists, link managers' bonuses to environmental
performance, and set in motion a measurement system that enables
the company to continually improve its performance. Environmental

excellence might be years away. But having a vision—and a system to implement it—is the key to a socially responsible company.

SOCIAL RESPONSIBILITY VERSUS SOCIAL MARKETING

Of course, some companies toe a fine line between social responsibility and social marketing. They use the *image* of social responsibility as a means of increasing market share by capitalizing on what appears to be a public willingness to embrace "good" companies. And as awareness of socially responsible business issues develops among both companies and the public, there is a concern in both sectors that such exploitation may grow.

Paul Hawken, co-founder of Smith & Hawken, a highly successful retailer of gardening products and author of several books on business responsibility, believes there is a self-descriptive aspect of such corporate disingenuousness. "You see tobacco companies subsidizing the arts, then later you find out that there are internal memos showing that they wanted to specifically target the minorities in the arts because they want to get more minorities to smoke," he says. "That is not socially responsible. It's using social perception as a way to aggrandize or further one's own interests exclusively." Hawken says these companies are not just fooling the public into thinking their actions are "responsible"; they're also fooling themselves.

More than a few companies have attempted to create an image of responsibility by employing slick advertisements that often leave the viewer or reader wondering what business the company is really in. However misleading such ads may be, their underlying premise is vital to understanding the importance of social responsibility: the marketing and advertising world has come to recognize that how companies operate is a key consideration for today's consumers.

The marketers are right: there is genuine concern about the impact of companies on the social and physical fabric of our world. Companies as well as consumers are beginning to vote with their pocketbooks, seeking out companies with whom they share values. They recognize that business itself has contributed to many social and environmental ills facing society. Companies may not have created these problems on purpose; they evolved as companies used people, capital, and other resources in the pursuit of productivity and profits. For a long time, neither the public nor business leaders generally recognized or acknowledged the links between company actions and such things as a deteriorating environment, abandoned inner cities, and employee stress and burnout.

Some company leaders are finally beginning to recognize these links, as well as the impact they have on the lives of their employees, customers, and neighbors. They recognize that in the aftermath of the "Reagan Revolution," in which the government opted out of areas in which it had previously been of service, Americans are looking increasingly to the corporate sector to rush in where legislators and regulators now fear to tread. The public wants industry to help with, say, education and training for the unemployed and dispossessed, or finding cost-effective, market-driven solutions to pollution their industry creates. Some companies are rising to the challenge, stepping in to fill the void left by a decade or more of federal government neglect. Often they help themselves in the process.

All of these links, which we'll examine more thoroughly in chapter 3, have created a growing community of companies that recognize that the impact of business goes far beyond the next quarterly report. They understand that socially responsible programs are more than a means for philanthropy—they are vital to recruiting and retaining quality employees and ensuring their safety, health, and productivity. They view social responsibility as key to protecting future consumers, ensuring an unwavering pool of qualified workers, and a steady market for future products. Through their policies and programs, through the way they conduct daily business, these forward-thinking companies respect the tremendous power business exercises in shap-

Businesses that master and embrace change can accomplish great things for themselves, their people, and the communities in which they do business. As leaders, they have the power to bring about complete shifts in the way they conduct business—which, in turn, enables them to thrive, to become known as an employer of choice for thousands of people, and to be a valued and respected member of society at large.

—John Martin,
president and CEO, Taco Bell

ing our daily lives, our communities, and the world—both today and for decades to come.

THE NEW BELIEFS

Most socially responsible business practices are predicated upon some fundamental beliefs about the world, especially the world of business. Among them:

• Employees function best when they do meaningful jobs at fair wages in healthy working environments, are empowered to have a say in how they do their jobs, are respected for their individual contributions and needs, and enjoy a healthy balance between work and family life. Their performance is further enhanced by their employer's willingness to invest in their continued personal and professional growth. The autocratic, authoritarian, abusive workplace, where employers rule by tyranny and intimidation, is not good for business.

• Companies function best over the long run when located in healthy communities where the quality of life includes such factors as a below-average crime rate, adequate education and health care facilities, pools of qualified workers, robust economic activity, a healthy environment, and viable cultural and community institutions. When one or more of these do not exist, there is a higher likelihood that companies will find it more difficult to attract and retain qualified employees, and may face increased taxes or regulatory burdens resulting from deteriorating conditions.

• Companies that treat the natural environment with respect throughout their operations usually reduce their output of waste, achieve higher-quality products and services, and maximize resource efficiency, including their capital resources. Moreover, they generally face fewer costs of regulatory compliance, pay lower insurance rates, experience reduced incidence of costly litigation, and enjoy higher loyalty from their customers, both individual consumers and business-to-business clients.

• Company must take a longer view of their operations. Short-term, quarterly-based management decisions frequently distort the true costs of doing business, both for companies and society. A growing number of decisions must be made with a broader perspective—of time as well as of the groups affected. That sometimes means forgoing short-term gain in favor of longer-term benefits.

• Corporate reputation will take on ever greater importance. A growing corps of customers—individual consumers as well as businesses and the public sector—is beginning to view company reputation and performance as criteria for their purchases. This is especially true of corporate and institutional customers, many of which have purchasing policies that give preference to products manufactured in a way that does not exploit workers or unduly harm the environment, including companies that do not engage in unethical business practices, discriminate against certain groups or classes, or support oppressive governments.

Each of these beliefs creates a new set of challenges for companies trying to remain competitive into the twenty-first century. Together, they portray a business climate changing in significant ways. No longer is it enough to offer a quality product or service at a competitive price. No longer is it sufficient to obey the law and pay your taxes. Tomorrow's successful companies increasingly will be asked to take a hard look at the impact of their operations both within and beyond their institutional walls, more carefully scrutinizing the impact of a variety of policies on employees, customers, communities, and society as a whole.

I get concerned when social responsibility is nothing more than writing a check to the right cause or telling your customers that you are politically correct in this way or that way. Responsibility in the whole spectrum of relationships has to include how it is you behave with one another in your own workplace, how you behave with one another in a competitive fashion, and how you collaborate with outside vendors. Responsibility has to be the attitude of all participants, at least those of us who are intentional about it. We have to be responsible in all our relations.

—TOM CHAPPELL,
CEO, Tom's of Maine

This new climate presents opportunities, too: for companies to improve productivity and morale, create motivated and committed workers, and help ensure an abundant supply of future employees and customers—all necessary ingredients for continued prosperity. There are opportunities for socially conscious business leaders to rise to the top of their companies, or to build entire new enterprises on the foundation of doing well by doing good. In the marketplace, social responsibility can provide a winning edge in an increasingly competitive environment. "The good news is that we now have a statistical basis to support what many of us have known or at least believed for years, namely that business practices such as employee stock and profit participation, energy conservation, waste minimization, worker education, diversity, and empowerment are the foundations and building blocks for stronger gross and net margins," says Gary Hirshberg, president and CEO of Stonyfield Farm, a New Hampshire–based yogurt maker. "We can now conclusively say that these practices not only don't hurt but utterly enhance the bottom line."

A DYNAMIC AND CHANGING WORLD

As one begins to examine the subject of socially responsible business, the questions come fast and furious: How does a company change its corporate culture to reflect more socially responsible values? Which comes first: social mission or bottom line? Is there an inherent conflict between the two? How do today's business people hang on to their social visions when they're besieged by all the worries of running a business?

Will it cost more money to implement socially responsible policies? Must a company reinvent itself to become socially responsible? If so, how will this affect a company's ability to be competitive? Should a company do everything at once or effect change more incrementally? Are there different challenges in inculcating social responsibility in a startup company, compared to a mature organization with established communication flows?

To be socially responsible, must a company forgo short-term profits in favor of longer-term investments? How might that affect a company's market value and stock price? How will these ideals affect a company's relationship with its customers? How do you measure success?

And, perhaps most fundamentally: Why should companies even

play a role in trying to help employees, families, and communities prosper? Isn't that the responsibility of the individual, government regulation, social agencies, religious and other institutions?

Some of these questions have ready answers, though the specifics may differ for every company. Other answers are more difficult to come by. In any case, the questions themselves never seem to go away completely, even for companies whose day-to-day operations are thick with socially responsible activities. That makes sense. One common theme among all successful companies is the need to continually assess their direction, goals, successes, and failures, both in business and in society.

Among the biggest challenges facing most of the companies that have embraced a socially responsible vision is simply staying abreast of this nascent and still-evolving business philosophy. The state of the art is ephemeral at best, as companies continue to innovate and as the sheer growth of the movement brings forth a diversity of management values and styles. There are more than a few collections of "best practices" in print describing exemplary companies and programs, issued by organizations such as the Social Venture Network and The Conference Board, some published for a relatively small circle of companies that belong to one of several associations and networks. Some of these collections—often samplings from company mission statements, employee handbooks, and marketing materials—are updated frequently to reflect the latest information and innovations.

This fleeting nature of socially responsible programs makes any attempt to present the bleeding edge of socially responsible business practices challenging, and that is not our sole intent with this book. The simple reality is that by the time this book comes out, some of the newest strategies and proposals profiled in these chapters will have caught on; in no time, they will become commonplace. That's unavoidable in a world where things are changing and growing at a dizzying pace. But the underlying visions behind these practices do not change. Many date back centuries.

Throughout this book, we will link the best and brightest examples of socially responsible policies with their underlying social and business rationales. We believe that without such a solid foundation even the most well-intentioned socially responsible practices will have limited duration and impact. Mere anecdotes won't inspire change for individual companies and business practices. It is too easy for business leaders to dismiss anecdotes, saying, for example, that what works for "them" is fine, but it won't necessarily work for "us."

Corporate social responsibility is not a politically correct set of standards or a simple platform of achievement. Rather, it is a continuous improvement process. A responsible company must regularly ask better and tougher questions about the impact of all its operations on the bottom line, its employees, communities, and the environment.

—GARY HIRSHBERG,
president, Stonyfield Farm

No company today has the luxury of making changes or initiating programs without regard for bottom-line impact: the costs, benefits, risks, and implications for both short- and long-term strategy and competitiveness. Throughout this book, our lodestar is that *one of the most socially responsible things most companies can do is to be profitable*: providing sustainable jobs at fair wages for their employees, solid returns for their owners and investors, and prosperity and sustainability for the communities in which they operate. Without such viability, even the best-designed and well-executed efforts will be for naught.

There is no question that the ideals and philosophies presented in this book are controversial. Make no mistake: No matter how fast the move to socially responsible business may be growing, most of the corporate world is by no means practicing these ideals. The overwhelming majority of companies have not yet embraced the notion that businesses have a responsibility to anyone but their owners, though a surprising number of these companies have one or two enlightened policies in place. But most of these companies lack a broader vision of social responsibility.

A LOOK AHEAD

In the chapters that follow, we will look more deeply into the visions, strategies, and programs inside socially responsible companies. The goal is not to present the definitive list of what's out there so much as a representative sampling of what's possible. Keep in mind that while the overriding rationale behind socially responsible business applies to any company, this is not a world in which "one size fits all."

To succeed, any corporate initiative must reflect the organization's size, sector, and culture. A cookie-cutter approach can be likened to the chair designed for the "average" person: it tends to be too big for half the population and too small for the rest. Similarly, these strategies and programs must be tailored to each organization and sector if they are to truly "fit."

In the next chapter, we will look at the origins of the move toward social responsibility in business, then meet some of the business leaders setting the pace for the rest of the corporate world in addressing these issues. In chapter 4, we will examine some of the tools socially responsible companies are developing for themselves, including the growing efforts to measure the impact of their programs and policies on their financial performance, in response to the confluence of forces demanding such accountability.

In subsequent chapters, we will examine four key areas in which companies are making a difference:

- the environment
- the workplace
- the community
- the international marketplace

In each of these areas, we will look inside companies and programs. We'll learn what works and what doesn't, benefiting from the insight and inspiration of individuals and companies that have broken ground in building new relationships with their employees, their customers, and society. Throughout, we will also offer "best practices" from companies of all sectors and sizes, which we hope will provide ideas and inspiration on how similar programs might work in your organization.

Learning from others' successes and failures is one key to integrating socially responsible thinking into company operations. There's no better lesson than a real-life one, and you are encouraged to contact the individuals and companies discussed in these chapters to learn more about them. Not all companies will readily share everything, but many will be willing to offer some insight into their programs and practices.

Here are some other things to keep in mind as you read this book:

- Be patient. Implementing socially responsible programs requires change, and that can take considerable time and effort. Don't expect

> Our position as the world's leading media and entertainment company could not have been reached—and could not have been sustained—solely from business success. It rests equally on our tradition of social responsibility and community involvement. At the core of this enterprise is the determination to make a difference as well as a profit.
>
> —GERALD M. LEVIN,
> *chairman and CEO, Time Warner Inc.*

that new programs will immediately be successful and embraced by everyone in the organization. Take it one small step at a time. Social responsibility tends to spread: your success in one area will make it easier to try something in another.

• The process never ends. Social responsibility is about continuous improvement; it is not a standard of accomplishment. Even companies with acknowledged leading-edge policies and practices are continually reassessing (and, when possible, measuring) their efforts, making changes to reflect their findings and changing business conditions.

• Everyone must participate. Successful social responsibility initiatives require participation from the top down and from the bottom up. While they require leadership, they can neither be mandated from the top without the rest of the company's participation and cooperation, nor conducted at the grass roots for long without top-management support (although many good ideas can and do originate at all levels of employees).

• Do what's right for your organization and its culture. A program that works in one company—or even another division of your company—won't necessarily translate directly into your operation. It may take creativity and flexibility to mold a program to fit your organization's unique way of doing things.

• This is not an add-on program. Social responsibility should be viewed in the company as part of its culture and fabric. That usually requires that an overall philosophy and commitment be articulated in a company's mission statement, employee handbook, marketing and sales materials, and other communications with employees, customers, investors, and the media.

• Don't rest on your laurels. As socially responsible programs mature and become more widespread, what seems effective and appropriate today could be inadequate tomorrow. That means continuously revising your goals and improving your effectiveness, as well as keeping up on what other companies are doing.

• It is difficult, if not impossible, to do everything "right." No one's perfect. No matter how hard you try, your company will still have some areas that need room for improvement. But don't let that inhibit your efforts. Simply getting started is what's key.

Chapter Two

The Birth of a Notion

"You can't do business in a society that's burning."

—WILLIAM C. NORRIS,
founder, Control Data Corporation

A great many of the ideas and practices behind socially responsible business have coalesced only in recent years. In 1992, companies practicing—or considering practicing—socially responsible ideals got their first trade association, Business for Social Responsibility, or BSR. The association emerged from a group of companies that found themselves spending a great deal of time sharing their socially responsible practices and supporting one another's efforts. They recognized that there was no voice for their sensibilities among existing business organizations. Helen Mills, an early BSR organizer whose company, Soapbox Trading Company, is the largest franchisee of The Body Shop retail chain in the United States, tells of a letter she received from a local chamber of commerce, urging her to fight mandatory recycling in suburban Washington, D.C. "It made my blood boil," she says. "That's when I knew we needed a group that speaks to the other side."

BSR was launched in June 1992 by fifty-four company leaders, including those from Stride Rite, Reebok, Ben & Jerry's, Stonyfield Farm, Working Assets, and the Calvert Group. The organizing committee of BSR was formed at a meeting of the Social Venture Network (SVN), a group of individual entrepreneurs, business leaders, non-profits, academics, and others. SVN is an internal group that deals only within its own membership and does not generally address the outside business world. In contrast, the mandate of BSR is to give voice to the idea of socially responsible business, informing both the larger business community and the public policy makers in Washington, D.C., and state capitals. BSR eventually merged with some older existing groups, such as New England Businesses for Social Responsibility, and then spawned a still-growing network of local chapters around the country. By the time of its first national conference in October 1993, it had emerged as a full-fledged national coalition, with more than 750 member and affiliated companies.

The idea of socially responsible business long predates BSR, however. The notion of balancing companies "doing good" for their employees, the environment, and society against their own immediate interests dates back to the first corporate charters, special protections, and privileges granted by monarchs to spur economic development—and to perpetuate their own sovereignty. In exchange for serving the common good, companies were given the right to do such things as issue stock, own property, sign contracts, and accumulate assets and debts, all with limited liability for the company and its owners. If they failed to obey the law or "do good," the government could revoke the corporation's charter—at least they could until the early twentieth century.

The issue of the relationship between business and society—especially with regard to healing society's ills or caring for the underclass—actually began in the United States with the advent of the Industrial Revolution, though some of its philosophical underpinnings date back to the Quakers. The Industrial Revolution dramatically changed American society, taking its citizens from their rural roots to urban life, often to these individuals' disadvantage. The builders of the New England mill towns that began to spring up in the early 1800s recognized that providing food and shelter to employees would benefit both employees and the company. Some mill towns became showplaces of industry, demonstrating how business's and society's interests and concerns could and should be harmoniously merged. The city of Lowell, Massachusetts, was testament to the policy of recruiting young women from rural areas and providing them "with living quarters and resources to meet their social, religious, and intellectual needs," according to Thomas M. Vetica, one of a growing number of academics who have written theses on the subject of business and social responsibility. But not all such paternalism turned out to be in employees' best interests. In many company-built communities, employers set wages, hours, production processes, and even machine speeds. Children were sometimes separated from their families and made to work long hours under inhumane conditions. Some company towns eventually took total control over their employees' lives, virtually enslaving them, the exact opposite of the intentions of their founders. Union organizers who tried to interfere with company policies were all but driven out of town.

Not all these efforts' outcomes were bad. The mill towns' brand of paternalism spread to other parts of the country and became a basis for the philanthropy of early large-scale industrialists, such as Julius Rosenwald, who took over a nearly bankrupt Sears, Roebuck & Co. and turned it into what for decades was rural America's most successful retailer. (Rosenwald launched the 4-H programs as a means of assisting American farmers' technological advances and long-term profitability.)

Some company towns were highly successful. In the late 1880s in upstate New York, George F. Johnson, in his early twenties, convinced his boss, Henry Endicott, to build a leather tannery outside the Binghamton city limits; Endicott owned the Lester Brothers Company boot factory in Binghamton. The then-radical idea was that large manufacturing plants should be sited outside the crowded towns. By 1894, the two had become partners in the Endicott-Johnson Company. By the time Johnson became president of the company in 1920, he had put into practice his plan of providing workers with quality homes at affordable prices and modest interest rates. Many of the homes are still standing. Under Johnson's brand of benevolent paternalism, Endicott-Johnson became one of the largest shoe makers in the country.

Housing was only the beginning of Johnson's benevolence. He provided free medical care for employees and gave each of their children a free pair of shoes every Christmas. He built recreation centers and parks, with free boating and swimming. The George F. Johnson Pavilion, built during the Depression, attracted famous-name performers, from Tommy Dorsey to Frank Sinatra. Binghamton boasts the largest collection of operating merry-go-rounds in the world— six—all donated by Johnson. As word spread of the company's reputation, immigrants, especially Eastern Europeans arriving at Ellis Island, sought out the factory. Legend has it that they arrived at their port of entry with hand-written signs hanging from their necks reading: "Which way, E.J.?"

George Johnson joined Andrew Carnegie and other early captains of commerce who recognized that companies had a special interest in spreading their wealth. Carnegie, for one, was a believer in the idea of "trusteeship": The principal purpose of being rich was to do good. Vetica points out that the philanthropy of early industrialists, many of whom owned and controlled their enterprises, is responsible for the sustained growth of several charitable institutions, including the YMCA and the Community Chest. By the 1920s, such philanthropy had become one of the primary channels of expression of social concern. A decade later, the Internal Revenue Service considered corporate contributions to charities to be a legitimate business expense. (Up to that point, the government considered charitable contributions as legitimate expenses only when some benefit other than goodwill returned to the corporation.) Some industrialists focused directly on their own employees' welfare. Henry Ford took that route—albeit not without great self-interest—when he raised workers' pay so that they could afford to buy one of his cars. But neither Ford nor Carnegie nor many of their colleagues had unblemished records in the way they treated employees or the communities where their companies operated. Many were heavy-handed robber barons who destroyed people's lives in the name of business. Ironically, they helped define what was socially responsible at the time: the amount of money a company gave away at the end of the year.

THE GREAT DEBATES

As the idea that businesses had a role to play in minding society's ills began to catch on, some individuals questioned openly whether executives were up to the task. For example, Wallace B. Donham, writing about "The Social Significance of Business" in the *Harvard Business Review* in 1927, observed that

> The social responsibility of the business man ... is inescapable. Yet in one respect the business group is less favorably situated to solve these problems than the legal group. . . . Our usual training in business, still carried on mainly within industry itself, is too narrow, too much specialized in the particular concern; it gives too few points of view on the

social importance of business. No profession can really develop which does not have an intellectual content shaped broadly by many men, and this condition does not yet exist in business. There are professional men of business, but business as a profession is developing rather than already in existence. It is peculiarly difficult to make the individual business man understand his opportunities and his responsibilities in harmonizing his economic and social obligations, because there has been inadequate analysis and inadequate statement of the problem.

Following World War II, the debates over the responsibility of business in society intensified. By then, corporate philanthropy had already become part of the social fabric. And the growth of government regulators and public interest watchdogs—from the Federal Communications Commission and the Federal Trade Commission to the American Civil Liberties Union and the Sierra Club—spurred new interest in business ethics, the standards by which to judge corporate and individual behavior within the moral framework of business and society. Between 1969 and 1972, what has come to be called the Big Four regulatory agencies—the Occupational Safety and Health Administration (OSHA), the Equal Employment Opportunity Commission (EEOC), the Consumer Product Safety Commission (CPSC), and the Environmental Protection Agency (EPA)—were all founded. "This was a whole new world for managers," says Donna J. Wood, professor in the University of Pittsburgh's Katz Graduate School of Business. "They had no idea this kind of thing was possible. And all of a sudden they're hit with four enormous regulatory agencies making lots and lots of demands for information and for corrective action. It cost huge amounts of money and took a lot of time to figure out and sort through." Ironically, the government's new quest for detailed information about business operations made many companies gun shy about disclosure in general, fearing the consequences they faced if that information didn't paint an acceptable picture. That only whetted the appetites of regulators and activists, who sought even greater disclosure.

Something else happened during the 1970s that shifted—perhaps even derailed—the debate over the social responsibility of companies for a time. "There was a period of development in our thinking where we sort of lost track of the ethical roots of social responsibility and moved into social *responsiveness*—the idea that companies had to be responsive to social demands in order to survive," says Wood. "That's quite different from the concept of social responsibility. Once they began to focus on responding to a changing environment, the topics that were studied in the field shifted from what companies could do to make this a better world to what companies could do to ensure their own survival." The result was a new emphasis on corporate political action, public affairs, and lobbying, and ultimately the birth of such terms as "cause-related marketing" and "strategic philanthropy." As a result, says Wood, "the people who were supposed to be articulating and defining social responsibility forgot what it was and moved on to responsiveness. The whole field foundered for about ten years."

The responsibility-versus-responsiveness debate was far from the hottest. The conflict that continues to dominate discussion has to do with what is the real purpose of business in society. Early business ethicists argued that the function of business had grown beyond the mere provision of goods and services to society. They said that business should become a social agent with responsibility to society, including those sectors of society outside the reach of pure commercial transactions. Of course, that belief was far from universal. Most vocal on the subject was the economist Milton Friedman, who argued that business's sole purpose is to generate profit for shareholders. He maintained that companies that did adopt "responsible" attitudes would be faced with more binding constraints than companies that did not, rendering them less competitive.

"What does it mean to say that the corporate executive has a 'social responsibility' in his capacity as businessman?" wrote Friedman in the *New York Times Magazine* in 1970.

If this statement is not pure rhetoric, it must mean that he is to act in some way that is not in the interest of his employers. For example, that he is to refrain from increasing the price of the product in order to contribute to the social objective of preventing inflation, even though a price increase would be in the best interests of the corporation. Or that he is to make expenditures on reducing pollution beyond the amount that is in the best interests of the corporation or that is required by law in order to contribute to the social objective of improving the environment. Or that, at the expense of corporate profits, he is to hire "hardcore" unemployed instead of better-qualified available workmen to contribute to the social objective of reducing poverty.

In each of these cases, the corporate executive would be spending someone else's money for a general social interest. Insofar as his actions in accord with his 'social responsibility' reduce returns to stockholders, he is spending their money. Insofar as his actions raise the price to customers, he is spending the customers' money. Insofar as his actions lower the wages of some employees, he is spending their money.

Friedman argued that such actions in effect turned executives into public employees or civil servants, levying "taxes" (in the form of corporate money allocated to social causes) and making "expenditures"—a part of "the socialist view that political mechanisms, not market mechanisms, are the appropriate way to determine the allocation of scarce resources to alternative uses."

Friedman concluded: "The difficulty of exercising 'social responsibility' illustrates, of course, the great virtue of private competitive enterprise—it forces people to be responsible for their own actions and makes it difficult for them to 'exploit' other people for either selfish or unselfish purposes. They can do good—but only at their own expense."

Friedman's perspective was far from universally shared by business leaders. In 1979, for example, declaring Friedman's profits-are-everything philosophy "a dreary and demeaning view of the role of business and business leaders in our society," Quaker Oats president Kenneth Mason wrote in *Business Week* that "Making a profit is no more the purpose of a corporation than getting enough to eat is the purpose of life. Getting enough to eat is a *requirement* of life; life's purpose, one would hope, is somewhat broader and more challenging. Likewise with business and profit."

Mason continued: "The moral imperative all of us share in this world is that of getting the best return we can on whatever assets we are privileged to employ. What American business leaders too often forget is that this means all the assets employed—not just the financial assets but also the brains employed, the labor employed, the materials employed, and the land, air, and water employed." He went

---

Profit is not the legitimate purpose of business. The purpose is to provide a service needed by society. If you do that well and efficiently, you earn a profit, perhaps an enormous profit.

—James W. Rouse,
founder, The Rouse Company

on to "encourage, not evade, discussion of those problems that arise when the activities of business conflict with the needs and concerns of society."

Two years later, the Business Roundtable, a venerable association of corporate executives, issued a "Statement on Corporate Responsibility." It acknowledged the need for growing corporate involvement in social issues, although it also cautioned against expecting that companies could be counted on to step in where government was opting out. "Many people believe that corporations are generally concerned only about profits and not about the impact their operations may have on society," it stated. "At the same time, it is clear that a large percentage of the people now measures corporations by a yardstick beyond strictly economic objectives." That yardstick, concluded the authors, included a company's product pricing, quality, and advertising; the fair treatment of its employees; its workplace health and safety practices; plant openings and closings; its record of environmental impacts; its role in the community; and its philanthropic practices. The document determined that "economic responsibility is by no means incompatible with other corporate responsibilities in society," and offered several recommendations, including one to consider "what can be done to assure that the company's larger role in society is understood by management, employees, and other constituencies."

But these were just well-intentioned words. Action was slow in coming. And the debate involved only big companies. Smaller firms didn't enter the picture until later.

So far, relatively few companies have focused their attention on saving the world, or even their own communities, although the number and breadth of programs aimed at easing society's problems— from homelessness to handgun violence to human rights violations— has grown dramatically. Many more companies have focused their social visions on their own employees and employees' families. These companies recognize that making workers more secure in their jobs and homes, providing them flexibility to balance their lives, and giving them the chance to participate in their communities helps guarantee a happier, healthier, more loyal, and more productive work force.

To some observers, these cultural changes signal nothing less than a transfer of responsibility for individual and public welfare from the public sector to the private. It would not be the first such transfer of power. Four hundred years earlier, social responsibility shifted from the church to the state, as government replaced religious institutions as society's predominant force. At the dawning of the twenty-first century, business appears the next likely candidate to carry this mantle. "There are many that now feel that the corporations are the most powerful institutions on the planet and with power comes incumbent responsibility, but also the efficacy of getting things done," says Thomas N. Gladwin, a professor at New York University's Sloan School of Business. "The most powerful institutions in any society must take responsibility for the welfare of the whole of the society."

Not everyone sees it that way. Professor Donna Wood views Gladwin's analysis as "a peculiarly American way of looking at things." In most other countries, she says, government has taken different approaches to dealing with social problems. For example, "the Japanese, when they first started making massive moves into American investment, got blindsided by the demands that they get involved in charitable giving. They thought this was really weird. It wasn't because they were stingy, greedy, money-grubbing capitalists. It was because they couldn't understand why it should be business's job to do what the government should be doing, and what the government in Japan does do—protect the social welfare." Besides, says Wood, there are good reasons not to invest all one's hopes in business to solve our social problems. While it may be true that business has amassed a great deal of power and wealth, she says, "It's not clear that you want business's modes of operations, financial values, and emphasis on efficiency directing our social welfare policy."

Wood isn't making a case that companies don't have a responsibility to care about social issues, or to act upon that concern. Her point is that the corporate approach and bottom-line values, however profitable, are not always the best way to tackle tough social problems. Companies' contributions may be more valuable when made in concert with government or the nonprofit sector, providing the brand of leadership and skills that only the for-profit business sector can offer.

So the debate continues: What *is* business's responsibility? To make profits? To "do good"? A combination of both? A simple answer is unlikely. But as we shall see, there is clear support for the idea that companies can operate in a way that strengthens their various communities, internal and external, and still provides solid, sustainable returns for their shareholders. They can do so, they should, and eventually they must.

THE GRAND OLD MEN

In some ways, the debates among Friedman, Mason, and others over the viability and appropriateness of socially responsible business were academic. By the end of the 1970s, a corps of modern business executives already had proved that the melding of morals and management worked, and worked well. Some, like IBM's Thomas Watson, Herman Miller's Max DePree, Cummins Engine's J. Irwin Miller, Levi Strauss's Walter Haas, and Stride Rite's Arnold Hiatt, represented a generation that came of age during the Depression, served in a world war, and saw their companies flourish during the expansive postwar era. As Friedman and others argued on, these business leaders practiced their socially responsible visions and philosophies every day, with great financial success. For them, the debates were nothing more than a sideshow.

Herman Miller's Max DePree is an exemplar of this generation. DePree, whose father started the company in 1923, and who himself was CEO from 1980 to 1987, preached the gospel of enlightened leadership. In addressing management meetings, words like "assets" and "profits" scarcely graced his lips. Instead, he talked of "being open," of "covenantal relationships," and of "meeting personal goals." "We're going to inhibit our own growth if we don't help everybody gain a good knowledge of the value system and the culture of this organization," was a typical DePree pronouncement. His convictions stem from his Dutch Reform background, which emphasized hard work, fairness, and the belief that individuals need to reach their highest potential. At Herman Miller, those beliefs came together in "participatory management," now a forty-year tradition, with all employees owning stock and having a say in how the company operates. Almost from the beginning, DePree's policies and beliefs have dominated the company's operating credos, from employee education to energy efficiency.

William C. Norris is another exemplar. One of the genuine pioneers of the computer era—he helped develop the forerunner of the modern digital computer to break enemy codes for the Navy during World War II—he is best known for Control Data Corporation, the company he founded in Minneapolis in 1957 by selling 625,000 shares of stock for a dollar each. By the early 1980s, the company employed nearly 60,000 people and generated annual revenues of $4 billion.

At the core of his company's operating principles was a policy of "addressing unmet societal needs as profitable business opportunities." According to James C. Worthy, Norris's biographer, "Norris was genuinely distressed at the extent of human misery brought explosively to light by the riots across the country and in Minneapolis during the summer of 1967, and he determined to do what he could to relieve the conditions that had led to those events." He also sensed that he could do so in way that reached beyond mere charity, that would have a sustainable impact and not require constant funding. Moreover, he saw that some of the "unmet needs" represented potential markets for Control Data, or at least a more stable environment in which to operate. "You can't do business in a society that's burning," he declared.

Following the 1967 riots, Norris decided that as a major employer, Control Data had an obligation to start hiring African-Americans in significant numbers. For him, providing jobs to the disenfranchised was a matter of business survival. By the end of the year, despite predictions of failure among his own staff, Norris had opened a new plant in Minneapolis' inner city to build computer components. The Northside plant, as it came to be known, became one of the company's most efficient and productive manufacturing facilities. Another pet project, called PLATO (for Programmed Logic for Automated Teaching Operations), a computer-based instruction system, aimed to use the new technologies to revolutionize the educational system.

Control Data became a computer industry powerhouse, reaching $5 billion in revenue in 1984. But it wasn't to last. As the computer industry began to shift to minicomputers and microcomputers, Control Data missed market trends and began to falter. By 1985, the company—which by now included such divisions as the Ticketron ticketing service and the Arbitron audience-measurement service—hit the skids. In mid-1986 the company fell into default on some bank indebtedness, its stock price plummeted, the company was restructured, and Norris retired. Some criticized Norris for his attention to external projects, for putting society's "unmet needs" before the company's.

Today, Norris calls this criticism "nonsense, a complete misapprehension." He points out that relatively few company resources were allocated to PLATO and other Norris projects, and that his community-based initiatives helped build the company as well as attract and retain employees. His faith in the power of business to turn society's unmet needs into profitable business opportunities remains unshaken. "The best hope is that there are always a few people who are willing to look ahead and take risks," he says.

Another grand old man of social responsibility is James W. Rouse, one of the most successful developers in U.S. history, who believed that "the surest road to success in our ventures is to discover the authentic needs and yearnings of people and to do our best to serve them."

The people's "needs and yearnings" ranged during Rouse's half-century-long career from the growing needs of suburbia during the postwar boom years—in 1958, Rouse opened the first privately developed enclosed regional shopping center in America, which he dubbed a "mall"—to the changing needs of cities. As early as the 1940s and through the 1980s, Rouse was deeply involved with crusades to rehabilitate slums and crumbling downtowns of America's northeastern cities. Rouse may be best known for his restoration of historic but decaying urban landmarks, which he renovated and turned into highly successful "festival marketplaces." Among his company's flagship restoration projects are Boston's Faneuil Hall and Quincy Market, Baltimore's Harborplace, and New York City's South Street Seaport.

But Rouse's passion—and, in some respects, his greatest legacy—may not lie in those glitzy tourist attractions but in the low-income housing projects he seeded in the inner cities. Before his retirement from The Rouse Company in 1979, Rouse had taken an interest in affordable housing for the poor and the homeless.

In 1973, Rouse met two Washington, D.C., women who asked his help to rehabilitate two rat-infested buildings. Impressed with the women's determination—they had already put down a nonrefundable $10,000 deposit—he personally bought the buildings for $625,000 and arranged for another $125,000 renovation loan. Ultimately, he set up a nonprofit organization, Jubilee Housing, which devised a creative formula to allow low-income residents to rent the units and to eventually become self-sustainable—that is, residents' rents would cover operating costs. Every six months for seven years,

---

People who have a good environment, education, and opportunity make better neighbors, employees, and customers than those who are poor, ignorant, and oppressed.

—COUNCIL ON ECONOMIC DEVELOPMENT, 1971

the rates for able-bodied tenants went up by small increments. The increases encouraged tenants to get jobs, improve their earning potential, and find their own nonsubsidized apartments, thus making room for new tenants.

That experience led Rouse in 1982 to establish the Enterprise Foundation, which he seeded with $1 million in Rouse Company stock. He intended it to be a catalyst for tenant activists, church groups, block associations, and other self-help nonprofit associations. The foundation helps these groups raise money, acquire and rehabilitate housing, manage the properties, and develop social support services that may be needed by low-income residents. After more than a decade, the foundation has built or renovated more than 10,000 housing units.

"In The Rouse Company we had three corporate goals," Rouse told a Business for Social Responsibility conference in 1993. "The first was to improve the physical environment and the quality of life of the American city. The second was to provide for the growth and fulfillment of the people working in the company. The third was to make a profit. We used to say this as a publicly owned company, to our shareholders, in our annual reports. We would say that if we achieve the first two goals, the third would take care of itself. We even went so far in one report to say that profit is not the legitimate purpose of business. Profit is a reward for a product or service well produced. If you fulfill those first two goals, profit will come. If we saw in business that profit was a reward and not a purpose, it would take profit to the bottom line where it belongs, and not to the top line."

BUSINESS REINVENTS ITSELF

Unfortunately, the Rouses, DePrees, and Norrises were relatively few and far between. The vast majority of business leaders saw little need for such direct involvement in workplace or community affairs, especially with the growth of government and private social service agencies, both in Washington, D.C., and around the country. But by the 1980s, a number of forces came into play that helped bring the issue of socially responsible business to the fore.

One of those forces was the blossoming of the consumer movement, which led to increased scrutiny of companies by a wide range of national and grass-roots groups. Corporate social responsibility had become a favorite thesis topic in business schools, yielding a rich lode of definitions and analyses of corporate behavior. The rise in litigation against companies, spurred in large part by the Ralph Nader–inspired public interest movement that had reached into nearly every college campus, was also providing peeks (via court documents) into the sometimes less than flattering machinations of corporate decision making. And the efforts of the environmental movement provided additional insight into companies' operations and decision-making processes.

At the same time, several small but fast-growing companies were starting to make their voices heard on a range of social issues. A small Vermont ice cream company called Ben & Jerry's and a British-based retailer called The Body Shop were among the more visible examples of companies that became noticed by the media—albeit as quirky "alternative" companies that deigned to call attention to society's problems. Eventually, that label gave way to grudging acceptance that these companies could indeed operate under their leaders' ideals while enjoying astonishing growth in sales and profits. Moreover, as many larger companies were paring their work forces to become more lean and competitive, their smaller counterparts were creating millions of new jobs. Some big companies began breaking themselves into smaller, decentralized units, hoping that a small business approach could foster creativity and productivity. That gave further credibility to the role of small business as an innovator.

The impact of the Reagan-Bush years—in which government gave business a freer hand than previously allowed to conduct business without government interference—engendered in some business leaders a sense that companies needed to step in to protect the average citizen. Even some executives with socially responsible visions thought Reagan's hands-off policies were in society's—and business's—long-term interest. Still, whether due to Reagan's policies or those of his predecessors, or merely the realities of the time, some company executives contrasted what appeared to be an alarming array of crumbling institutions—including weakened federal and local government agencies once charged with protecting those institutions—with the wealth they and their shareholders had amassed over roughly the same period, and recognized an inherent imbalance. More important, they also recognized that business represented the only institution with adequate resources and expertise to turn things around. Business, for some, seemed to be the last great hope.

Despite Reagan's oft-stated goal to get the federal government off business's back, government's role as business regulator did not end during the Reagan era. OSHA, EPA, and other agencies joined with Congress to continue pressing for new laws to protect workers and the environment. Some of the workplace laws took over the role of the unions, which by the 1980s had become virtually extinct in certain industries. Labor membership in 1985 stood at only 17 million members—less than 18 percent of the U.S. labor force—compared with just over 22 percent a quarter century earlier, the lowest level since the Great Depression.

The Reagan and Bush years saw the creation of millions of jobs and the expansion of the U.S. economy. But many of these jobs were low-skilled and low-paying, without benefits or the stability of the past, undermining the financial security of many Americans. During a period in which Americans' overall real income growth dipped, there were multi-million-dollar executive bonuses and unprecedented "golden parachutes" for CEOs affected by mergers and acquisitions. In 1994, a report by President Bill Clinton's Council of Economic Advisers called the widening gap between rich and poor over the previous decade "a threat to the social fabric that has long bound Americans together and made ours a society with minimal class distinctions."

Some observers concluded that the Friedman-Reagan philosophy—that a "rising tide" of corporate profits would raise all of society's "ships"—was fallacious at best. Given the chance to allocate an abundance of profits, companies opted—with Wall Street's enthusiastic help—to benefit shareholders and executives rather than investing in employees, environmental protection, or community problems to help ease epidemics of drug abuse, unemployment, illiteracy, racism, failing education, inadequate training, or other pressing issues plaguing their communities.

It wasn't just money, it was also power. During the Bush administration, a White House Council on Competitiveness, chaired by Vice President Dan Quayle, became a means for business to undo federal environmental and occupational health and safety laws. Reagan had a similar group during his terms, chaired by George Bush. Both councils' original purpose was to ensure that no federal regulation unduly inhibited U.S. industrial competitiveness. This concept had merit—government regulation *was* strangling competitiveness in some industries. But critics charged Bush and Quayle with using the council to circumvent the legislative process to undo laws intended to protect the public and the environment. Under Quayle's leadership, for example, the council turned around a host of laws and regulations enacted by Congress or the regulatory agencies, doing virtually all of its work in closed sessions, unaccountable to public scrutiny. Among other things, the group tried to make wetlands more accessible to oil drillers and land developers. It relaxed rules that required biotech-nology companies to get government approval before creating new life forms. And it proposed more than a hundred changes to weaken the Clean Air Act of 1990. What was done in the name of getting government off the back of business seemed to some more like put-ting government in business's back pocket. The council's efforts ben-efited relatively few companies, said the critics, potentially to the detriment of the environment and employee health and safety, while adding to public cynicism about big business's willingness to play by the rules.

All of this—government's hands-off approach, business's growing impact, the media's and the public's perception of government's role, seemingly excessive profits, and the unprecedented rises in home-lessness, drug abuse, and other social problems—helped to foster a subtle shift in public perception of business. By the beginning of the 1990s, the tone of media coverage of business had changed: from what had been an almost breathless accounting of multi-billion-dollar mergers and acquisitions and record-breaking sales and profits to a more circumspect examination of what the decade had wrought on the nation. As some of the 1980s' most successful business figures—Ivan Boesky, Michael Milken, and Charles Keating among them—were carted off to serve prison terms, and government agencies attempted to sift through the ruins of banks and savings and loans, what had been dubbed the go-go decade seemed to lose some of its luster.

This is not to say that all business was perceived as inherently evil, or that no business leaders cared for their employees or communi-ties. For years, an impressive list of companies comprising the major business sectors—manufacturing, service, finance, and retailing—im-plemented policies that improved the lot of their workers, their communities, and the environment. (Not all of these were voluntary: for example, several employee benefits and policies were born of contract negotiations with unions, which for the past century had produced the majority of employee benefits.) Corporate philan-thropy had long been a major pillar of support for the nonprofit sector. As you will see throughout this book, a handful of the most

"The Good Corporation" Is Alive and Well

Several decades after Milton Friedman's heyday, skeptics still question whether companies can be socially responsive and still remain viable. *Newsweek* economic writer Robert J. Samuelson, in a 1993 article headlined "R.I.P.: The Good Corporation," offered a eulogy to corporate caring amid unprecedented layoffs at International Business Machines Corp., or IBM. The giant computer maker, he said, was "our ideal of what all American companies might become. They would marry profit-making and social responsibility, economic efficiency and enlightened labor relations." IBM, he said, "seemed to do everything right." And yet the opposite happened—not just at IBM but elsewhere. Striving to stay competitive, companies laid off workers, encouraged early retirements, and cut fringe benefits, including basic health insurance.

Of course, IBM did not "do everything right," not by a long shot—and it continued its socially responsible policies when times got tough. (Samuelson fails to mention that while IBM lost $5 billion in 1992, it was America's top corporate donor at $120 million.) But the company failed miserably in some of its strategies and business decisions. Among other things, it virtually gave away the market for personal computer operating system software to Microsoft Corporation and other companies, opting out of what grew into a multi-billion-dollar market that today reaches more than 85 million computers worldwide. IBM spread itself too thin, missing tremendous market opportunities. It lost market share to Apple Computer, Inc., whose user-friendly Macintosh captured a significant piece of the PC pie. And it didn't remain competitive with the makers of the PC "clones" it inspired. Much of this, critics say, resulted from IBM's rigid, autocratic, and hierarchical style, which reduced the company's ability to respond flexibly to a rapidly changing market.

It was not being a "good corporation" that resulted in unprecedented massive layoffs by IBM in 1993. It was bad management, a disease no socially responsible program or policy can cure.

effective and forward-thinking programs and policies date back generations.

A TORCH IS PASSED

What changed by the early nineties was the recognition by business leaders that the business and social issues of the day demanded more than isolated approaches from a few companies or a program here and there. This wasn't born of any single incident or epiphany. Rather, it seemed the logical evolution of all that had preceded it: the growth of socially responsible business practices, the success of companies with social responsibility strategies, the growing need for new solutions to old problems, the inability of government to play a sufficient role in addressing society's needs. What was clearly needed was a change in philosophy, an overarching vision that companies become more involved, not just within their walls, not just with their wallets, but by transforming their culture to embrace some new notions of "social responsibility" that integrated daily business and the bottom line with their impact on the lives of employees, customers, communities, and beyond.

At the moment, the baby-boom generation that currently controls the White House is poised to step into leadership positions at many of the largest companies. Weaned on the free speech movement, the civil rights movement, Vietnam, and Watergate, boomers grew up in the 1960s, came of age in the 1970s—railing against big business, big government, and every other authoritarian institution—and rose up through the ranks during the 1980s. Each of these decades contributed significantly to the boomer philosophy. In the 1960s, business ethics and corporate responsibility first emerged as public interest issues, with pressure coming from outside companies mostly in the form of shareholder resolutions advocating a variety of social and political issues. By the 1970s, government came on board with renewed vigor and powers, promoting environmental responsibility, occupational safety and health, consumer product safety, automobile safety, and other vital issues. Ralph Nader sounded his call for consumer activism, inciting thousands of local, regional, and national efforts to bring accountability to previously unaccountable business and government institutions. And the 1980s brought new resolve on these issues, as national government leadership and policies attempted to weaken the role of government, granting new freedom and power to business to strengthen its impact on the social agenda.

Today, survivors of these decades-long battles—and others of the Boomer generation who chose to stay far from the front lines—are beginning to emerge from this amalgam of experiences to occupy corner office suites at major companies. So far, only a few have reached the top. (Just under 100 of the nation's 1,000 largest companies have a CEO who is forty-six or younger, according to a 1992 survey by the *Wall Street Journal.*) But the inevitability of aging promises to quickly increase the power of that generation: In 1992, nearly 400 of the *Fortune* 1,000 had a CEO who was expected to retire within five years. "The new CEOs will have critical impact on American business over the next twenty-five years and on the economic-revitalization measures favored by fellow Boomer Bill Clinton," reported the *Journal* just after the 1992 presidential election. "The corporate policies they foster will shape debate on social issues ranging from family leave to health care."

The ideas behind socially responsible business are not universally embraced by the boomer generation, of course. Far from it. And many of that age group, by choice or circumstance, work outside the world of big business, opting instead for smaller companies or entrepreneurial endeavors. While small business has generated several socially responsible business leaders, they are relatively few and far between. As with the rest of society, there is a sizable proportion who find little currency to the notion of caring corporations and socially responsible businesses.

But with the election of Bill Clinton and Al Gore, the subject of business's responsibility in society has once again been emphasized by national leaders. The ideals of socially responsible companies parallel the administration's political agenda. Their stated agenda of rebuilding America through a cooperative effort that emphasizes each individual's value and the hard work of both individuals and institutions for the common good, and their espoused ideals— family and medical leave, community investment, individual involvement, diversity, lifelong learning, improved education, increased opportunities—all are consistent with socially responsible philosophies.

So it was not without significance that Bill Clinton was the keynote speaker at the first annual BSR conference in 1993. "You have found a way to live the rhetoric of my last campaign: 'Putting People First,' " he told the assembled guests in a Washington, D.C., hotel ballroom.

"I am convinced that BSR has proved that the future of the American private sector, the triumph of free enterprise, will be in proving that we can actually do right by our employees, do right by our customers, do right by our bottom lines, if we are enlightened and do the right things."

Chapter Three

The New Leaders

"I feel very lucky to be in business. It's not a right, it's a gift we're given."

—DEBBIE AGUIRRE,
Tierra Pacifica Corporation

At first glance, Jack Stack does not appear to be someone on the cutting edge of capitalism. A self-deprecating, boyish-faced executive who was once expelled from missionary school for excessive drinking and later fired by General Motors for playing poker on the job, he heads a company that remanufactures car, truck, and tractor engines for companies such as Chrysler and General Motors. His favorite haunt near his company's Springfield, Missouri, headquarters is the local Steak & Brew, where he is known to invite guests to settle into the red-leather banquettes to hear tales of how he quietly turned a cash-dry, poorly performing engine factory into one of the most successful business ventures of the late twentieth century.

"The most important thing that we should worry about is building a beautiful company," says Stack, president of Springfield ReManufacturing Corporation (SRC). "It should be a natural course of events. It shouldn't be a big goal. It shouldn't be a separate program. It shouldn't be a self-interested responsibility. It's something that we should do as good corporate citizens."

Stack didn't start out trying to build a "beautiful company." In 1968, at age eighteen, he hired on as a mailroom clerk at International Harvester's plant in Melrose Park, Illinois—his father, a foreman at the plant, got him the job—where he began climbing the corporate ladder. At age twenty, he was put in charge of a purchasing department that made $200 million in acquisitions a year. In less than a decade he became head of the least productive of Harvester's seven divisions, a perennial money-losing operation that produced heavy-duty truck engines, without much regard for quality control. Prodded by top management to turn the division around, he used everything from free pizza and beer to $500 bets about who could beat whose productivity.

But Stack offered his workers more than just beer, bets, and bribes. The wager competition helped him to see that the more his employees understood about his division's needs and goals, the more they were willing to work to meet them. He recognized that if he told people half-truths, he'd get half-efforts. And by giving them the complete truth, he'd get the best each employee had to offer.

That philosophy was put to the test in 1972, when Stack learned at a management meeting that the company faced a huge financial penalty if it failed to meet an upcoming deadline for shipping tractors to the Soviet Union. His back-of-the-envelope calculations told him that he was 800 tractors short, had 20 days left, and was producing about five tractors a day. Things didn't look good. His colleagues agreed that the less they talked about this predicament, the less blame there would be to go around.

Stack disagreed. He laid out the situation for his assembly-line workers, challenging them to exceed the minimum quotas for which they had been striving. Suddenly realizing that what they did mattered, the workers' productivity zoomed—to more than fifty tractors a day, a tenfold increase. By the deadline, Stack and company had shipped 808 tractors.

That episode confirmed a fundamental truth Stack had learned about people: They just want a chance.

"Every time there was a new fad or a new program, it was always introduced to us that if we all went out and learned this, we would change the world," says Stack. "In the early days it was management-by-objective. We evolved into material requirements planning. And then the Japanese came along and we all got scared to death, so we learned quality circles and Just-in-Time systems. Then we all learned statistical process control.

"What I began to realize is that we didn't feel people had the intellectual ability to understand what they really needed to do, and what was right. So we had to go down there and teach them. But things didn't change. We still downsized, we still laid people off, and we still didn't do well as a business." He recognized that something more was needed to bring out the best in people.

In 1979, the company shipped Stack off to Springfield, to run its troubled Springfield ReNew Center, a $20 million operation that rebuilt automotive engines. The operation, which employed only 170 workers, was hemorrhaging cash to the tune of about $300,000 a year, due in part to the dreadful morale of its employees, who had invited both the United Auto Workers and the Teamsters in to organize the facility.

The unions never succeeded at the plant, and Stack gradually began to turn things around. He asked employees' opinions, shared financial data, and offered bonuses for those who met financial targets. In the meantime, however, his parent company, International Harvester, started into a nose dive. When Stack learned the company had advertised to sell the Springfield shop, he brought together his top managers to try and buy the plant. Harvester wanted $8.9 million; he and his thirteen managers came up with less than $100,000 in assets.

Stack persuaded a manager at a troubled California bank to grant a loan enabling them to buy the company. With a debt-to-equity ratio of 89 to 1 (leveraged buyouts typically have a debt/equity ratio of 2 to 1), a loan interest rate of 18 percent, $90,000-a-month interest payments, and only $100,000 in available cash, the deal represented what Stack calls one of the most shaky leveraged buyouts in history.

The new company, named Springfield ReManufacturing Corporation, took over in early 1983. Stack began applying his open-book policy, sharing financial and production data with all employees. To make the data meaningful, Stack put everyone, even at entry level, through training courses to help them understand balance sheets, profit-and-loss statements, and other financial reports. This was no mean feat. When he began to teach others about the financial ins and outs of business, he was surprised to learn how unprepared most people were to understand the information. Many lacked fundamental math skills. He realized that before he could educate his employees about common stock and retained earnings, he would first have to help them master long division and compound fractions. Eventually, that obstacle was overcome.

Over the years, and without formal schooling, Stack had picked up a great deal of common-sense wisdom about what he came to call the Great Game of Business, which he began sharing with SRC's employees. His essential philosophy was startling in its simplicity: The more employees learn, the more they can do. He served up "The Higher Laws of Business," a set of folksy adages (Law #2: "It's easy to stop one guy, but it's pretty hard to stop 100." Law #7: "When you raise the bottom, the top rises"). Each of these is the foundation for a deeper Stack truth about how people are motivated to exceed everyone's expectations.

"When I went to school, they told me that to make a product, you needed labor, overhead, and material," he says. "What's been interesting here is to see that there's a fourth element. There's labor, overhead, and material, but there's also intellectual capacity. Intellectual capacity is something that we've scrapped out of the job— just like we scrap out a part that we made wrong. I think allowing a person to sit at a drill press and watch them drill a hole in a forging, then try to measure it to make sure that it falls within the bar chart for statistical process control—you're leaving a tremendous amount of value in that person's mind sitting in that chair. When you can capture that into that forging or into that work order, the value of the product is just absolutely incredible."

If Stack's "Higher Laws" sound like just so much common sense, that common sense has sent SRC's employees—and its earnings—to ever-growing heights of success. Revenues that first year grew by 20 percent, to over $15 million. Ten years later, in 1993, revenues hit $85 million and were still growing. The work force has expanded sixfold since 1983, to 750 employees at 13 SRC-operated plants.

And all those employees can clearly read the company's financial statements, as well as their own stock-ownership accounts, which tell them that shares of the company, after three stock splits, have climbed from 10 cents up to over $18 each, making the employees' stock fund worth about $5.5 million, up from a mere $6,000 at its inception in 1983. As probably any SRC employee can tell you, that amounts to a more than 9,000 percent annual growth rate over ten years.

Beyond that, SRC has spun off more than a dozen new businesses, enterprises conceived of and operated by former SRC employees, in which Stack's company holds some interest. The spin-offs are part of a strategy "to transform SRC into a diversified collection of enterprises and an ongoing business incubator," as Stack puts it. He garners satisfaction and strength from seeing his progeny come into their own in the "Great Game of Business." The employee-owners have the opportunity to acquire the spin-off businesses sometime in the future, whenever they choose to do so.

The benefits of Stack's open-book workplace don't end at the company door. Employees take their enlightenment and empowerment out to their families and the community. "What we call the Great Game of Business is a whole series of small wins," says Stack. "It's making people feel proud about themselves—that they are doing something, that they are accomplishing. That turns on a light inside of them. And they say, 'We don't want to lose that light.' " As a result, SRC employees are among the city's highest per capita contributors to community causes, and among its most dedicated volunteers. "We see people going out and getting involved because they got this glow on, they got this luck, and they don't want to lose it," says Stack. "The way you don't lose it is you go out and you share and help."

For Stack, bringing out the best in employees at work provides the root for a whole host of socially responsible contributions. "If we're going to change the society, if we're going to make a difference, if we're going to be responsible, we've got to get our house in order first," he says. "We've got to use the millions and millions of people in the work force to create a movement. Maybe the press only want to talk to the CEO, but down in the ranks, that's where the change has to occur. What you really need to do is to get people to accept social responsibility—the fact that they do make a difference. The fact that they can contribute to a better community, and they start right within themselves."

A few years ago, it would have been easy to dismiss Jack Stack as an isolated case of a triumph of empowerment over ennui. No longer. Stack's passion for the power of people to perform sets him amid a growing corps of business leaders dedicated to the proposition that business can and should be more than an eight-hour-a-day warehouse of human labor toiling for the benefit of a relative handful.

Where does this new breed of leaders come from? What qualities do they bring to the table that enable them to do business with a broader vision than their colleagues?

There's certainly no universal set of answers. Some, like Jack Stack, came up through the ranks, garnering their business savvy on the job. Others struck out on their own early on, growing their small, entrepreneurial shops into successful enterprises. They represent liberal philosophies and conservative ones, poor upbringings and substantial ones, broken homes and loving, supportive families.

Still, there are some threads that tie many of these leaders together. "They have a deeper understanding of themselves, their customers, their human enterprises, and the connection that their company has to a larger society," observes psychologist Robert H. Rosen, president of Healthy Companies, which studies and advises large and mid-sized companies on organizational health and performance. "They understand the basic principles of human development, that people are the core of what they do, the engine that drives American business. They are the levers that drive a company's competitive advantage. They understand what makes them tick, why they're different, the relationships that people need to have to work hard, and what they want from their relationship to the company." Most important, says Rosen, these leaders understand "how you leverage all that toward a goal and a set of results that adds value to the people that are in the company and to the owners of the company at the same time."

As Rosen observes leaders, he sees them arriving at socially responsible ideals in different ways. "Some leaders get there out of their own development," he says. "Some leaders are either born with it or they bleed in midstream in their life: they have a crisis and grow out of it a different person. And they get it. They understand that their success and other people's success are tied together, and that building these kinds of organizations will in fact help them, society, and people who work for them."

BODY AND SOLE

Arnold Hiatt is an embodiment of Rosen's notion that personal success is linked to making others successful. At age sixty-six, he bridges the gap between the old guard and the new wave, though he doesn't fit neatly into any stereotypes of socially responsible business leaders. Hiatt appears as he is: a mild-mannered, highly successful retired business executive, the product of a generation born and bred on traditional values of personal and business success.

Hiatt helped build the Boston-based Stride Rite Corp. into what is generally regarded as the country's most successful children's shoe company, what the *Harvard Business Review* has called "one of the few true success stories in the U.S. footwear industry." In 1967, Stride Rite—which first shipped shoes in 1919—acquired a small children's shoe company Hiatt had owned for fifteen years. The following year, Hiatt became Stride Rite's president, a position he held until his retirement in 1992. During his tenure, he set in motion a series of innovative programs and policies that made the company a model of corporate caring. In 1971, in a move that was considered radical for a captain of commerce, he introduced the first in-house day care center for both employee and community children at the company's Roxbury, Massachusetts, headquarters; in 1990, after Stride Rite moved its headquarters to Cambridge, the first in-house *intergenerational* day care center was launched on-site, bringing children together with elderly people who needed daytime supervision.

Today, nearly one hundred kids and senior citizens mix daily on the fourth floor of the company's relocated headquarters building in Cambridge. But day care was only a part of Hiatt's legacy. He implemented the nation's first corporate no-smoking policy. He helped create a Stride Rite Scholars Program at Harvard University (Hiatt's alma mater) and Northeastern University, offering scholarships to students who do volunteer work in the inner city. He started a mentoring program, in which Stride Rite employees tutor inner-city students two hours a week for a year—on company time. And early on he offered one of the most liberal family-leave policies in corporate America. When *The New York Times* announced Hiatt's retirement as Stride Rite's chairman in 1992, it called Stride Rite "a sort of guinea pig for corporate America," and Hiatt "one of the nation's best-known corporate do-gooders."

None of Hiatt's efforts seems to have put much of a crimp in Stride Rite's profits—indeed, Hiatt would say they were major contributors. During Hiatt's twenty-four-year stint at the company, Stride Rite's market value grew from $36 million to $1.5 billion, increasing earnings every year between 1971 and 1992, with the exception of a blip in 1984, when Stride Rite acquired the venerable Keds line of sneakers. (During Hiatt's reign, Stride Rite also acquired Sperry Top-Sider, which quickly rose in popularity among the legion of "preppies.") From 1984 to 1992, Stride Rite's financial performance ranked among the top 1 percent of companies listed on the New York Stock Exchange. If you had bought $10,000 worth of Stride Rite stock in 1984, your investment would have been worth $156,000 eight years later when Hiatt retired—a 36 percent compounded annual increase.

This combination of business acumen and progressive management has turned Hiatt into a kind of founding father of socially responsible business, a distinction he declines with his characteristic modesty. In fact, Hiatt doesn't even like the term "social responsibility." As a founding board member of BSR, he led an unsuccessful campaign to have the group's name changed to "Business for *Corporate* Responsibility." "I wish there were another way of communicating whatever it is we mean when we talk about social responsibility," he says, sitting in his office overlooking Boston Harbor. "The words become trite or abused, or maybe mean different things to different people. I find it easier to talk about values and vision. I guess if I had to make a distinction between a company that has social responsibility as a point of view, as opposed to a company that doesn't, I would characterize the first company as taking a broader view of what the role of business is and not separating stockholders and the bottom line from employees and the community."

One hallmark of Hiatt's success in implementing workplace and community programs was his ability to get past such natural barriers, to "sell" them to his board of directors—like most boards, a group whose natural tendency is to see such programs as a distraction from the business of making shoes, and profits. He persevered, making a business case for his ideas and innovations. "When we introduced child care for the community in the inner city in our Roxbury facility in 1971, it was considered somewhat alien to the corporate mission, which I could understand," recalls Hiatt. "But as employees participated, sent their children to this day care center that we supported, right in the Stride Rite facility, they began to feel pretty good about the company. They went from distrust to feeling that maybe this company cares, and in subtle ways a commitment to the company became more extensive."

By demonstrating increased employee commitment—and the resulting ability to recruit and retain the best people, inspiring loyalty, productivity, and innovation—Hiatt helped board members see the benefits of day care. Says Hiatt: "It's really the stockholders who empower us. They provide us with the capital. They have an expectation that there is going to be a return on their capital. That's something none of us can ever forget. Some business people forget what their mission is. You hear about arrogant managers who are no longer mindful of what their true role is. If those traditional business people recognize that they are custodians of other people's capital, then they can maybe become more reflective on how to improve return on investment. By just cutting costs indiscriminately? One way is to address needs in the workplace, like day care. Improving morale improves productivity as well.

"It all comes back to my sensitivity to the words 'socially responsible.' I think it's important to stay away from any kind of vocabulary that is in any way suggestive of righteousness or even morality. That's not to suggest that the traditional business person is immoral or amoral, but morality has not necessarily been a part of the culture or the development of the corporate mind. I don't know how you can teach ethics, but there are other ways of developing a sensitivity to what I think is a broader mission. It isn't by talking about ethical behavior. It's talking about economic rationales for doing what you do."

Reflecting on his career at Stride Rite, Hiatt views initiatives like day care and intergenerational care centers as the things that sustained him. "They gave some meaning to my life. I told the board I'd stay on for seven years when I took over the presidency. But there was always a reason why I had to stay: I was in the middle of an acquisition, I had to turn Keds around, or we were starting the retail division. But just doing the same things didn't give me enough satisfaction. For me it was self-serving. I've said, and I mean it, Ivan Boesky was half right when he said, 'Greed is good.' I say, *enlightened* self-interest is better because it's *my* interest, satisfying some needs of mine as well. But that process didn't in any way interfere with satisfying the needs of the stockholders or the community or the employees. They reinforced one other because there was a mutuality of interest."

THE BIG POWER OF SMALL BUSINESS

When Helen Mills was eight years old, she and her sister operated a candy stand in their Atlanta neighborhood. During times of slow sales, Mills would haul out her father's cane fishing pole and attach a sign on the hook: "Candy." As cars passed, she would dangle the sign in front of them in the hopes of reeling in business.

Mills has been hooking customers ever since. An indefatigable owner of two thriving businesses—the Mills Group, an employee benefits and insurance-counseling firm, and Soapbox Trading Company, which operates five franchises of The Body Shop retail chain—she is also one of the leading advocates for socially responsible business practices.

This mix of dogma and doggedness is vintage Mills, a self-described workaholic who lives to work—and loves to work. In describing Mills, her friends, family, and business associates all refer to her zest, humor, and drive. "She has an unstoppable energy and joie de vivre which has driven her forward since she came out of the womb," says Mary Ann Mills, her younger sister and business partner. "She idles at a very high pace." Business for Helen Mills is far more than merely a means of making money. Rather, it is a vehicle for interacting with people and companies, and influencing both through her vision and values.

As she looks around, she is generally heartened by the changes in attitudes she sees taking place among business leaders. But she is also concerned about what she considers to be antiquated business attitudes toward employees. "As an employee benefits consultant, I sit in the executive planning sessions, human resources departments, and boardroom discussions of how companies will spend their money and what employees, in executives' minds, deserve or need," Mills says. "And I'm fascinated with how they go about the internal struggle of whose dollar is going to pay for it—will it be the corporate dollar or the employee dollar? Companies are really behind the eight ball in how they perceive their employees' value to the corporation. They don't understand what employees' contributions are. They look at them more as a cost center instead of a very productive asset. As we move toward the millennium, looking at the productivity of these employees and the company as a whole is going to be extremely important."

Mills has strived to set a good example in her own relationships with employees. She runs her consulting business on a philosophy of "I'll take care of you if you take care of me," she says. "It's a very symbiotic environment, where a person comes to me and says, 'Helen, I'm getting ready to have my second child and I'd like to work three days.' I say, 'Okay, let's figure out how we can do it.' And we do it. There's no firing them to make room for another full-time person; we accommodate. I know that I get 110 percent out of that person every single minute of every day that she's on the job. You can't trade that for anything. It's having a family, a connected kind of environment."

The bigger challenge comes in her five retail stores, an environment not known for its commitment to retaining employees. Of Soapbox Trading's sixty or so employees, about a quarter of them work full time. In 1994, nine of them celebrated their five-year anniversaries with Mills's company, an astonishing longevity record in an industry that often experiences 200 percent annual turnover.

Mills doesn't seem surprised at this feat. For her, it is the logical result of treating employees with respect. "We invest in our employees through training, and by addressing their problems through employee assistance programs to help with all the stresses of living," she says. "It doesn't matter whether it is financial or work-related. Companies must ante up to take care of many of the personal needs of employees in order to have a work force. It is those values that permeate and penetrate every facet of business. I'm talking about quality of life, quality of the product, quality of communications within an organization. And considering the human aspects of all these things."

Mills's two private enterprises have created a platform for her public life as mentor and role model supporting women and minorities in small business, and as an advocate for social responsibility. She is an active member of such groups as BSR, the Points of Light Foundation, the Social Venture Network, the National Association of Women Business Owners, the Ms. Foundation, and an advisory committee member of the U.S. Small Business Administration—all organizations that help entrepreneurs and companies flourish and link them with the needs of employees, communities, and the environment. She has been called to testify before Congress on health care. These activities are where the salesmanship Mills mastered while building two successful enterprises is called into action. She frequently makes presentations or keynote speeches on behalf of these groups, and often can be found selling executives on one or more of their philosophies or programs, spreading her vision of business's potential in helping fill society's unmet needs. By doing so, Mills has served a vital role in the growth of socially responsible business, bridging the gap between the business and nonprofit worlds, and between big companies and small ones.

As the first and largest franchiser of The Body Shop stores in the United States, Mills's Soapbox Trading Company has helped set the standard for other franchisees. "It is very important that our companies succeed," she says. "Anita Roddick [who founded the entire chain] calls The Body Shop a grand experiment. I don't know that it's an experiment; I think it's a necessity. Every consumer dollar spent there is another vote of success, another demonstrable step in the progression to say that a company can have principles and profits at the same time. They are not mutually exclusive terms."

Being at the front line of sales, Mills is convinced that consumer support for socially responsible businesses will be crucial in persuading company leaders of the importance of addressing the needs of employees, communities, and the environment. She knows that employees respond, too. "It's part of being an American citizen. It's part of our heritage, the American values. Wouldn't you want your company to be as good a citizen as you expect yourself to be? And if you think about [the fact] that you're investing eight to ten hours a day at your company—in some cases fourteen to sixteen—wouldn't you want it to be a place you were proud of?"

The greatest barrier, she says, is executives' fear of change. And Mills spends an inordinate amount of time, both personal and professional, trying to convince business leaders that change is not only important, it is inevitable. "You look at the major corporations who have been digging their heels in, spending millions of dollars on lobbying, trying to get congressmen, the tax code, everything, to try and protect their approach to business, instead of taking that money and investing it in research and development and their people. Companies are not going to be able to fight the change. The market is going to push, push, push. If you are spending all your money trying to keep things the way they were, forget it. You are going to lose."

Ultimately, says Mills, company leaders must recognize the tremendous power they wield by making incremental but meaningful changes in their policies and practices. "There are choices that we make all down the line," she says. "Simple little things that impact profoundly when you begin to aggregate them. We are doing the convenient things. Now it's time to do the thoughtful things."

THE VALUE OF VALUES

Robert Haas, chairman of Levi Strauss & Company, has been known to hole up in the mountains of California for several days at a time with employees to talk about such intangibles as empowerment, diversity, values, and "psychic ownership." It is all part of Haas's vision to mix the "hard stuff" with the "soft stuff."

"In the past," he says, "we always talked about the 'hard stuff' and the 'soft stuff.' The soft stuff was the company's commitment to our work force. And the hard stuff was what really mattered: getting the pants out the door. What we've learned is that the soft stuff and the hard stuff are becoming increasingly intertwined. Values are where the hard stuff and the soft stuff come together. A company's values—what it stands for, what its people believe in—are crucial to its competitive success. Indeed, values drive the business."

Values have helped drive Levi Strauss in a big way. In 1984, when Haas at age forty-three took over the helm of his family's company after spending years working there in a variety of positions and departments, he experienced what he later admitted was "stark terror": "We were a company in crisis," he recalls. "Our sales were dropping, our international business was heading for a loss, our domestic business had eroded its profit base, our diversification wasn't working, and we had too much production capacity. I had no bold plan of action."

A decade later, Levi Strauss—the company started in the 1850s by Haas's great-great-granduncle, the young immigrant for which it is named—has turned around. Today, with annual sales approaching $6 billion, it is the world's largest apparel maker and one of the world's five most recognized brands. One of the company's product lines, Dockers, has generated annual sales of close to $1 billion. To put that in perspective, Levi's as a whole took 125 years before its sales reached the billion-dollar mark.

Beyond the financial success are the respect and plaudits Levi Strauss has received in almost all aspects of business. The company's employees have been imbued with a sense of vision and empowerment rarely seen in a business of this size. The company's overall employee benefits package is, according to *Money* magazine, better than that offered by any other American company. Levi Strauss is an acknowledged leader in philanthropy, community involvement, and corporate environmentalism. It has set the standard for ethics among business, both domestically and internationally.

Haas is quick to credit these successes to the change in attitude of his company's 36,000 worldwide employees. But such dramatic changes require more than changed attitudes. They require a vision, and a bold one at that. In the case of Levi Strauss, that bold vision came when Haas recognized that the top-down, authoritarian, hierarchical organizational model that had been the norm at his and most other large companies wasn't working. What was needed, as he described it several years later, was "an enormous diffusion of power." In a word, empowerment.

"If companies are going to react quickly to changes in the marketplace, they have to put more and more accountability, authority, and information into the hands of the people who are closest to the products and the customers," says Haas, a former Peace Corps volunteer, Harvard business school graduate, and White House fellow. "That requires new business strategies and different organizational structures."

But structure and strategy aren't enough, says Haas. What's also needed are values. "It's the *ideas* of a business that are controlling, not some manager with authority," he says. "Values provide a common language for aligning a company's leadership and its people."

As a result, Levi Strauss has become a values-driven company, beginning with a corporate "Aspirations Statement," a 1987 initiative Haas headed to define the shared values that will guide both management and workers. "We all want a company that our people are proud of and committed to," the statement begins, "where all employees have an opportunity to contribute, learn, grow, and advance based on merit, not politics or background. We want our people to feel respected, treated fairly, listened to, and involved. Above all, we want satisfaction from accomplishments and friendships, balanced personal and professional lives, and to have fun in our endeavors."

From there, the Aspirations Statement goes on to define the type of leadership necessary to make the aspirations a reality: diversity and recognition, communications and empowerment, ethical management practices and "new behaviors."

Levi Strauss's aspirations are not mere window dressing. Consider the approach Haas took to a small group of minority and women managers who approached him in the mid-1980s to talk about what they felt were barriers keeping them from rising in the organization. Though the company had a longtime commitment to equal employment opportunity and employed a relatively high number of women and minority managers, Haas decided to organize an off-site retreat. He paired ten senior managers, all white and male, together with either a woman or a minority manager for two and a half days of discussion that tapped the reservoir of frustration that existed among the managers. That event led to sixteen additional such encounters between white male managers and women or minorities, and to a series of monthly forums held by the company's executive management committee and small groups of fifteen to twenty employees, which continue today. Originally, the forums were to focus on matters of race and gender, but they have expanded to cover a broad range of workplace issues.

Haas recognizes that his company's future competitiveness depends on the ability of Levi Strauss employees to trust one another and to respect the firm for which they work. That strategy can be seen in an unprecedented affirmative action policy, which became a role model for other companies when it offered benefits to gay partners of employees and unmarried heterosexual partners.

Haas's vision of employee well-being is part of his company's effort to push decision making increasingly farther down the line. "The fact is, we can no longer compete solely on the basis of cost," he says. "U.S. businesses interested in achieving enduring success must invest in their people and involve them in running the enterprise. In other words, those of us in the corner office will have to relinquish power and transfer greater responsibility to our front-line people—those who design and produce our products and who serve our customers. That is how America will continue to compete."

Haas's belief in empowerment seems to be working. The company is in the process of reinventing itself to take advantage of dynamic changes in the apparel business. As a result of the growing empowerment, says Haas, "We will be able to make changes to existing products—adding a new color, a new finish, or whatever—with a lead time of thirty days from when we have the idea until it's in the store. We can have a completely new product in the stores in ninety days from the time the idea is created. Currently, it takes anywhere from seven months to a year to create a new product."

This is the essence of Haas's strategy: Make your employees a success, in all senses of the word, and they will make your company successful, too. "The most visible differences between the corporation of the future and its present-day counterpart will be the makeup of its work force, relationships of its people," stresses Haas. "Not the types of products they make or the equipment they use in factories—although these certainly will be different. But *who* is working, *how* they will be working, *why* they will be working, and *what* work will mean to them."

SWEET SUCCESS

Elliot Hoffman's company is Just Desserts, a San Francisco–based bakery whose breads and pastries are found in 600 northern California restaurants, hotels, and supermarkets, as well as the company's ten owned-and-operated retail stores. Founded in 1974 by Hoffman, his wife Gail Horvath, and a friend, the company began with a cheesecake recipe Hoffman used to bake a cake for Horvath's twenty-fourth birthday. After deciding to start a baking business in their home, they sold their Volkswagen Bug to raise the necessary $500 of startup capital. Today, Just Desserts has grown to nearly 400 employees, $15 million in annual sales, and an enviable reputation.

Growth and success are the least of what make Hoffman a standout in the world of business. Just Desserts is often viewed as a model for balancing equality, diversity, and financial success. As he tours his company's 31,000-square-foot plant, he points with pride to the assemblage of employees representing a range of backgrounds and lifestyles. "From the beginnings, we were pretty clear that we didn't care where you were from, what color, race, or age you were, whether you are gay, lesbian, straight, man or woman—any and all opportunities are open to you as long as you did your job well and got along with your co-workers," he says.

A quick look around the plant is telling. On the main baking crew there's Phuc from Vietnam, who's been with Just Desserts for twelve years; Tika from Indonesia, a ten-year veteran; and Mike—"the white guy from New Jersey," as Hoffman calls him—an employee for fifteen years. There's Miguel and Javier from Mexico, and Micki and Sala—"lesbians, falling in love by the ovens," says Hoffman.

"I like to think that Just Desserts is one of those emerging-yet-imperfect models of what business can be, now and into the future," says the forty-seven-year-old Hoffman. "It's not utopia. We have our disagreements like everyone else. But it's not over race or culture. We have learned to live and work with each other. I'm very proud of the level of human respect at Just Desserts."

Hoffman grew up in the Bronx. His father was "a very community-involved person," and caring for community has become part and parcel of Hoffman's passion as well. "It's either in my genes or it's part of my own attempt to live up to my father's standard," he says. Just Desserts has become a leading force in San Francisco for community involvement and social change. The company sponsors the Garden Project, a highly successful, innovative post-release program that helps former prisoners at San Francisco County Jail use gardening to make the transition back to society. The project's aim is to empower its "students" by helping them to heal the environment, their communities, and, ultimately, themselves. (More about the project in chapter 8.) Hoffman tries whenever possible to hire disadvantaged youths from the Hunter's Point neighborhood surrounding his plant. He is the driving force behind several projects that bring local businesses together to solve local problems—from education to homelessness to drug abuse. And he serves on the San Francisco Chamber of Commerce, standing out as a contrapuntal voice of entrepreneurship and social vision amid a choir of mainstream business interests.

His socially responsible efforts aren't all focused outside the company. Hoffman pays his workers well—he studies industry averages, then makes sure he betters them—and offers all workers liberal benefits. Everyone, from Hoffman on down to line workers, gets the same generous health plan. And everyone—again, from Hoffman on down—is expected to put in time on the bakery floor, mixing dough, packaging brownies, or doing whatever else is needed.

For Hoffman, it's all part of a very natural way of doing business—and living one's life. "I would say that I have a spiritual sense of things that has no national boundaries, no color or gender boundaries, just human beings. And I have a very strong sense that humanity has a great potential." He scoffs at the notion that his vision is a product of the flower-child generation. "To be frank with you, one of the attitudes that I picked up in the sixties was actually detrimental to our business. That was the idea that profit was inherently evil—a four-letter word. We were just fortunate that we made money in spite of ourselves. I finally got to the point, after a few years, when I realized that money, in and of itself, wasn't bad. It was merely a matter of how you made it and what you did with it. Profit wasn't the end, it was the means. And profits made by paying people as little as you can get away with were not the kind of profits we would be proud of. Taking profits and merely stuffing one's pockets without regard to anyone else is not the wisest and best use of profits.

"My own passion for my fellow man and woman pervades my being, and I do what I can to share that passion in our community," says Hoffman. "Hopefully, my leadership style is reflective of that passion. As working people, we and our employees spend nearly half of our waking hours in our world. Why can't it be fulfilling and have meaning? Shouldn't our workplaces be the kind of environments that we want to spend our work lives in? Certainly, we at Just Desserts have our workplace challenges and issues, but clearly our heart and passion is there to continually improve."

BUILDING BRIDGES

That Debbie Aguirre finds herself at the top of something called a "socially responsible business" comes as no surprise to her. The idea that companies should give something back to the local community is to Aguirre as much a part of doing business as cost estimating and project scheduling. "I feel very privileged to be allowed to play in the Great Game of Business," she says. "And it's a very fun game. Giving something back is my little way of saying thank you and that I am very appreciative of that."

Aguirre is the first to admit that she is something of an anomaly: in a field dominated by white males, she is a Hispanic female who is founder and president of Tierra Pacifica Corporation, a young and growing construction and engineering firm based in southern California. Her company, founded in 1992, develops primarily public projects, things like libraries and fire stations. In addition to that, it focuses on building affordable housing for both public and private developers. In 1994, its second full year of business, Aguirre expected the company to see about $10 million in revenue.

Aguirre, who grew up in the Los Angeles area, didn't expect to go into the construction business. In fact, growing up, she didn't have much direction at all. "It was naturally assumed that I would marry young and have a brood," she says. "I think I was probably unimaginative and couldn't quite come up with anything. I had never really thought about a career." For a time she considered teaching, but was discouraged, partly by the low wages. Then her mother suggested real estate, which turned out to be "a perfect fit."

Her career path eventually led her to work for a large national developer. As a real estate generalist, Aguirre acquired a broad range of experience. "My job was to go out and find a piece of land, put together the concept of what we were going to build, work with the cities, finance, build, project-manage, lease, and perhaps dispose of the property." One particular part of that process became her passion. It has to do with a process called "exaction." In many California cities, as in other parts of the country, developers are required to give something back whenever they build a project of significant size. In exchange for permission to erect an office building, for example, a developer might be expected to build a park or a day care center.

At one project, in Thousand Oaks, north of Los Angeles, Aguirre managed construction of a 160-unit apartment building. "The exaction that came to play in this particular project was that the city wanted a senior day care center built," recalls Aguirre. "So the city manager called one day and introduced me to a nonprofit senior care provider and said, 'I think it is a very good idea for the two of you to meet and see what you can do.' It was very obvious to me what they wanted. And over a period of meetings, it was determined that I could donate some land to them and build them a shell of a building." Over time, the exaction portion of Aguirre's construction projects became more fulfilling than the principal project. "They were more in alignment with what my core beliefs were," she says. At times, she found that balancing the two aspects of a development project—the principal project and the exaction—created some internal tension: while her primary role was to get the best deal possible for her employer, deep inside she also wanted to get the best deal possible for the community. This internal tug of war eventually led her to quit her job. "I realized that what I had been doing was placating the part of myself that knew and believed very firmly in making the world a little bit better every day. But it's not the ethic that I had been trained with in my corporate career."

While considering her next move, she was offered a job running a newly formed banking consortium that specialized in affordable housing. She took the job, got things up and running, but left after a year. "I realized very quickly that working for a nonprofit board of directors was not my cup of tea. I wanted action, and what I got was policy and procedure and a lot of different people's agendas."

She decided to start Tierra Pacifica, and things soon blossomed. Within a few months, Aguirre's fledgling company formed a long-term joint venture with a large construction company that provided some operating capital and the ability to leapfrog into much bigger projects. Today, Tierra Pacifica employs thirteen full-time workers.

For Aguirre, having her own business is an opportunity to realize her notion of the importance of community—both her community of employees and subcontractors and the larger communities in which she develops projects. "We have a corporate commitment that every time we do a job we will leave something behind in that community," she says. "For example, we did a single-family project in a local coastal city when we first started our company. We identified a number of existing social service agencies and we went to those agencies and tried to determine what their needs were. We were lucky enough to find a battered women's shelter close by that was in particular need of goods and services. We held a food drive, asked for the participation of a number of local retailers, stores, as well as our own subcontractors. In that particular case there were thirty-six different subcontracting firms on the project. We had carpenters and plumbers and electricians and each of those were small companies who had a labor force they would bring out. We held a food drive to refill the pantry at this battered women's shelter. We asked for baby clothing and diapers as well as canned goods. And we presented them with a check as well as the food we had accumulated."

In effect, Aguirre has instituted her own system of exaction to feed her own needs as well as the community's. "I feel very lucky to be in business," she explains. "It's not a right, it's a gift we're given. So the way we look at this is that when we go into a city and we build something, we pay a fee and we hire local people, and that contributes to an economy. But what we want to do as our way of giving thanks is to say, 'Let us do a little something for your community that will last hopefully beyond the time that we are in your community working.' So in my mind, I would like to see a map of southern California and other places where we work and see a little pin in every place we've given a little bit. If our firm does that and other firms do that, it lessens the need of government and other agencies to participate."

Why bother? Why not forgo the charity work, make more money, and hire more local community members with the profits? For Aguirre, the answer has to do with a balance in her life between business and the rest of daily living. "If we were dealing in a world that was only about business, that would be fine," she explains. "But my world is not only about business. No one's world is only about business. Business is what we do to earn our money. Granted, we spend the majority of our time here, and it is because I spend the majority of my time working in business that it's important for me for it to be as well rounded as possible and for it to include all the values that I hold near and dear."

For Aguirre, business is also about helping—customers, employees, communities, and others. "If 10 percent of the companies in the United States did this, we could have a huge impact. Would it make a difference? Yes, clearly it could make a difference in the quality of our lives. Could it make enough of a difference? I don't know. But I don't know if that's really the point. The point is that by doing this we take our power back and we are no longer hopeless and helpless about the lives that we lead."

Aguirre sees the participation of the business community in improving people's lives as an inevitable evolution. "Business is undergoing a transformation that is just as large as when we moved from the Victorian age into the industrial age," she says. "I don't think we're even going to see the end for perhaps another decade or so. Things are moving very fast for us right now. We're undergoing a tremendous amount of change. And we're having to absorb an awful lot of data to adjust to that change. And I think social responsibility is a part of that. We are recognizing that government cannot solve our problems. We are recognizing that the quality of our life is diminishing, that our communities are diminishing. We have watched our family structure change. It's a reality. We can't go back."

Chapter Four

Beyond the Bottom Line

"Our success will be measured not only by growth in share-holder value, but also by our reputation, the quality of our constituency relationships, and our commitment to social responsibility."

—LEVI STRAUSS & CO.
business vision statement

How do you measure success? In business, there's only one real way: the bottom line. Of course, there are many "bottom lines"—pre-tax profits, return on assets, stock price, return on equity, sales growth, earnings-to-assets ratio, and many more. In all cases, the end product is some quantifiable result that can be tracked, compared, and otherwise analyzed.

So, how do you measure the success of being socially responsible? There are no universally accepted social accounting systems yet developed along the lines of the Generally Accepted Accounting Principles, to which the financial community faithfully adheres. For all the academics researching and theorizing on the topic, there are no workable models from which to borrow. Still, a number of companies consider their socially responsible programs and policies successful, in business as well as nonbusiness terms. When asked to describe their success, these business leaders may point to both the tangible (increased sales, reduced energy costs, higher stock price, increased employee retention, fewer product defects) and the intangible (higher customer loyalty, improved employee morale, increased goodwill). But for the time being, they must rely more on anecdotal than empirical evidence.

What's needed is a new language and a new system of accounting, a broader balance sheet. Regulators, shareholders, employees, community leaders, the media, and consumers are all taking a deeper interest in the many impacts of businesses and industries, leaving some companies scrambling for the tools and language to respond.

The challenge to companies to account for the impact of their operations—both internally and externally—is one of several streams of influence affecting business these days. Together, these streams seem to be converging into a formidable current, leaving companies to ponder a strategy: Do they go with the swift flow, accommodating each of the many demands for policy changes, new programs, and disclosure? Do they paddle upstream, resisting such efforts? Do they wait, drifting for a while, in the hopes that calmer waters lie ahead? Or do they adapt, steering a course that allows them an expeditious journey to their destination?

In this chapter and the next we'll examine some of the more formidable streams of influence affecting companies, including

- the growing demands for companies to account for their impacts on their workers, the environment, and on society;

The bottom line follows everything else. We say in our company that profit is like breathing; it's required. So we don't pay a hell of a lot of attention to it. What we pay attention to is creating an environment, setting up the circumstances and the goals, so that people can do the work that produces the bottom line.

—JAMES AUTRY,
former president, Magazine Group, Meredith Corporation

- the demand for companies to adopt formal mission statements integrating a policy of socially responsible ideals;
- investors' concern over the links between financial performance and company social and environmental responsibility, and their growing leverage to impact company policy; and
- consumers' concern about the social and environmental performance of companies, and their willingness to vote their conscience in the marketplace.

Not all of these are a factor for every company, and each affects companies differently. It is in the aggregate that we believe these forces will have long-term impact on the way companies do business in coming years.

ACCOUNTING AND ACCOUNTABILITY

Considering any socially responsible policy or program rationally requires companies to get a firm handle on things: to be able to translate the many tangibles and intangibles into the traditional language of profits and productivity, and to use this information as a means for making strategic decisions.

Traditional accounting methods tell us how to track the *costs* of company initiatives, but not necessarily the *benefits* to a company. For example, we know how to account for the cost of training, but we haven't yet developed an effective means for plugging in the value to the company of the smarter, better-qualified employees that result

> If you were to ask people at Ben & Jerry's why they work here, 80 to 90 percent of them would tell you because of the social mission, even if they can't fully define to you what they think that means. The people who work here are highly motivated. They know there is an aspect to their job that goes beyond the day-to-day task. They feel they are part of a greater good.
>
> —LIZ BANKOWSKI,
> *director of social missions, Ben & Jerry's Homemade*

from training, or the resulting productivity and innovation—let alone from such benefits as having safer neighborhoods for employees to live in, or cleaner water for them to drink, or less stress about child care. Yet all of these outcomes of corporate programs inure to the benefit of companies, in the form of increased motivation and productivity, decreased absenteeism, fewer health claims, reduced turnover and training costs, increased employee retention, decreased fines and penalties, and lower materials costs through greater efficiencies.

"When you look at a balance sheet, labor is viewed as a cost," says Robert Rosen, president of Healthy Companies, the Washington, D.C., firm which advises large and mid-sized companies on organizational health and performance. "Salary is a cost item. Benefits is another cost item. When somebody gets sick, it's a greater cost item. Worker compensation programs, disability claims, turnover, absenteeism— all cost items. Our accounting systems are set up to measure people, our principal asset, as depreciating costs, not appreciating assets. So many of our internal measures of success don't capture the value that the company has in such things as enhancing organizational learning, the health and well-being of a worker, or in cultivating commitment because you treated that person's family well in a time of crisis."

The best developed measurement systems center on environmental performance. Most large and many small manufacturing companies now routinely conduct environmental audits to assess their regulatory compliance, measure their emissions of everything from waste paper to hazardous chemicals, or identify opportunities for improvement. Perhaps more common are simple cause-and-effect calculations of company efficiencies or pollution reductions based on specific initiatives or investments. For example, Niagara-Mohawk, an electric utility serving most of upstate New York, set up a program to find markets for its waste and scrap. With a $640,000 annual operating budget and a staff of about seventy-five, the department earned more than $7 million in a single year by recycling some of its waste and selling surplus materials. Similarly impressive statistics abound throughout corporate America—among both large and small companies—a testament as much to the ability to calculate tangible savings as to companies' environmental efforts.

Increasingly, companies are being able to attribute hard cost savings to some of the "softer" areas of business. As we shall see in chapter 7, companies such as Fel-Pro and Aetna have quantified huge financial returns to their companies from such factors as increased employee motivation, productivity, and retention. "Our experience shows that there is a significant return to the company in employee performance, commitment, and productivity from our socially responsible strategies," says Elliot Lehman, chairman emeritus of Fel-Pro, which makes automobile parts. "We increase our competitiveness with these strategies and policies."

Back on the environmental side, a few companies are using life-cycle assessments, which attempt to measure the "cradle-to-grave" environmental impact of a product, process, or company—from its inception through its manufacturing, sale, use, and ultimate disposal. But even this tool is in its nascent stages, involving equal parts art and science, and is far from widely accepted, despite years of development by task forces involving academics, scientists, corporate managers, and government researchers. And while life-cycle assessments are now being put to use in some companies, it will be a while before the process achieves any reasonable level of standardization. So it seems even less likely that there will soon be a generally agreed-upon means of measuring and valuing some of the so-called softer aspects of the social impacts of business.

In the meantime, several academic studies have generated some compelling bottom-line evidence of the payoff for social responsibility. In 1992, for example, Stephen E. Erfle and Michael J. Fratantuono, economics professors at Dickinson College in Pennsylvania, analyzed the links between companies' social performance and their profitability. Their finding: A positive correlation exists between financial performance and several dimensions of social responsibility.

The two economists linked financial performance with social performance by comparing eight standard measures of companies' economic performance with ratings given those companies by the Council on Economic Priorities (CEP), a New York–based research group. Since 1986, CEP has compiled ratings of thousands of consumer products, based on their manufacturers' records on a variety of social issues, including environmental performance, advancement of women, promotion of minorities, charitable contributions, community outreach programs, research conducted on animals, military sector involvement, nuclear power involvement, and disclosure of information. CEP gathers information from media reports, questionnaires filled out by the companies themselves, and other sources, such as the Center for Science in the Public Interest, labor unions, and outside advisers. Companies then have a chance to review, correct, and otherwise comment on their ratings before the data are released.

The fruits of these labors are published in an annual paperback guidebook called *Shopping for a Better World*, intended for use by consumers who want to base purchases at least in part on these social issues. It is an imperfect rating system—for example, some environmentally questionable products may get high environmental ratings because the companies that produce them generally don't pollute—but the book has won popularity not only with the public but with many in the business sector. Some companies that rated poorly in one or more areas have approached CEP to seek ways to improve their ratings in subsequent editions.

Erfle and Fratantuono's study attempted to test the hypothesis that "strong social performance is associated with strong financial performance." They reasoned that "good social performers may find it easier to win concessions from workers, draw customers, and, given the reduced probability of costly government-imposed sanctions, attract investors." To test this, they compared companies' ratings in *Shopping for a Better World* with their bottom-line results. They assumed their findings would demonstrate, and perhaps measure, the financial costs to companies for their highly regarded social performance.

The two economists did not find significant costs; instead, they found that being socially responsible at worst had no financial impact and in some cases had a strong positive financial payoff. This was most evident in the environmental category. Compared to the bottom-ranked companies, the top-rated companies were found to have

- 16.7 percent higher operating income growth
- 13.3 percent higher sales-to-assets ratio
- 9.3 percent higher sales growth
- 4.5 percent higher return on equity
- 4.4 percent higher earnings-to-assets ratio
- 3.9 percent higher return on investment
- 2.2 percent higher return on assets
- 1.9 percent higher asset growth

The study also concluded that companies rated highly for community outreach also had significantly higher return of equity, return on investment, and operating income growth. Overall, a positive relationship exists among five dimensions of social performance: environmental performance; promotion of women; promotion of minorities; charitable contributions; and community outreach programs. (There was at least one interesting surprise: Erfle and Fratan-tuono concluded that "firms which tend to have women on the board of directors or at the VP level or higher also tend to have lower growth rates." They had no explanation for this.)

THE LINK BETWEEN SOCIAL RESPONSIBILITY AND PROFITS

The Erfle-Fratantuono study is only one of a growing number of efforts by academics in recent years to discern a link—or lack there-of—between social responsibility and corporate performance. And although the evidence to date is mixed, there is some compelling evidence that an empirical relationship exists. In 1994, Elissa Sheri-dan of Levi Strauss & Company amassed a comprehensive collection to date of these studies. A sampling:

• A 1988 study at the University of Massachusetts, which linked financial performance to *Fortune* magazine's ratings of corporate rep-utations—gathered from surveys sent annually to 8,000 executives—found that firms low in social responsibility had lower returns on assets and stock market returns than those rated highly in social responsibility.

• A 1993 study at Wright State University in Dayton, Ohio, found that managers believe corporate actions have an effect on perceived market share. Participants filled out a questionnaire asking them to rate the perceived effect of a number of socially responsible issues on their organization's market share. Of the nine issues, corporate ac-tions related to environmental pollution, corporate philanthropy, and disclosure of social information were perceived to have the greatest effect.

• A 1993 study at Rutgers University examined the relationship between workplace practices—such things as promotion systems, incentive systems, grievance procedures, and labor-management par-ticipation—and financial performance of 700 publicly held firms. Us-ing an index of "best practice" prevalence, the study concluded that the 25 percent of firms scoring highest on the index performed substantially higher on key financial performance measures than lower-rated companies. For example, firms in the top 25 percent had an 11 percent gross rate of return on capital, more than twice as high as the remaining firms.

• A 1994 study at Florida International University that tried to link social performance with financial performance found a significant positive relationship between social responsibility and growth in sales, return on assets, and asset age. Corporate social responsibility was also significantly related to free cash flow and debt to equity over the long term.

• A 1994 study that tracked companies' financial performance with their workplace reputations found that those with a broad reputation for good workplace practices overwhelmingly had higher price-to-book valuation ratios than their industry peers. The study, by the Gordon Group of Waban, Massachusetts, also found that companies with substandard reputations on workplace issues had lower price-to-book and price-to-sales valuation ratios than companies well regarded for these practices. Moreover, concluded the researchers, "a large portion of companies with the worst reputations on workplace issues are either taken over or experience bankruptcy."

Professor Donna Wood of Pittsburgh believes these efforts to measure the financial impact of social responsibility will continue to grow and become more comprehensive, and finds precedent in the world of environmental auditing. "I remember reading papers from 1970 to the effect that it wouldn't ever be possible to come up with a calculus of environmental costs and benefits, that it was just too complex and we didn't understand enough about it," she says. "And then in 1970 there was an interesting little paper published in *Fortune* by an economist who had spent some time trying to sort out how to understand environmental costs and benefits. He went and asked people how much they would pay to go fishing in an unpolluted stream or river. He tried to figure out how much more often people had to dry clean their clothes in major cities than they do in small towns because of the smog. How real estate values decline around industrial areas. And how often you have to paint your house because of acid rain. It was only the beginning, and over the next twenty-five years people have really jumped on the environmental costs-and-benefits bandwagon because it's become clear that you can sort this stuff out; it's just complex. And you can assign a value to natural resources, recyclables, and energy being used. So I'm not sure

The Walker Study

In 1994, the first annual Walker: Reputation and Social Performance Assessment presented a strong case for socially responsible business practices. The national study, based on interviews with 1,037 households, was conducted during April and May of 1994 by Walker Research, a business unit of the Indianapolis, Indiana–based Walker Group, a research firm that specializes in measuring the impact of social responsibility on the bottom line.

Among the study's findings:

- Twenty-six percent of potential investors say social responsibility and good corporate citizenship are extremely important to their investment decisions.
- Thirty-nine percent of current or previous investors say they always or frequently check on business practices and values before investing. Twenty-one percent say they always do.
- While quality, price, and service are still the most important determinants for a purchase by consumers, 92 percent of consumers are much less or somewhat less likely to buy from a company that is not socially responsible and not a good corporate citizen. Seventy percent say they won't buy from this type of company even if the product or service price is substantially discounted.
- Eighty-eight percent of the public is much or somewhat more likely to buy from a company that is socially responsible and a good corporate citizen, all other things being equal.
- Thirteen percent say they always or frequently seek information about a company's practices or ethics before purchasing.
- Thirty-five percent say they always or frequently avoid a product or service from a company perceived to be unethical.

The Walker Study (continued)

- When asked to name the top factors considered when rating a company as a prospective employer, respondents most frequently cited employee treatment, ethical business practices, product or service quality, financial history, and customer service.
- There was a direct and positive relationship between an employee's perception of a company as being socially responsible and that employee's job satisfaction.

Concluded Walker Research: "The study shows that not only does being socially responsible pay off today, but also that the public's interest in corporate reputation and social responsibility is growing and will be even more important in the future."

that we might not be in the same situation with other costs and benefits of business activity. We're just twenty or twenty-five years behind what's happening in the environmental area."

For years, some in the accounting profession have been examining ways to link social accounting to the current system of financial accounting—the Generally Accepted Accounting Principles. During the mid-1970s, there was a major effort to create social audits of companies, pushed by companies like Bank of America, Arco, Dayton Hudson, and others. In 1975, Arthur Andersen, the large accounting firm, compiled an internal document called "Social Impact Planning and Reporting." It proposed guidelines for measuring and reporting costs and benefits in such areas as environmental protection, energy and mineral resources, human resource utilization, land resources, consumer protection, and civic participation. These reflected the dominant social concerns during the early seventies. The document went into substantial detail about how Arthur Andersen's staff might create measurements and reporting of "social impact" for its clients in anticipation that such accountability would be in demand among American corporations. But the report was never intended for distribution outside the company, says Ralph Estes, professor of ac-

Putting Your Best Foot Forward

Human history is the experience of individuals confronting the world around them. Timberland participates in this process not just through our products or through our brand, but through our beliefs that each individual can, and must, make a difference in the way we experience life on the planet. As a team of diverse people motivated and strengthened by this belief, we can and will deliver world-class products and service to our customers and create value for our shareholders around the world.

The Timberland boot stands for much more than the finest waterproof leather. It represents our call to action. Pull on our boots and make a difference. With your boots and your beliefs, you will be able to interact responsibly and comfortably within the natural and social environments that all human beings share. When confronting the world around you, nothing can stop you.

—From the Timberland Mission Statement

counting at the American University's Center for Advancement of Public Policy and author of *Corporate Social Accounting.*

Other efforts to create systems to measure the impact of socially responsible practices ended after only a few years, says Wood, "probably because nobody in business was confident that the information would be used wisely or well by external constituencies." Many were concerned about what might happen to the information when it fell into the hands of public interest organizations, shareholders, or other constituencies. The accounting field was quiet on the subject until the social investing movement came along during the 1980s and started asking questions about company operations.

One recent effort to gauge the social impact of companies comes from the U.S. Department of Labor, which in 1994 issued a "discussion guide" aimed at helping investor and business groups "examine the usefulness of alternative corporate performance measures based on workplace practices." The idea of the guide was to provide investors, directors, and managers with new tools for evaluating a company's long-term financial performance. According to the introduction, the Labor Department guide was based on the premise that "in the 1990s, companies are finding that they can achieve superior financial results by developing a superior workplace. The preliminary empirical evidence suggests that a positive correlation [exists] between innovative approaches to workplace practices and company performance."

The guide focuses on ten workplace issues "most often mentioned as indicators of firm performance":

- training and continuous learning—whether and how much companies are spending on initiatives to enhance workplace skills;
- employee participation—how much workers are involved in such areas as designing products and processes, hiring, and generally setting their work and quality performance goals or operating schedules;
- access to information—the extent to which employees at any level enjoy access to financial and operating information, and whether they are trained to use this information;
- organizational structure—what efforts have been made to organize people into cooperative teams, and to generally shed layers of management;
- employment security—strategies used to reduce costs during periods of economic downturn;
- supportive work environment—whether the company provides for flexible work schedules, child care, and other "family-friendly" programs;
- product and service quality—the way quality is measured, and whether employees can rapidly modify the work process to correct problems;
- compensation linked to performance—the use of reward and incentive programs, including the consideration of team performance in determining compensation;
- worker-manager relations—the overall relationships, as well as the way disputes are resolved; and
- strategic integration of workplace practices and policies—how human resource practices are integrated into the company's long-term business strategies.

Each of these ten "discussion points" is the basis for both empirical and anecdotal evidence linking workplace policies with financial per-

What We Believe

We believe that both human beings and nature have inherent worth and deserve our respect.

We believe in products that are safe, effective, and made of natural ingredients.

We believe that our company and our products are unique and worthwhile, and that we can sustain these genuine qualities with an ongoing commitment to innovation and creativity.

We believe that we have a responsibility to cultivate the best relationships possible with our co-workers, customers, owners, agents, suppliers, and our community.

We believe that different people bring different gifts and perspectives to the team and that a strong team is founded on a variety of gifts.

We believe in providing employees with a safe and fulfilling work environment, and an opportunity to grow and learn.

We believe that competence is an essential means of sustaining our values in a competitive marketplace.

We believe our company can be financially successful while behaving in a socially responsible and environmentally sensitive manner.

—TOM'S OF MAINE STATEMENT OF BELIEFS

formance. That the federal government has attempted to demonstrate the links—and has created a model for investors to assess companies' potential long-term performance—is a significant milestone on the road to integrating these so far "softer" aspects of the workplace with the "harder" realities of financial performance. The Department of Labor is interested in demonstrating the links between corporate policies and financial performance because it wants these socially responsible companies, which create jobs, to succeed.

Still another pioneering effort comes from Ben & Jerry's Homemade, the Vermont-based superpremium ice cream company whose products have gained a reputation for mixing dogma with dessert. In 1992, the company hired author and entrepreneur Paul Hawken to produce a social audit of the company. Hawken was given unprecedented access to Ben & Jerry's employees, records, and documents. The report, which included criticisms of some company policies, was published uncensored in the annual report along with traditional financial data—a first, although many other companies conduct such assessments for internal consumption.

Clearly, it will take time for companies and the accounting profession to come to consensus on what to report and how to report it. As academics join with accounting professionals and progressive companies, a consensus will likely emerge, but it could take years.

The focus of the activist community in pressuring companies on social responsibility has been less on *accounting* than *accountability*. "We need a corporate accountability system that reports benefits and costs to all stakeholders, not simply those that affect stockholders," says Ralph Estes. "The key issue is to recognize that a successful business is one that does not exploit one stakeholder for the benefit of another, but rather serves its entire set of stakeholders. If it can't do that, then it shouldn't be in business." Estes lays blame for the lack of attention paid by companies to their social impact to the types of accountability mandated by government, dating back to the Securities Act of 1933: "The philosophy behind this legislation was not to dictate to corporations that they would offer only high-quality financial instruments. Rather, the philosophy was that we would require you to fairly report essential information about the instruments that you wanted to sell to the public. Let the marketplace do the regulating once they have the information. And that has been the philosophy that has been followed ever since. But we have only done it with respect to financial investors. We haven't done it with respect to workers, customers, communities who give substantial benefits to corporations, and with respect to the national society."

A lot of that accountability already exists in U.S. law, albeit in piecemeal fashion. A host of acts and agencies are involved: the Community Right to Know Act, the Worker Right to Know Act, and the disclosure and reporting requirements of the Equal Employment Opportunity Commission, Federal Trade Commission, Securities and Exchange Commission (SEC), Federal Communications Commission, Interstate Commerce Commission, Food and Drug Administration, Environmental Protection Agency, and other agencies—as well as their counterparts on state and local levels and, in some cases, in the international arena.

Estes, in essence, would like to see many of the disclosures mandated by government rolled into a single offering. His radical proposal involves reconstituting the SEC as the Corporate Accountability Commission, "with a mandate to develop content and rules for a comprehensive annual corporate report, supplemented by ad hoc periodical disclosures as necessary."

In Estes's grand vision, information on company operations would be self-reported, much as it is now for financial data. He maintains that companies already have the bulk of this information on hand, requiring few new efforts. Indeed, such a system could actually reduce paperwork by consolidating reports and making them more efficient to produce. "It might bring some rationality to all the disclosure that now goes to Washington," Estes suggests. "You might be able to reduce the cost to corporations." That may be a dubious proposition in a system where, despite years of "paperwork reduction" efforts and a renewed emphasis on "reinventing government," form filling remains a boom industry. But it is hard to dispute Estes's assertion that the current system of corporate reporting borders on the anarchic, with little logic and virtually no interagency coordination.

Voluntary self-reporting already is being done in the environmental arena. For example, the CERES Principles is a set of ten goals for corporate environmental excellence promulgated by a coalition of environmental and socially responsible investment professionals. The principles commit companies to conduct annual audits and complete a CERES-designed disclosure form, which is made public. Signatories—companies ranging from General Motors and the Sun Company to a few dozen small businesses—place themselves in the public spotlight, with all their environmental foibles illuminated.

CERES's disclosure protocol, if it continues to be embraced by large companies, could become the foundation for company reporting on other issues, such as workplace practices and community involvement. If so, it could go a long way toward Estes's vision of a uniform reporting standard for business, albeit a voluntary, nongovernmental one.

A MATTER OF POLICY

Not all companies are waiting for appropriate accounting systems to emerge in order to establish social responsibility as a priority. Several have set forth their commitments to their employees, their commu-

Our Declaration of Interdependence

Our Mission Statement reflects the hopes and intentions of many people. We do not believe it always accurately portrays the way things currently are at Whole Foods Market, so much as the way we would like things to be. It is our dissatisfaction with current reality, when compared with what is possible, that spurs us toward excellence and toward creating a better person, company, and world. When Whole Foods Market fails to measure up to its stated Mission purpose, as it inevitably will at times, we should not despair. Rather, let us take up the challenge together to bring our reality closer toward our vision.

Whole Foods Market is a dynamic leader in the quality food business. We aim to set the standards of excellence for grocers. We are building a business in which quality permeates all aspects of our company. Quality is a state of mind at Whole Foods Market.

We recognize that our success reaches far beyond the company by contributing to the quality of life renaissance occurring here on earth. We are willing to share our successes and failures, our hopes and fears, and our joys and sorrows with others in the quality food business. Moreover, we have a responsibility to encourage more people to join us in the quality food business, to adopt higher standards of excellence, and generally contribute wherever and whenever it makes sense to the quality of life renaissance. The future we will experience tomorrow is created one step at a time today.

The success of our business is measured by customer satisfaction, Team Member happiness, return on capital investment, improvement in the quality of the environment, and local and larger community support.

Our ability to instill a clear sense of interdependence among our various stakeholders (the people who are interested in and benefit from the success of our company) is interconnected with our desire and efforts to communicate more often, more openly, and more compassionately. Better communication equals better understanding and more trust.

—From the Mission Statement of Whole Foods Market

nities, the environment, and others in their mission and policy state-ments. A few companies specifically refer to multiple bottom lines—several quantitative measures of social and financial performance they use to measure success.

One of the more visible efforts to integrate social goals into a mission statement belongs to Ben & Jerry's. In its factory tours, pack-aging, annual reports, and other communications, Ben & Jerry's pro-motes its three-part "Statement of Mission," quoted here in its entirety:

> Ben & Jerry's is dedicated to the creation and demonstration of a new corporate concept of linked prosperity. Our mission consists of three interrelated parts:
>
> - Product Mission—to make, distribute, and sell the finest-quality, all-natural ice cream and related products in a wide variety of innovative flavors made from Vermont dairy products.
> - Social Mission—to operate the company in a way that actively recognizes the central role that business plays in the structure of society by initiating innovative ways to improve the quality of life of a broad community—local, national, and international.
> - Economic Mission—to operate the company on a sound financial basis of profitable growth, increasing value for our shareholders, and creating career opportunities and financial rewards for our employees.
>
> Underlying the mission of Ben & Jerry's is the determination to seek new and creative ways of addressing all three parts, while holding a deep respect for the individuals, inside and outside the company, and for the communities of which they are a part.

In its simplicity, Ben & Jerry's mission statement encapsulates the fundamental and oft-quoted principle of socially responsible busi-ness: Doing well by doing good. Key to its success is the single word "interrelated," contained in the preamble. Since its founding in 1978, through its astronomical growth into a $140 million-a-year company, Ben & Jerry's has generally managed to balance those three objec-tives, albeit not without sacrifices and inner turmoil. As much as any company, Ben & Jerry's has attempted to demonstrate that profit-ability can accompany a proactive agenda.

But how do the dealings of an idealistic and highly profitable ice cream maker operating out of bucolic Vermont relate to the larger, hardscrabble world of business? Is Ben & Jerry's an anomaly among enterprises, a quirk in the system? Or does it represent a forward-thinking vision to which other companies could and should aspire?

Those are questions a lot of other companies—not to mention a gaggle of inquiring reporters—have asked in recent years, as these out-front companies have come under intense scrutiny of their idealism and their success. In the case of Ben & Jerry's, the inquisitors include both the curious—looking to see how a few scoopfuls of Ben & Jerry's unique corporate culture might be dished out at their companies—and the cynical—those determined to prove Ben & Jerry's to be everything from an aberration to a fraud. Mainstream media, which once touted Ben & Jerry's as a new business sensation, have been among the toughest critics, variously grilling and skewering the ice cream makers about everything from their phenomenal financial success ("proving" that the company could be socially responsible only because it could afford it) to the company's lackluster 1993 performance in the stock market despite rising profits ("proving" that socially minded initiatives are bad for investors).

Officials at Ben & Jerry's tend to shrug off such coverage, although they admit to finding it somewhat frustrating. "We have tried to be very honest about what we are and what we're not," says Liz Bankowski, Ben & Jerry's director of social missions. "We are not a model of an environmental company. There are a lot of interesting things we have done, but we have never said we are that. Somehow our external reputation gets ahead of us, and we're always trying to reel it in.

"I think we are the only company in America that does a social performance audit in our annual report that takes some real hits at us," she continues. "In fact, in a *Newsweek* article, which was critical of us, the negative information came directly from our own social performance audit. If you're going to say that you strive toward some notion of social responsibility, you have to accept that as part of the contract. Obviously, you're not perfect, it's always in increments that you do these things. But the expectations will always be greater than that which you can deliver."

Ben & Jerry's isn't alone in being held to a higher standard than other businesses. A handful of other companies promoting socially responsible philosophies and practices have been similarly scrutinized, their inevitable faults held up for all the world to see. And while no one seems to have conclusively proven or disproven any of these companies' ideals or intentions, the debates rage on with seem-

Daring to Be Different

Calvert dares to be different, if being different makes good business sense. The organization prides itself on its individualistic, unconventional, and nontraditional approach to the businesses in which it chooses to be. Independent thinking will be valued and encouraged as long as it benefits the organization and is not voiced just for the sake of being independent. We firmly believe that the more heterogeneous and diverse the organization is, the more creativity and entrepreneurial spirit it will possess. Therefore, we will hire and promote individuals based on potentials demonstrated, accomplishments, creativity, ambition, willingness to learn, and flexibility. We will constantly encourage risk taking and recognize creativity, hard work, and initiative even if the end result is not successful. In a more complex and sophisticated world, high levels of creativity and entrepreneurial spirit will be required to excel. Our experience has proven that freedom to be oneself actually promotes higher levels of personal commitment and responsibility than does the more conventional, highly structured organization.

—FROM CALVERT GROUP'S STATEMENT OF SHARED VALUES

ingly increasing intensity. Meanwhile, Ben & Jerry's and their social-minded brethren continue to grow—and, more often than not, prosper.

Ben & Jerry's is only one of dozens of companies that has integrated social responsibility into its mission statement. There are many others, from smaller niche firms to large national companies. A few examples:

• **Valley Plastics,** a $750,000-a-year manufacturer of component parts in Santa Rosa, California, sends its customers and suppliers a five-part set of "Guidelines for Good Stewardship." Among other things, the guidelines commit the company to maintain a high level of quality in its products and services while offering a full set of benefits to employees, provide training of job-enhancing skills, engage in community activities, be environmentally responsible, act with honesty and integrity—and in general to "consider the short- and long-term effects that our actions will have on real people, and never let the promise of greater profits cloud our better judgment."

• **Herman Miller Co.,** the $850-million-a-year Zeeland, Michigan–based manufacturer of office furniture, promotes its "Herman Miller Mandate." Besides underscoring its commitment to high product quality and customer service, and to "appropriate financial results" that enable "future vitality," the mandate acknowledges an "obligation to perform in a manner consistent with our values." That includes a belief that "all career employees should be able to own stock in the corporation. We believe that participative ownership, practiced with fidelity, can make this an exceptional company." It further recognizes that "we are more than participating owners in our company: We are also members of families and communities. We are committed to the nurture, support, and security of the family."

• **Levi Strauss & Co.,** the world's largest apparel manufacturer, with sales approaching $6 billion a year, offers a three-part mission statement, aspiration statement, and business vision. The business vision states in part that "Our success will be measured not only by growth in shareholder value, but also by our reputation, the quality of our constituency relationships, and our commitment to social responsibility."

• **Quad/Graphics,** a Pewaukee, Wisconsin–based company that has grown since its founding in 1971 into the largest privately held printer of magazines and catalogues in the United States (among the more than five hundred publications it prints are *Time, Newsweek,* and *U.S. News & World Report*) commits in its mission statement "to be good neighbors, improve our environment, offer our services to community projects, have attractive grounds, and provide employee opportunities to all, including disadvantaged groups." It further states that "each employee should be treated as an individual, allowing room to develop their full potential and upgrade their skills and capabilities through continuing programs of education and training."

• The **White Dog Cafe,** a 164-seat restaurant in Philadelphia— named by *Condé Nast Traveler* magazine as one of the fifty American restaurants worth a journey, and by *Inc.* magazine as one of "the best small companies to work for in America"—publishes a set of goals dealing with product excellence and workplace satisfaction. They also commit the company to "making a difference" by using the business "as a vehicle for social change, promoting a more just society and world community, incorporating our values into every aspect of our work"; and profitability, "never neglecting the first three goals to achieve higher profits, nor jeopardizing the financial health of the business to maximize other goals."

More about some of these companies in later chapters. For now, what's important to note is the fundamental acknowledgment through their mission statements that there is more to business life than simply making money. They certainly don't try to make a case that making money is unimportant. Rather, they attempt to demonstrate that there are salutary and increasingly vital benefits to business and society from recognizing what goes on inside their walls and beyond the direct products or services in the larger universe in which they operate. Among other things, these companies understand that their "products" also include the kinds of corporate cultures they engender and the legacy those cultures will have on the world around them.

Ultimately, of course, mission statements are only as good as the actions that back them up. Without such action, they represent hollow statements whose benefits are usually short-lived. Over time, those whom the mission statement is trying to impress—customers, employees, investors, or anyone else—will see past the rhetoric to the reality.

Chapter Five

Forces for Change

"If you run afoul of something and you're going to go down like a rock, companies that... haven't spent a lot of time working on their reputation are going to go down faster."

—JOHN GILFEATHER,
managing partner, Yankelovich Partners

The calls for socially responsible mission statements and changes in accounting and accountability are only two of the streams pushing companies to take a harder look at their performance and practices. Another force for change is investors. Individual and institutional investors—including the endowments and treasuries of universities, churches, cities, states, and the pension funds of millions of workers—have made socially responsible investment one of the biggest financial phenomena of the 1990s.

This is not exactly new. As long ago as the 1920s, some churches warned against investing in "sin stocks"—alcohol, tobacco, and gambling. The trend grew in the 1960s, when some investors began to recognize that their money was being used to produce napalm for use in Vietnam, to do business in apartheid-torn South Africa, and to underwrite discriminatory hiring and promoting practices at home. Now, a wide variety of social investment "screens"—investment criteria established by investors or their representatives—include such factors as charitable donations, environmental protection, military contracts, community outreach, family benefits, gay rights, and minority advancement. In the early 1990s, mutual funds promoting socially responsible investing, or SRI, were among the fastest-growing investment vehicles around.

Until a few years ago, SRI was the country cousin of the investment world, a pair of Birkenstocks in the pinstripe-and-Gucci world of Wall Street. Conventional wisdom in the investment community had it that, like oil and water, money and ethics didn't mix. And the sluggish financial performance of some of the stock funds that screened out investments deemed socially irresponsible was taken as proof of that wisdom. More recently, SRI funds have cleared the credibility hurdle of performance, often tracking and sometimes out-performing such mainstream benchmarks as the Standard & Poor 500, and being tracked by investment research services such as Morningstar and Value Line. The big brokerage houses—Merrill Lynch, T. Rowe Price, and Dreyfus Corp.—have established their own funds in order to attract what they see as a niche market of investors with a social conscience.

All of these houses are trying with varying degrees of success to replicate what the Calvert Group has made its stock in trade. Calvert was not the first sponsor of socially responsible mutual funds. That honor belongs to Pax World, established in 1971. Calvert's first social investment funds were launched in 1982 by Calvert founders D. Wayne Silby and John G. Guffy, two friends who met at the University of Pennsylvania's Wharton School of Business. Even in 1982 the idea of screening investments for social considerations was considered odd. But Calvert managed over the next twelve years to develop a family of seven funds with nearly $1.5 billion in assets under management for some 130,000 shareholders. In 1984, Silby and Guffy sold Calvert to Acacia Mutual Life Insurance Co.

In general, the SRI community's long-term, buy-and-hold approach to investing is in sharp contrast to many traditional investors' notoriously short-term view, says Steve Schueth, vice president for socially responsible investing for the Calvert Group. That view gives little weight to such longer-term initiatives as employee training, community involvement, and pollution prevention. Moreover, a host of government and institutional requirements of publicly traded companies—10K filings with the Securities and Exchange Commission, for example—force management to keep its eyes trained firmly on the current quarter instead of on the coming quarter century. "Wall Street is incredibly shortsighted and does not look at building a business," says Matthew Patsky, vice president of equity research at Robertson, Stephens & Company, a San Francisco investment banking firm. "They don't understand building a business as well as most business people do."

Like Schueth, Patsky represents a new breed of financial professional who sees currency in determining what makes some socially responsible companies so successful—and how to identify those diamonds in the rough that will be the next Starbucks, Reebok, or Celestial Seasonings. "What I have found is that over time, the companies that are going to succeed are the companies that have adopted what have been labeled socially responsible criteria into their business practices," he says. "I say that because I think that over time, if you are not empowering your employees, if you are not caring about the community and the environment, you are not going to survive as a company." Stan Sorrell, the president of Calvert, agrees: "Companies with the most responsible policies and practices will do better over time—better for investors and for all of us as members of a vibrant, healthy society. There is no doubt in my mind that responsible corporate operations are good for businesses."

Patsky wishes there were more publicly traded companies placing their socially responsible policies in a public light: "One of the problems I see with socially responsible businesses is that the majority are privately owned and have no interest in going public. What they have in effect said is, 'I am running my business the way I want for the long term, I don't want to deal with the public markets.' But if they're not very public and visible, they are not spreading the gospel, helping the cause of encouraging people to develop businesses in a socially responsible manner. They have to be willing to make noise."

Patsky and Schueth are part of a sizable industry of services targeted at socially responsible investors: newsletters like *Clean Yield* and *Franklin Insight*; research and screening services, offered by professional brokerage houses as well as nonprofits such as CEP and the Investor Responsibility Research Center; socially responsible investment funds, such as those offered by Franklin Research, Working Assets, and Progressive Asset Management; the Social Investment Forum, an 1,100-member nonprofit group dedicated to promoting the concept and practice of SRI; even a stock index—the Domini Social Index (DSI), created by the Boston corporate accountability research firm Kinder, Lydenberg, Domini & Co. The DSI tracks the returns of 400 "clean" companies, using primary screens that eliminate companies engaged in military contracting, alcohol and tobacco, gambling, and nuclear power, as well as secondary screens that judge a company's policies on the environment, product quality, employee relations, and hiring and advancement of women and minorities. During a four-year period from its inception on May 1, 1990, through March 31, 1994, the DSI, which its creators call a "market-capitalization weighted common stock index," climbed 63.7 percent, outpacing the Standard & Poor 500 index, which grew by 52.4 percent during the same period. Steve Schueth says that the DSI has given credence to the notion that socially screened stocks can do well. "It is very impressive because there aren't a lot of managers who can say they have outperformed the S&P 500 on an annual basis, let alone on a three-and-a-half-year basis," says Schueth.

Kinder, Lydenberg, Domini & Co. (KLD) is one of many companies that offer reports profiling major companies on their socially responsible policies and practices. Each of the 650 or so reviews offered by KLD covers a company's strengths and failings in major social issue areas: community, employee relations, environment, product, women/minorities, military contracts, nuclear power, and "other." Also included is an editorial analysis of company actions. The reviews are updated annually.

The world tracked by KLD and others is growing like kudzu. All told, SRI watchers are bullish: According to the Social Investment Forum, SRI equity mutual funds now manage some $25 billion, as well as another $625 billion of investments screened for pension funds and other institutional investors (the bulk of which were screened for investments in South Africa, though those investments are expected over time to shift into other screens). While that's still a relative drop in the $371 trillion bucket of securities investments, the fast growth represents nothing short of a revolution.

So, how have all these socially invested dollars changed the way companies operate? The answer is not much—at least directly. But that's not the only point of SRI. "I don't think that simply buying or selling—or not buying and not selling—stocks and bonds has any direct impact on corporations," says Calvert's Steve Schueth. "What has the impact are things that go along with owning stocks."

One of them is the proxy resolutions voted upon by companies at their annual meetings. Calvert works with other groups, such as the Interfaith Center on Corporate Responsibility (ICCR), to jointly file a resolution on some social issue—say, for a company to disclose information that would indicate whether it is giving equal treatment in hiring, paying, and promoting women and minority employees. The resolution is then sent to every registered share-holder.

ICCR is a coalition of nearly 250 Protestant and Roman Catholic institutional investors, including denominations, religious communities, agencies, pension funds, dioceses, and health care corporations. Through its efforts, investors sponsored or co-sponsored 230 resolutions at 155 companies during the 1993 annual meeting season. At the meeting of May Department Stores, for example, the Sisters of Charity of St. Elizabeth, New Jersey, joined with seven other groups to sponsor a resolution calling for the company to produce an equal employment report disclosing the gender and racial composition for each of nine job categories for three years, as well as a summary of affirmative action programs and other related information. Identical resolutions were filed at Chevron, GTE, Texaco, Time Warner, and Weyerhaeuser. Meanwhile, the Congregation of Passion, Holy Cross Province, co-sponsored a resolution calling for Zenith Electronics to provide "a comprehensive report describing our Company's maquiladora operations" along the Mexican border. It also called for the company to "respect fundamental principles of safe environmental practices, adequate health and safety standards for workers, and compensation which would provide for a dignified quality of life for workers."

None of these resolutions passed, but that's not the point. "You rarely get a majority," says ICCR's Diane Bratcher, "but it represents a significant statement of dissent within a corporation." More common is that company management will sit down with these dissident investors to discuss what changes might be required for the shareholders to withdraw their resolution, or agree not to resubmit it the following year.

Schueth tells the story of a large West Coast–based supermarket chain—"a company that we'd known for some time and liked a lot, but we had some questions about their equal employment opportunity policies and practices and record. We asked them for information and they refused to give it to us. We filed a proxy resolution in 1993. Once we filed that, they immediately were willing to sit down and talk to us. By the end of that conversation, they gave us the information we were looking for, in return for which we pulled the proxy. They've continued that dialogue, and are continuing to supply us with information. And we're pleased with the progress that they're making. They're not perfect yet, but they are moving in the right direction and we think we had a major impact. And the way we got their attention was through the proxy."

PENSION POWER

The real players in the investment world are pension funds, which, with holdings worth more than $4 trillion, represent the richest pool of investment money in the nation. Increasingly, pension funds are using their investments as a tool for social change—and improved financial returns.

The $80 billion California Public Employees Retirement System, or Calpers, the nation's largest pension fund, has been the most active investor. Calpers has gained fame and increased its fortune in recent years by using its shareholder clout to push for changes in the corporate suites at companies facing financial problems, such as American Express, General Motors, IBM, Kodak, Sears, and Westinghouse. The fund has purchased large stakes—up to 10 percent—of these companies' stocks, in some cases becoming their largest stockholders. With that kind of clout, they have pushed for a host of changes.

Traditionally, pension funds would purchase small amounts of stock in hundreds of companies, buying and selling them at every rise or dip in prices. Holding even one share would enable them to introduce resolutions at annual meetings, a process that, if persistent, might lead to negotiations with management that could result in policy changes as a condition for withdrawing a ballot measure, or agreeing not to submit future ones.

That's the old way. The new way is called "relationship investing," so called because pension fund officials hope to develop constructive, long-term relationships with the managers of targeted companies. In relationship investing, pension funds take large investment stakes—perhaps 10 percent or more—with the intention of holding on to the stock for years. (With such large holdings, they cannot easily sell off shares without disrupting the market, making the funds so-called permanent investors.) Fund managers or their representatives then seek to improve corporate performance, and boost investment returns, by forming long-term advisory relationships with the management and directors of the companies they choose. Holding such a large stake, a fund is likely to be a company's largest investor and gives it the right to have a say in company operations—perhaps enough to topple a CEO or board member with whom fund managers are dissatisfied.

With relationship investing, pension fund managers need no longer content themselves with the role of passive shareholder. Instead, they can position themselves to flex their muscles on everything from executive compensation to the environment to hostile takeovers. As key shareholders, representatives of pension funds can command a regular audience with a company's directors and management to discuss the company's long-term plans to gain market share and profits. In some cases, pension funds are pooling resources to make large stock purchases. In 1992, the Securities and Exchange Commission relaxed its rules, making it easier for giant investors to discuss investments without making filings and disclosures.

Clearly, the strategy has made CEOs and company directors nervous. Pension fund activists already have claimed credit for the forced 1992 resignation of Robert C. Stempel as chairman of General Motors Corp. Supporters of relationship investing point to this and other actions as evidence that shareholders finally have a weapon to wield against seemingly monolithic corporate management. Many critics, however, wonder whether fund managers possess the qualifications to wield such power. Among those likely to raise questions are top executives of target companies, who argue that pension funds have become too influential and lack the expertise to help management improve corporate performance. Others have questioned whether even the best-run funds are properly staffed and equipped to dispense advice on business policies that have a far-reaching impact on corporations, stockholders, communities, and employees.

Such criticism was muted by a study commissioned by Calpers and released in 1994. The study found that shares of companies the fund had pressured to improve operating performance did much better than the rest of the stock market, including stock price and dividends, improving the investment results for its almost 1 million workers and retirees.

The pressures by institutional investors on companies to act more socially responsible may grow as new measurement systems are able to track the financial performance of companies with socially responsible policies and programs. If such a link can be successfully established, the common stock certificate may become a potent weapon, not just for large investors but smaller ones, too. In any case, the efforts by Calpers and other activist investors have given fund managers renewed vigor to pursue their agendas with management, in the hopes that good corporate policies will result in good investment returns over the long run. As Calpers board president Bill Crist told *The Washington Post* in 1993: "We are in corporate America's face and intend to stay there."

WHAT KEEPS "GOOD GUYS" FROM BEING GOOD

Calpers and their investor brethren may find that being bigger doesn't necessarily make the going any easier in fomenting organizational change. There are a variety of institutional barriers to change, barriers that may reward companies for making moves that often fly in the face of the ideals of social responsibility.

The fundamental problem has to do with the legal precept of company directors' responsibility to maximize shareholder profits. "While some boards of directors will behave socially responsibly, they don't have to," explains Lawrence E. Mitchell, professor of law at George Washington University. So, he says, company directors need not concern themselves with the impact of their operations on their employees, the environment, or Third World cultures. In effect, they say, "I am constrained by law to maximize stockholder profit. Everything else is outside of my field of vision."

"Once you've done that," says Mitchell, "you've basically absolved directors and managers of any responsibility, any moral accountability for their actions beyond profit maximization for stockholders. That is to say, to put it in the language of grade-B World War II movies, 'I was only following orders.' And as long as they're only following orders, we can't hold them legally accountable and we can't hold them morally accountable. They don't feel morally accountable because it isn't their problem."

That brings us back to the importance of measurement and accountability—how to identify, in no uncertain terms, the costs and benefits to various company actions. Without proper measurement tools, socially responsible policies will be subject to this kind of criticism.

Most directors aren't quite so callous, of course. Mitchell classifies company directors into one of three categories. The first sees shareholder profit maximization as an excuse "to profit at the expense of everybody else, to externalize all the costs and profiting on everybody else. And not have to feel bad about it." The second group, the biggest, are those who want to be socially responsible, but feel the law constrains their ability to do so. A third category are the truly committed directors, those who say, "I'm a person and the fact that I work for this corporation doesn't change that. I still have to behave as I would in my entire life, considering all the different roles I play in society and my entire moral context."

So, Mitchell says, what keeps the "good guys" from acting like good guys is that they may be put at a competitive disadvantage, at least in the short run, because they appear to sacrifice short-term profit for longer-term gain; without adequate measurement systems, no one knows for sure. "It permits and encourages directors and managers to externalize the cost of stockholder maximization onto all these other third parties. If it's cheaper to do business by dumping stuff into the environment, maltreating your employees, selling substandard products, or setting up a company town and shutting it down when it's no longer profitable to operate—then guess what? They're going to do that. And unless there are broader laws that prohibit that, there's going to be no check on that. The stockholders will receive all of the benefit and the third parties will get dumped on."

Ironically, Mitchell foresees the rise of institutional investing as exacerbating the institutional barriers. Many pension funds, for example, are already underfunded, meaning that they pay out more each year in benefits than they take in through employee contributions or investment yields. According to a 1994 *Wall Street Journal* estimate, state and local pension plans alone are more than $125 billion short of the money they will need to meet their pension promises. Adding in federal civilian and military employees, the underfunding—the gap between what has been salted away and what will be required—is $1.24 *trillion*, says the *Journal*. Mitchell says that as fund managers anticipate cash shortfalls, they are inclined to lean on company directors to pay out dividends that might otherwise be reinvested. Directors, knowing that these big investors have the power to oust them from office, often capitulate. Pension fund managers are rewarded for meeting their fiduciary responsibility; moreover, many are compensated based on the returns they generate. In the meantime, the action has pushed money out of the corporation, possibly setting the stage for cutbacks, layoffs, reduced investment, or other moves that can have an adverse impact on employees or the larger society.

It's a tough problem, with no simple solution. Mitchell and others who follow these issues believe the answers lie in more than a change of consciousness. It could take a restructuring of securities regulations and tax law to create the proper incentives for companies to concern themselves with more than the price of their stocks.

CONSUMERS: THE REALITY OF PERCEPTION

Investors are by no means the only ones who are letting companies know of their concerns about ethical business practices. Consumers are also making their voices heard by writing letters, calling toll-free customer service lines, and, most important, voting with their dollars. The green consumer movement may be the most visible example of individuals attempting to boycott companies—from Exxon to McDonald's to General Electric—whose policies did not appear to be in the best interests of the environment. But there have been dozens of other boycotts focusing on other social issues—against companies whose products include cigarettes and liquor (the "sin stocks"); against companies known to discriminate against women, blacks, or gays in their hiring practices; against companies with subsidiaries in the weapons-manufacturing business. At the same time, there are grass-roots efforts to *support* companies whose policies mesh with customers' values.

Companies that don't sell directly to individual consumers aren't being let off the hook. In fact, business-to-business customers may be among the most potent forces in the marketplace. A growing number of companies—as well as federal and local government agencies, universities, and other institutions—have established procurement policies that give preference to products and companies that meet certain specifications, sometimes even allowing purchasers to pay slightly more for such goods. So far, the vast majority of purchasing

---

We did a number of consumer focus groups. It became evident to our customers that we weren't just using coriander in our deodorants because it was the right thing to do from a marketing standpoint. It really was based on a fundamental belief that nature is beautiful, deserves our respect, and that it offers all the solutions to our personal care needs if we take the time and attention to find them. If we are careful and selective with nature, we can find those and use them on our bodies. It related much more to what we make.

It turned out that one plus one equals three. The credibility of what we make was enhanced by what we believe. It really was very interesting. For some customers, they were intrigued by what we believe. They said, "That's the kind of company that I want to support, let me look again at what it is that they make."

—KATHRYN M. SHISLER,
group product manager, Tom's of Maine

policies focus on environmental issues: products containing recycled materials, for example, or fewer hazardous ingredients. But in a few notable cases, companies are looking to other issues, including the overall reputation and performance of the companies.

Such policies handily demonstrate the potential power of business to affect significant behavioral change in the marketplace, perhaps even more quickly than government regulations. After all, companies can skirt, dodge, appeal, stonewall, or simply ignore environmental regulations, but losing a few key customers can really ruin their day. The customer is always right, and if the customer suddenly discovers that doing good for society makes bottom-line sense, its policies become the law of the land. The penalties for noncompliance could be severe.

Individual consumers are a force to be reckoned with, too. In small but significant numbers, they are prodding companies to change, using both carrots and sticks. Even some of these boycotts' organizers admit that the impact of the campaigns is debatable. But the effect on the management of target companies often is disproportionate to the financial hit the boycott may be causing. The boycotts a few years back against McDonald's and the tuna industry are cases in point. By all reports, the boycotts—to protest the use of polystyrene hamburger "clamshell" packaging and fishing practices that harm dolphins, respectively—affected as little as 1 percent of the marketplace, yet both efforts prevailed.

The reason: Perception won out over reality. Which is to say that the mere idea of ill feelings by the public about these companies' products was sufficient to motivate them to change. In the case of hamburger boxes, McDonald's executives describe the intensive research that had gone into evaluating their environmental impact, compared to other packaging alternatives. Nevertheless, when the company announced the move away from polystyrene in October 1990, McDonald's president said, "Our customers just don't feel good about it. So we're changing." In the case of tuna fishing, the major companies in 1990 announced a ban on tuna fishing that harmed dolphins. In making their announcement, the companies said nothing about protecting dolphins, or even "saving the earth." They spoke instead of "consumer pressure," despite the relatively tiny number of shoppers actively involved.

These are not isolated examples. Consumer boycotts have led to a number of changes in corporate policy. Activists claim credit for General Electric's 1993 decision to sell off its nuclear reactor business, following years of protests and demonstrations against the company, including an Academy Award–winning documentary lambasting the company's nuclear operations. (G.E. denies the activists had anything to do with the decision.) Several major cosmetics companies have agreed to stop using animals in testing their products or ingredients after boycotts led by groups such as People for the Ethical Treatment of Animals.

If a relative handful of disparate, outspoken voices can move markets and badger boards of directors, company executives ought to be downright fearful of Working Assets, which has harnessed the activism of 200,000-plus customers of its phone and financial services for political and social causes. Indeed, activism is one of Working Assets' products—along with offering discount long-distance telephone service (by buying excess capacity of major carriers at deep discounts and reselling it), Visa credit cards, and a travel service.

A portion of Working Assets' profits—as well as funds received from asking long-distance customers to voluntarily "round up" their bills to a higher dollar amount, to the tune of as much as $50,000 a month—are divided among three dozen or so nonprofit groups "building a better world," as the company puts it. Included are groups working in the areas of human rights (Amnesty International, Family Violence Prevention Fund, National Minority AIDS Council), peace building (the African National Congress, Center for Economic Conversion, Global Fund for Women), the environment (Defenders of Wildlife, Indigenous Environmental Network, Institute for Local Self-Reliance), and "economic justice" (the Association of Community Organizations for Reform Now, the Federation of Southern Cooperatives, YouthBuild USA). In 1993, the company donated more than $1 million to this pool of organizations.

None of this giving seems to have hurt Working Assets' growth. In fact, it is a key part of the company's marketing efforts. Revenue has jumped from $2 million in 1991 to $35 million in 1993, as its customer base grew from 5,000 to 130,000—and continues to grow by 1,000 new customers a month. In 1993, the company was named one of the 500 fastest-growing privately held companies in America by *Inc.* magazine, boasting 125 percent annual growth.

Working Assets may represent the purest form of what social responsibility can do to build a business. Their prices are competitive with other discount phone companies. What draws in business is the company's unique brand of activism. For starters, customers' monthly service bills (printed on 100-percent post-consumer, recycled paper) double as a bill of fare for social change.

In a given month, bill inserts might ask customers to take direct action on selected issues—to prod Congress or the President to take (or not take) a particular action, or to register one's displeasure with a particular company or government policy. Example: "Cracker Barrel, a national restaurant chain, fires employees for being gay or lesbian," advised one message in late 1993, referring to the firing of eleven gay and lesbian workers and the general antihomosexual employment policies of Cracker Barrel Old Country Store. "Tell CEO Dan Evins to adopt a nondiscrimination policy. Bigotry is bad business." (Cracker Barrel also was the target of the New York City Employees Retirement System, holder of 1 percent of its stock, which pushed to get an antidiscrimination question on the company's proxy ballot. Cracker Barrel eventually rescinded its public opposition to hiring gays.) Whatever the issue, Working Assets customers are urged to call key politicians or business people (the company provides free three-minute calls to these phone numbers on select days, with discounts to those numbers on all other days) or to send a company-generated "CitizenLetter" by checking the appropriate box on the bill's payment remittance form; the letters cost $3 for one or $4.50 for two.

Does it work? Get yourself mentioned in a Working Assets communiqué and be prepared to field 25,000 calls and letters a month. Recipients of such deluges include the CEO of McDonald's (supporting vegetarian burgers), the head of the Environmental Protection Agency (opposing toxic waste incinerators sited near schools), and the chairman of the Federal Reserve (opposing redlining by banks). While it is unclear whether any of these actions has led directly to changes in company or governmental policy, it's hard to ignore the impact of such a protest, particularly when you assume that there's an even larger body of the public that feels similarly but doesn't take the time to write or call.

Building a business around social activism is far from the definition of a socially responsible business. But Working Assets plays a key role in the marketplace for corporate social responsibility. The mere existence of Working Assets and a handful of other companies that promote or sponsor boycotts, phone-calling, and letter-writing campaigns contributes to the daily drumbeat of messages received by citizens about the business community, and about specific companies: Is this company in sync with its customers' and communities' social needs and mores? How much does it contribute to social or environmental problems or their solutions? Does it need more regulations or enforcement of existing laws to persuade it to act more responsibly?

HOW THE PUBLIC VIEWS COMPANIES

A lot of these questions focus on companies' ethics, whether individual consumers think in those terms or not. And a company's ethics are a part of its reputation, which reflects on whether or not a company is perceived to be socially responsible. Individual companies' ethical reputations notwithstanding, the public's opinion of business leaders' ethics overall is not very good. For years, a succession of polls and surveys has indicated that the public is concerned with business ethics overall and is frustrated with business's response to a variety of social problems. A sampling:

- In 1985, 62 percent of Americans told *U.S. News & World Report* that white-collar crime "is a serious and growing problem that shows a real decline in business ethical behavior."
- The following year, when the American Institute of Certified Public Accountants asked, "Compared with ten years ago, would you say that the level of honesty and integrity in business dealings generally has been improving, getting worse, or staying about the same?", three times as many Americans responded that it was getting worse than said it was improving.
- In 1987, nearly two thirds of respondents agreed with the Roper Organization's statement that "American business and industry ... hoodwinks the public through advertising."
- In 1989, Times Mirror found 61 percent of the public believing that "U.S. business puts too much emphasis on profits in the short run."
- A 1990 *Working Woman* magazine survey found 56 percent

Citizenship has two elements: the behavior of the corporation as an entity and the behavior of individuals within that entity. The corporation's behavior should be such that, in everything it does, it adds to society in meaningful ways, making the world a better place and enhancing the climate in which we do business.

—HARVEY GOLUB,
president, American Express

responding that "American business ethics have deteriorated in the past ten years." A strong majority said they would not work for a company with a history of environmental accidents, insider trading, or worker accidents, or a law firm that defends known racketeers.

- According to a 1991 survey by Decision Research, only 7 percent of Americans believe companies are taking appropriate steps to protect the environment.
- In 1993, a survey on Corporate Ethics in America by the Society of Consumer Affairs Professionals in Business found that while 96 percent of *Fortune* 500 CEOs believe American corporations to be ethical, only 59 percent of their employees agreed. Two thirds of adult consumers surveyed said they give consideration to a company's ethics when deciding whether to purchase its products or services.

There is no doubt that most companies are aware of the messages the public receives from the media and others about business ethics. What's less certain is what companies are doing about it: how willing each company is to engage in the process of self-examination, open discussion, and, ultimately, actual changes in the ethics of their practices. Do they really mean what they say, or are they delivering highly visible lip service to the ideals of corporate responsibility?

THE MEDIA'S MESSAGES

Companies may sincerely believe that their messages promoting ethics and social responsibility are getting through, that a mere slogan is sufficient to convince the public of their devotion to the environment or other pressing social issues. But these message marketers often fail to recognize the competing messages the public hears—not from other companies, but from the menu of news stories, movies, TV shows, and other forms of news and information we receive on a daily basis. Media analysts and public opinion experts know that even small amounts of media coverage on the same topic, if persistent over time, can make an impression on the public's collective memory that rises to the forefront of consciousness when events warrant: a major plant closing, an insider-trading scandal, an environmental disaster, a landmark discrimination suit, and so on.

In other words, a steady stream of negative stories about business results in a sort of subconscious public vigil on business ethics and responsibility. Such day-in, day-out coverage may be likened to the steady dripping of water on a rock: over time, it won't likely move the rock, but it will nonetheless make an indelible impression. In the case of public perception of business, that impression is one of indifference to how companies treat their employees, their communities, and the environment.

That certainly has been the case with media coverage of the environment. Throughout the 1970s and 1980s, environmental issues continued to receive a steady level of coverage by the news media. When the level of coverage rose during the period leading up to the twentieth anniversary of Earth Day—helped by the *Exxon Valdez* oil spill and new reports about the severity of such matters as global warming and ozone depletion—the public needed little encouragement in making the environment one of the top concerns of the day.

The larger topic of socially responsible business issues will likely experience a similar rise in the public's consciousness. For years, Americans have been subjected to a steady diet of stories that depict business in general in a negative light. Thanks to the news media, there is a cache of images to be called upon at a moment's notice: Love Canal, gas lines, windfall profits, golden parachutes, the savings and loan scandal, political action funds, plant closings, "glass ceilings," recalled breast implants, and so on. Each of these serves as a ready reference for future stories, much as the Three Mile Island nuclear accident became the benchmark for future nuclear mishaps, and the *Exxon Valdez* accident the point of reference for most subsequent oil spills.

The public is listening. Individuals listen not just to what companies say and do, but to a wide range of other things that help them form impressions about the role of business in society. Each of us receives valuable information in our many roles in society: as citizens, employees, investors, community members, voters, and shoppers. All of that information helps us form impressions, thoughts, and images that aren't easily undone by a single advertising campaign.

Increasingly, the public is listening to companies—as well as to the entire business community—about their roles as corporate citizens. The small but steady stream of messages about the positive impact of socially responsible business will no doubt gradually add pressure for all companies to adopt these philosophies and practices. As public examination of business's role in society continues to grow, companies that hope they can get by with superficial words or deeds will likely be bypassed or outclassed by their more enlightened competitors.

DOES SOCIAL RESPONSIBILITY SELL?

None of this is to imply that companies "do good" solely because they were forced to by investors, customers, or the general public. As we said, most of the companies and programs profiled in this book came to social responsibility on their own, inspired by company leaders and line workers alike (or sometimes the result of negotiations with labor unions). These are the proactive companies that somehow came to recognize the benefits—tangible or intangible—that would result from their investments in social responsibility.

But the question remains: Does social responsibility sell? Does all of the hard work needed to transform a company into a socially responsible one pay off through increased sales or public support? It certainly does for companies who make social responsibility a part of their image. Ask consumers why they buy The Body Shop's cosmetics, Tom's of Maine's toothpaste, Stonyfield Farm's yogurt, or Working Assets' phone service, and a high percentage will undoubtedly tell you that they like the company's values at least as much as their products. But companies boasting their social responsibility in such a visible way as these are relatively small in number. Another group of companies—including Fingerhut, Herman Miller, Johnson & Johnson, Levi Strauss, Motorola, and Xerox—don't promote their social responsibility, but benefit from it anyway, after years of building trust among their various constituencies. For the much larger universe of companies, it is still difficult to measure how much social responsibility boosts sales.

Besides, what works for The Body Shop or Levi Strauss won't necessarily work for your company. And what works for you may not work for them. The key point is that consumers seem to want to support companies that espouse socially responsible philosophies—and back it up with socially responsible action.

But don't let consumers fool you. What they say and what they do are often different. Consider green consumerism. During the early 1990s, companies coming to grips with growing pressures to become more environmentally responsible faced a perplexing question. Would companies that retooled their products or processes in the name of planet Earth be rewarded through increased sales and customer loyalty? Public opinion polls indicated that would indeed be the case, but the actual evidence has been mixed. Paradoxically, strong public pressure for responsible environmental behavior isn't reflected in their loyalty at the checkout counter. A few companies, such as Church & Dwight (makers of Arm & Hammer baking soda) and Whole Foods (which operates a highly profitable chain of stores selling healthy and environmentally sound groceries) have prospered in the age of environmentalism; but their tales, and that of others, are mostly anecdotal.

Some insight may be found in a 1993 poll conducted by Roper Starch Worldwide for Cone Communications, a Boston-based marketing and communications firm. The poll focused on cause-related marketing, campaigns by advertisers to hitch their messages to a charitable or social cause. (The advent of cause-related marketing into the big-time world of Madison Avenue advertising is generally associated with American Express Company's 1983 promotion to donate a percentage of charges made by its cardholders to the Ellis Island/Statue of Liberty Restoration Fund. Since then, cause-related marketing has been the marketing vehicle of choice for countless companies ranging from fashion designers to financial institutions. But it's hard to call these efforts socially responsible based on our larger definitions.) Seventy-eight percent of the adults surveyed said they would be more likely to buy a product that is associated with a cause they care about. To do so, two thirds said they would switch brands and 62 percent said they would switch retailers. And just over half said they would pay slightly more for a product that supported a worthy cause.

But before you pick up the phone to call your advertising agency, it is important to understand that there is a gigantic leap between social *concern* and social *consumerism*. A few years earlier, a succession of polls indicated a very strong desire by consumers to choose environmentally improved products. Indeed, nine out of ten consumers said they would be willing to buy Product A over Product B, if Product A were kinder and gentler to the planet—and be willing to pay more for the privilege of doing so. But by the time their grocery carts reached the checkout stand, their purchases were remarkably similar to the way they had shopped prior to their "green" consciousness-raising. It turned out that there is something marketing experts call the "halo effect," in which respondents to polls give answers they think will make them look like angels (in the eyes of the pollsters, at least), as opposed to answers that truly reflect their attitudes and behavior.

Indications are that consumer responses tend to be influenced by the most recent commercials or advertisements they saw or read. In the Roper poll, companies that consumers mentioned as the most socially responsible included McDonald's, Anheuser-Busch, Ben & Jerry's, Coca-Cola, DuPont, Procter & Gamble, General Motors, and Kodak, each being named without prompting by between 6 percent and 8 percent of respondents. All except for Ben & Jerry's and Du-Pont rank among the nation's one hundred largest advertisers according to *Advertising Age*. Perhaps more significant, however, was that more than half the respondents couldn't name *any* company they considered socially responsible.

And so it is unclear how much social responsibility "sells" to the general public. Polls offer only modest help in understanding consumer concerns and habits—or which companies are doing the most "social good." They tell us little about how shoppers are likely to view companies whose socially minded efforts aren't heavily promoted and advertised. There is a strong likelihood that these quiet operators are among the truly committed companies, as distinguished from those whose efforts ebb and flow with the tides of marketing fashion. The evidence so far is mostly anecdotal. As it becomes more empirical, the uncertainty will fade.

THE REWARDS OF A WINNING REPUTATION

Each year, the editors at *Fortune* magazine assess "America's most admired corporations." The annual study asks more than 10,000 senior executives, outside directors, and financial analysts to rate the ten largest companies in their own industry on eight attributes of reputation—including their responsibility to the community and the environment. "You won't find it on the balance sheet, and it's not listed in a 10K or proxy," the *Fortune* editors noted in their introduction to the 1992 ratings. "If you ask the wizards on Wall Street how it figures into a company's net worth, be prepared for some mighty blank stares. But more and more companies are now coming to realize that when managed correctly, a good name can be their most valuable and enduring asset."

Some CEOs and advertising agency executives believe that over the next decade or so, corporate reputation will play an increasing role in corporate competitiveness, ultimately rivaling quality and brand name among criteria used by customers in selecting products and services. That reputation, in most cases, won't be built from a single carefully crafted marketing effort, or even a single socially responsible program. Rather, it will be built, little by little, from a myriad of company activities: product quality, treatment of employees, community volunteer programs, where and how products are manufactured, environmental record, corporate philanthropy, and participation in everything from Little League to Earth Day. That's quite different from the past, when reputation was based on how much money your company gave away. "Business is all about building relationships with people, both inside and outside your organization," says John Martin, the president and CEO of Taco Bell. "It's about listening and responding to the needs of others. A company's reputation today is built around everything it does—it's the sum total of all its actions. Organizations that are socially responsible are viewed as having integrity as well as quality products and services. That combination and balance is absolutely critical in business. It determines, in the public's mind, just who you are and what you stand for."

Measuring reputation, and linking it to financial performance, is a nascent but growing science. So far, the more than two dozen academic studies linking the two have produced equivocal results, says New York University business school professor Tom Gladwin. "There is a general belief that a fairly strong, well-developed corporate identity that shows caring and compassion is associated with superior performance long term," he says. "Over the long term, reputation is probably the only real asset that a company has."

The idea of reputation as a measurable asset is just beginning to take hold in some companies. "There's a link that people are increasingly seeing between reputation and financial success," says Levi Strauss's Bob Dunn. "There has to be a new accounting system that develops this because traditional accounting can't cope with what can't be measured."

While individual companies are figuring out how to do it, outsiders are increasingly focusing on how to measure reputation on a broader level. The Connecticut-based research firm of Yankelovich Partners has been tracking company reputations for nearly two decades, more recently determining companies' "corporate equity," an index derived from a complex algorithmic calculation and weighted scales of several aspects of reputation. In determining corporate equity scores, Yankelovich gauges awareness of a company, familiarity with its products and operations, individuals' overall impressions about the company, their perceptions about how the company performs, and whether the respondents would actually buy its products or engage in a number of other "supportive behaviors." The product of all this is an index, an assigned number that allows a company to compare its reputation with those of other companies.

The results, says Yankelovich managing partner John Gilfeather, show that companies with good reputations outperform other companies on a number of dimensions. Those companies that are seen favorably will find people more willing to buy their products, support them in a controversial situation, form joint ventures with them, recommend them as a place to work, or buy the company's stock. Moreover, the companies with the highest corporate equity scores consistently showed the highest price-to-earning ratios on their financial statements.

Yankelovich didn't measure social responsibility specifically. But Gilfeather sees reputation based on social responsibility as an increasingly visible part of the equation. More significantly, he sees a company's socially responsible reputation as insurance during tough times. "If you do something bad, you're going to get hammered," he says. "There's very little forgiveness these days. If you run afoul of something and you're going to go down like a rock, companies that are not well known, that haven't spent a lot of time working on their reputation, are going to go down faster." Fel-Pro's Elliot Lehman agrees. "I don't believe our company gets an order just because we are good guys," he says. "But when there is a choice, they come to us because we are good guys; it is a marketing plus."

There are plenty of those in business who believe that, and who see social responsibility as a factor in shaping that reputation. Among the believers is Steve Schuitt, human resources manager at Tom's of Maine, which manufactures natural toothpaste, deodorant, and other personal care products. He sees the benefits of reputation firsthand— for example, in "the caliber and quantity of job applicants we get. When we're perceived as the socially responsible company that we are, immediately people who have common values are attracted. So it enables us not only to find competent employees, which is a goal of every corporation, but we also have applicants who increasingly have values that are socially responsible. They're concerned about

> We should take pride in the values we uphold. The merits of applying high moral and ethical standards may well be a matter of belief. I believe it is the right thing to do—and I also believe it is good business. Sound long-term customers want to do business this way, the best employees want to work under these conditions, quality suppliers favor these kinds of customers, and suppliers of capital find these relationships rewarding.
>
> —DWIGHT C. MINTON,
> *CEO, Church & Dwight Co., Inc.*

how companies treat their employees, the environment, and the communities. They're attracted to Tom's of Maine. It enables us to see a better group of applicants whose values, again, are more in sync with ours."

Not all potential employees are so committed, and the majority of shoppers don't yet vote for reputation with their dollars—at least, not consciously. Still, few executives will tell you these days that reputation isn't a factor in remaining competitive. A few will say that it is *the* key to competitiveness. There is little doubt that companies' social performance will help shape their reputations—both internally, among employees, and externally, among the other stakeholder groups—as the many issues surrounding social responsibility move to the forefront.

TO THE VICTORS GO THE SPOILS

Marketers are aware that there are pockets of consumers in all demographic groups ready, willing, and able to respond to socially aware companies and messages. One big challenge is finding them.

It is more likely that socially conscious consumers will find the companies. If your company is socially responsible, a portion of the public will seek you out, and perhaps tell their friends about you as well. They will be helped along by any of several national and local efforts dedicated to helping consumers vote for social change every time they open their wallets. The Co-op America Business Network is one small example of a network formed in part to promote socially conscious companies. Each year, the group publishes its *National Green Pages*, a directory of its business members. To join, companies must sign a pledge of social and environmental responsibility, promising to continually improve their practices. A Co-op America board-appointed committee reviews each applicant, who must be approved by the full board of directors. While companies don't need to be perfect to be accepted—"We look for companies that go beyond industry standards in their practices," says one spokesperson—about 4 to 5 percent of applicants get turned down. Most of its members are small, entrepreneurial businesses.

Another promoter of "good" companies is the Council on Economic Priorities, the group that publishes *Shopping for a Better World*. Its Campaign for Cleaner Corporations issues an annual list of "America's Dirtiest Companies" that gets considerable media attention. On the flip side, it issues "America's Corporate Conscience Awards" annually to showcase companies with good social policies. The awards—presented with much fanfare at a black-tie banquet at New York City's Plaza or Waldorf-Astoria hotels, replete with movie stars, politicians, and copious amounts of press—are given out in specific areas, such as charitable contributions, community action, employer responsiveness, environmental protection, and equal opportunity. Among the winners have been Avon, Dayton Hudson, Ford, Gannett, General Mills, Hallmark, IBM, Johnson & Johnson, Kellogg, Levi Strauss & Co., Pitney Bowes, Polaroid, Shorebank Corp., Stonyfield Farm, Stride Rite, and Xerox.

CEP's awards are only one example of the recognition being given to companies that attempt to do well by doing good. Another is the Business Enterprise Trust, or BET, a nonprofit organization founded in 1989 whose mission is "to tell some stories and create some heroes who have integrated some social concern with bottom-line performance," according to Kirk Hanson, the Stanford University professor who was its executive director during its first four years. BET was the brainchild of television producer Norman Lear, who had the idea of creating a sort of Nobel Prize for business. He recruited James E. Burke, formerly CEO of Johnson & Johnson, to chair its board of directors. Among BET's other board members are Berkshire Hathaway's Warren E. Buffett, *The Washington Post*'s Katharine Graham, Levi Strauss's Walter A. Haas, Jr., former United Auto Workers boss Douglas A. Fraser, and Labor Secretary Robert Reich.

BET describes its mission as one that "seeks to shine a spotlight on acts of courage, integrity, and social vision in business" by identifying "bold, creative leadership that combines sound management with social conscience." Each year, at a star-studded ceremony, it gives crystal sculpture awards to five individuals or companies that demonstrate a commitment "both to the long-term interests of the shareholders and to the needs of society." It focuses on acts that occur in "the normal course of business," as opposed to acts of philanthropy or volunteerism, and special emphasis is given to those who have not already been in the national spotlight for their deeds.

The BET offices on the Stanford University campus are filled with nomination packages—nearly a thousand were submitted during the first four years—showcasing individual and company efforts. Applications go through a multistage screening process, involving members of the business and academic communities, before being submitted to the board for final selection. Winners' stories are told through individual print profiles and video documentaries commissioned by BET. The videos are screened at the award ceremony. At the 1993 ceremony, hosted by TV journalist Diane Sawyer, the videos were narrated by veteran journalist Bill Moyers. Hillary Rodham Clinton made the ceremony's closing remarks.

The BET awards are notable in part for their diversity. Although winners include some of the "usual suspects" among socially responsible companies, they also have included G.E. Plastics, a division of the General Electric Company, for its innovative program to foster teamwork for both the company's and the community's benefit; four middle-management minority employees at Inland Steel, who pushed top management to promote greater sensitivity to workplace diversity and wider opportunities for minorities and women at their company; and the Prudential Life Insurance Company of America, which created the Living Needs Benefit option, providing terminally ill and permanently confined policyholders access to their life insurance benefits.

There are many other awards and citations given to national and local companies involved with a range of such socially responsible issues as education reform, environmental stewardship, community involvement, employee welfare, and minority advancement. There's the Points of Light Foundation, which gives awards to companies for community service activities. *Inc.* magazine now has a category for social responsibility in its annual Entrepreneur of the Year awards. Annual rankings by magazines as "the best place to work"—for minorities, women, working parents, and others—have become a staple of the publishing trade, and no doubt, a profitable way to boost circulation. The point is, companies like awards and will spend considerable time and money to get them. They see value in the form of pride inside their companies and the growing reputation they build outside. Awards perform a service to the social responsibility movement, elevating it—and the winning companies—to a more visible stature.

FORCES FOR CHANGE

And so the many streams have come together: the failure of government and other institutions to successfully address a variety of social and environmental problems; the growing understanding by companies of the larger role they play in society, and the clout they potentially wield to contribute to their employees, customers, communities, and others; the growing call for accounting and measurement tools to help both companies and outsiders measure the impact of companies on society—the positive impacts as well as the negative ones. There's the increased concern among stockholders, customers, employees, and others about the vision and policies of the companies with which they are affiliated; the ascension of a new generation of business and political leaders who understand the complex links between business and society; and the growing body of success stories among companies that have turned social responsibility into a competitive advantage.

Most companies won't be getting awards from BET or citations from CEP any time soon. These companies are the ones most vulnerable to pressures from investors, activists, the media, consumers, and competitors. Increasingly, companies that haven't yet accepted the need to think about social responsibility as a strategic value will find themselves falling behind. As awareness of social responsibility issues continues to grow, and proactive, people-oriented companies continue to further the state of the art for the entire business community, companies will be expected to do more and more: to invest in their employees, their communities, the environment, and the larger world. More than likely, company policies that are now seen as unnecessary luxuries or "ahead of the curve" will become expected, perhaps even required. Those that ignore the signals they receive will find themselves playing catch-up with their competitors in putting socially responsible programs to work.

Together, the confluence of these streams is having an impact, variously inspiring and prodding companies to look more deeply into their own operations to see where social responsibility makes good business sense. In a growing number of companies, business leaders are recognizing that their investment in the quality of their employees' and communities' lives will reap dividends—if not next quarter, perhaps next year, and for a long time to come.

Chapter Six

The Greening of the Bottom Line

"We have a firm belief that we're going to have a cradle-to-grave responsibility for our products. If you apply that principle to your products, you are not really selling products, you're renting them."

—WALTER ROSENBERG,
Compaq Computer Corporation

About 60 miles north of San Francisco, amid the seemingly endless acreage of vineyards that populate southern Mendocino County, there's a revolution going on. Fetzer Vineyards, a respected twenty-five-year-old winemaker based in Hopland, is going organic. No more petrochemical-based herbicides, no pesticides, no fertilizers. Instead, decaying grape skins and other natural matter fertilize the crops, and cover crops help attract "good" bugs that prey on "bad" ones.

Fetzer's goal is to become the first all-organic winery. That means that the 2.2 million or so cases of cabernet, chardonnay, gewurtztraminer, merlot, pinot noir, zinfandel, and other varietal wines it produces in a typical year will originate with grapes grown according to strict standards established by California Certified Organic Farmers, which certifies organic farming methods. Already, Fetzer is producing limited quantities of wine from organically grown grapes—about

25,000 cases a year in 1994, a number expected to triple in 1995. The two vintages produced so far—a red table wine and a chardonnay—have received an enthusiastic thumbs-up from wine critics.

And from environmentalists. Traditional grape growing is a chemical-intensive business, contributing to the more than 1.5 billion tons of pesticides used by U.S. farmers each year, some of which drain off croplands and into drinking water. The Environmental Protection Agency estimates that over 20 million pounds of pesticides a year enter the water supply; one study found at least seventeen agricultural pesticides in groundwater in twenty-one states. About half of all Americans rely on groundwater for their domestic drinking water. By switching to organic methods, Fetzer may play a small but significant role in reducing the flow of toxins.

The switch to organic came in 1992 after the Fetzer family sold the winery it had founded to Brown-Forman, the Louisville, Kentucky, based conglomerate that also owns Jack Daniel's whiskey, Hartmann luggage, and Lenox china, among other blue-chip brands. After the ownership change, the new management team assembled some Fetzer and Brown-Forman executives at a mountain resort "to talk about our values and what we held to be important for ourselves," says Paul Dolan, Fetzer's president and chief winemaker. That produced a mission statement, saying in part that Fetzer was "an environmentally and socially conscious grower." Going organic became part of that mission.

Like most larger winemakers, Fetzer doesn't grow all its own grapes. In fact, it grows only about 20 percent of the grapes it crushes into wine; the rest come from 150 or so farms scattered throughout California. Under Fetzer's plan, they, too, will become organic growers within a few years—or risk losing Fetzer's business. But prodding its own growers to become chemical-free is only a beginning. Dolan's goal is nothing less than persuading and prodding the entire California winemaking industry to kick its chemical habit.

Fetzer is on a mission "to do something good for the environment," says Dolan, who in 1991 was named "Wine Maker of the Year" by the Los Angeles Times. He's taking a new look at just about everything, from the way Fetzer's wine is made to the way its offices are designed and operated to the kind of paper and ink used to print wine labels. "I'm a fifth-generation winemaker and so I have a real closeness to the business," he says. "I see that this is a great opportunity to make a difference."

But make no mistake: this is also good business. By transforming itself into the industry leader on organic farming methods, Fetzer has harvested a bumper crop of favorable publicity. Its first 10,000 cases of organic wine, produced in 1993, sold without much effort. And Dolan sees a strong continued demand. Sales and profits were up during 1993, a sober year for wine sales, even though Fetzer had made a transition from lower-end table wines to higher-priced varietals.

More important is Fetzer's ability to make the transformation to organic without increased costs, and perhaps a slight decrease in costs over time. In 1989, the last year the winery used only traditional farming methods, its annual costs for pesticides and fertilizers were about $460 per acre. Its current annual costs for farming organically—including new equipment such as compost spreaders and weeding instruments—are between $450 and $500 per acre for the first three years of pesticide-free farming, dropping to about $400 per acre after that. Beyond these roughly comparable costs, there is the potential for indirect savings from reduced chemical exposure by farm workers, which could help keep them healthy and productive and cut Fetzer's medical and insurance costs. In addition to savings and increased revenues, Dolan and company are satisfied that their pioneering efforts will likely bring long-term benefits to California's environment and the health of their fellow citizens.

WHY COMPANIES ARE GOING GREEN

Like Fetzer, other companies are finding that there are significant dividends to be reaped from investment in reducing the environmental toll of their operations. The payoffs are both tangible and intangible: lower operating costs and increased profit margins, reduced oversight by regulators, increased customer satisfaction and loyalty, and increased competitiveness in the global marketplace.

Environmental performance may represent the most direct link between a company's socially responsible vision and practices and its impact on both financial performance and the well-being of society. The impact of environmental performance is often immediate and acute; so, too, is the financial impact of waste and pollution. Companies recognize this, and so does the public, which in recent years has taken an ever-increasing interest in companies' environmental performance. Federal and local regulators' interest has grown, too, as they have stepped up enforcement of environmental laws and offered

Environmental concerns are like a great river, a river that's getting bigger and stronger all the time. All Fuller is doing is getting out of the backwater and into the fast central flow of the river. A lot of companies don't see the river yet. When they do, we'll be way ahead.

—ANTHONY ANDERSEN,
CEO, H. B. Fuller

greater incentives for companies to reduce waste, energy use, and emissions. For companies, that means a dramatic shift in thinking about environmental issues, from a "command-and-control" mentality—the traditional government enforcement model—where pollutants had to be safely captured and neutralized before entering the environment, to a more proactive stance that recognizes that it is far less polluting—and ultimately less expensive—to avoid creating waste and pollution in the first place. Companies that have managed to redesign their products, processes, and policies to embrace environmental thinking are finding themselves a step or more ahead of both the regulatory curve and their competitors, and are being smiled upon by customers, suppliers, government agencies, and communities alike.

As a result, the notion of corporate environmental responsibility has shifted dramatically for thousands of companies. Until a few years ago, addressing environmental concerns was simply a matter of not breaking the law. Federal and state lawmakers offered few if any incentives to help companies "go green," and public concern and pressure were limited to a relatively small corps of environmental groups and community activists.

How quickly things have changed. Today, corporate environmental responsibility has become a bottom-line issue—as well as an expectation of regulators, customers, insurers, investors, community members, and other stakeholders. The change of pace has been dizzying. What only recently seemed cutting edge—corporate recycling, partnerships with environmentalists and regulators, purchasing policies favoring environmentally improved goods and services—can now be found in many companies and industry sectors. It wasn't long ago that a company could issue an environmental mission statement, initiate a modest paper-recycling program, perhaps ban polystyrene foam coffee cups from its premises, and stand a reasonable chance of making the nightly news or garnering a few column-inches in the *Wall Street Journal.* Now, companies that *aren't* doing these things are much more likely to find themselves fielding calls from reporters and activists compiling the latest in a never-ending series of corporate environmental ratings, which include annual "toxic ten" and "dirty dozen" lists issued by groups such as Citizen Action and the Council on Economic Priorities.

A socially responsible stance on the environment comes from the widest possible perspective, integrating environmental thinking into the core of company operations: product design and personnel policies, maintenance systems and marketing programs, accounting and advertising, purchasing policies and public relations, and so on. Environmental responsibility begins with a company's understanding of the links between the environment and these myriad aspects of their business—the resources used, the waste and pollution generated, and the opportunities to reduce both while improving bottom-line performance. These internal policies are part of a larger corporate vision that also includes leveraging a company's actions to influence others—competitors, customers, suppliers, employees, governments—to improve their environmental performance as well.

Still, the bottom line remains a key motivating factor. Nearly every environmental initiative involves two very simple ideas: minimizing waste and maximizing resource efficiency. Those two worthy goals embrace the entire range of a company's operations, whether in the manufacturing or service sectors: how a product is designed and manufactured or a service is delivered; the energy and other resources required to transport things to market and use them or keep them functioning throughout that product's useful life; how goods are ultimately disposed of—ideally, by turning them into raw material for other products. Such life-cycle, "cradle-to-grave-to-cradle" thinking is the backbone of the new environmental consciousness.

Another influence on this new mode of thinking is the growing body of knowledge on the larger economic value of the environment. Academic groups, such as the International Society of Ecological Economics, have tried, with varying degrees of success, to quantify such things as the value of a standing forest as opposed to its value when cut down and sold for timber or paper pulp. Already, several nations have attempted to incorporate environmental values into their national accounting schemes. In Norway, for example, the gross domestic product reflects the value of petroleum, mineral (copper, iron, lead, titanium, and zinc), forest products, fish, and hydropower resources, offset by negative values assigned to the discharge of selected air and water pollutants. France has been trying to create a national accounting system known as "patrimony accounting," intended to analyze and describe the natural environment in its three basic functions: economic, ecological, and social. Germany is attempting to quantify its "gross ecological product," employing statisticians and economists at its Federal Statistical Office to merge the country's natural resource accounts with its national income accounts. In 1994, the U.S. Department of Commerce's Bureau of Economic Analysis took the first steps in calculating a "green" gross domestic product, a move that over time could have widespread impact in determining how the government sets tax policy, for example, or allocates its financial resources.

As economists slowly learn how environmental concerns can be factored into accounting practices, companies will be asked, perhaps required, to translate these concepts into balance sheets, profit-and-loss statements, and other standard accounting instruments. This will mean analyzing each product or service for its inputs and outputs: the nature and amount of resources that go into producing it (as well as into operating the company itself) and the wastes and by-products that result from its manufacture, use, and disposal. Such requirements are not far off; already, the Securities and Exchange Commission is asking publicly held companies to account more accurately for the impact of hazardous waste cleanups and potential environmental liabilities on their balance sheets, a move that could have serious implications for the way some companies' stocks are valued. If federal accounting rules require your company to report a $350 million contingent liability for its role in creating a hazardous waste dump, it could have a profound impact on the attractiveness of your company to investors.

And so the bottom line is greening throughout some companies' operations, although "the environment" remains a discrete program, department, or initiative in most. At the head of the class are companies that have integrated environmentalism into their philosophies, mission statements, employee handbooks, accounting systems, and stakeholder relationships. While relatively few companies have managed to integrate environmental thinking successfully into every part of their operations, a solid core of companies are trying—and both companies and the environment are benefiting from their efforts.

FETZER'S ENVIRONMENTAL VISION

At Fetzer, "green" thinking is now part of every decision, from the way grapes are grown and harvested through sales, marketing, and the disposition of waste and by-products. In the middle, the environment has become part and parcel of relationships the company has with suppliers, customers, neighbors, and employees, leading Fetzer to forge new alliances, rethink old policies, and search out synergies. So, for Fetzer, the environment is not a value-added program. It is a way of doing business.

Paul Dolan sees few limits to Fetzer's environmental initiatives. And nearly all of them seem to have a salutary effect on company operations, from product yield to employee morale. "What we've found is that we're actually better farmers as a result of going organic," says Dolan. "We're closer to the ground. We're much more aware of what's happening in the vineyard. We've seen that by spraying so much, we were actually killing the microbiological life in the soil. I can remember as a young winemaker going out and tasting fruit to determine if it was ready for harvest. I could take one vine and it had all the spicy flavors of the sauvignon blanc and it was perfect. And I could go just ten feet away and taste another grape and it would be flat and insipid and wasn't at all right. Now I understand that there was less microbiological life in that part of the vineyard than in the other." That realization has shown up in the quality of grape yields. At the vineyard where Fetzer is growing organic, the grapes go into the company's best sauvignon blanc. During the days of chemical-laden farming, the grapes went into its lowest-end table wine.

Fetzer is working closely with its independent growers to help them make the transition to pesticide-free agriculture by the end of the decade, although Dolan has not set a firm deadline. The company has created educational programs, showing farmers how to implement organic growing techniques. Already, about 20 percent have converted; an equal number are farming organically but aren't yet certified. (Certification requires that land lie fallow or be farmed pesticide-free for several years to rid the soil of chemical residues.) But, says Dolan, "we're not interested in certification. We're interested in really eliminating herbicides and pesticides." Beyond that, Dolan believes the closer interaction between Fetzer and its growers is opening up overall communications and generally improving relations.

The company is educating competitors, too. Dolan regularly preaches the organic growing gospel in meetings and speeches,

which has produced both interest and action from other winemakers. Gallo, the state's largest winery, is currently farming 6,000 acres
organically—more acres than Fetzer, though a relatively tiny portion
of Gallo's behemoth operation. Sutter Home and Beringer are among
the other better-known wineries following Fetzer's lead by experi-
menting with organic growing techniques.

The company is also focusing on waste. Whenever possible, it is
trying to close the loop by turning waste into feedstock of one kind
or another. Already, the company's main plant in Redwood Valley
recycles 80 percent of its waste, on its way to its goal of 100 percent.
Plastic shrink-wrap is sent to China, where it is used in farm fields to
keep the weeds down. Glass wine bottles that used to be recycled are
now washed and reused. Dolan is looking into ways to reduce the
amount of glass used to manufacture each bottle, and is trying to
curtail use of gold inks in labels, because of the significant impact of
gold mining on water pollution. About 20,000 tons a year of grape
skins, seeds, and stems are sent to a compost pile, where they are
mixed with other materials—including wood shavings from Fetzer's
barrel-making operations and mushroom compost from a farmer
down the road—to create a nutrient-rich humus that is put back on
the vineyards.

Fetzer saves $5,000 a month from energy conservation efforts. Its
new office complex will be built to run on solar energy, with traditional electricity available only as a backup for phones and computers. In constructing the project, built by Fetzer's in-house
construction crew, Dolan is looking at the environmental impact of
such things as carpet fiber, the glues being used to put the windows
together, and timber sources.

Dolan sees all of these efforts as helping to put a positive image on
his industry. "There is so much negative press about alcohol, and the
wine industry is included in that," he says. "I view this as a greater
opportunity for us to look at how we're operating. We can change
the conversation about wine by changing the way we operate. So if
people start to hear that the wine industry is a leader in the area of
organic farming and we're making a difference in the environment, it
automatically changes how people perceive wine."

The financial returns, says Dolan, will come, though he declines to
speculate on how much, or when. At the very least, he says, "There
will be a lot more awareness about Fetzer, and I think our sales will
be better as a result of all this. And yet I'm not driven by that. I'm
driven by the fun of doing what we're doing."

To be sure, not all of it can be considered fun. A good deal of what companies must do to reduce their environmental toll involves hard work, painfully slow change, fighting considerable resistance up and down the line, and persistent communication with employees, customers, suppliers, communities, regulators, competitors, media, lenders, and, of course, environmentalists. But Fetzer has the right idea. Its "greening" efforts extend well beyond compliance with environmental laws, improving company image, or creating good, green profits. Rather, Dolan and company view their environmental efforts as a means of turning good business practices into an agent for change—in their region as well as their industry.

BEYOND COMPLIANCE

Hundreds of other companies, both large and small, are joining Fetzer in the quest to reduce their environmental impacts—and, usually, to improve their bottom lines. The most effective actions come from companies whose environmental vision extends beyond mere recycling, or beyond merely a single program, to embrace an environmental ethic that is integrated throughout company operations. As a result, many of the environmental benefits of these efforts percolate up and trickle down to affect suppliers, customers, neighbors, and others. A few brief examples:

• **Quad/Graphics,** the $700-million-a-year Wisconsin-based magazine and catalogue printer, has become a leader in the printing industry in its pursuit of environmental excellence. At its half-dozen printing plants, just about everything is reduced, reused, or recycled. For example, waste inks and press-cleaning solvents, many of which contain toxic heavy metals and air pollutants, have been eliminated or significantly reduced. Quad has invested in environmental research and development, leading to less-polluting inks as well as a new kind of ink-jet printer (used for putting subscriber addresses directly on magazines as they come off the press) that uses substantially less ink. The company has reduced solid and liquid wastes to a bare minimum and has set forth an aggressive effort to educate its employees, customers, community members, even competitors, on environmental matters. The effort has won the respect of its industry, the loyalty of its customers, and an impressive array of local and national environmental awards and citations.

The Earth as a Bottom-Line Issue

Enlightened environmentalism is a natural part of Quad/ Graphics' holistic approach to business. We're here to improve the quality of life for ourselves, for the communities where we live and work, and for all God's creatures. Underlying our day-to-day actions is our desire to make our surroundings better for our having been here. Our goal is to take better care of ourselves, our clients, our community, and our world.

Our goal is wise, balanced use of all resources, including financial ones. We conserve raw materials, and we continually minimize waste and reduce our effect on the environment by working with clients and vendors, testing new equipment, developing new manufacturing processes and materials, and making one another aware of the difference each of us can make. We are educators, within the company, in the community, and as leaders in the printing, publishing, and cataloging industries.

We are proactive in creating and maintaining an "environment for excellence."

We serve as a catalyst for community action and as a resource for legislators.

We don't just react to what happens; we help shape policy and events.

Giving loving care to Mother Earth *is* good business!

—FROM QUAD/GRAPHICS, INC.,
ENVIRONMENTAL MISSION STATEMENT

• **Stonyfield Farm,** the $25-million-a-year, New Hampshire—based yogurt maker, has set its focus on the survival of the family farm in New England, which it sees as fundamental to the region's environmental and economic future. Aside from implementing a wide range of environmental processes and practices in its own operations, it provides financial incentives and a training program to get local dairy farmers to use low-impact methods, and educates its customers about their benefits as well.

• **Valley Plastics,** a small northern California–based manufacturer of component parts for high-tech companies, has worked closely with suppliers, customers, and other regional businesses to eliminate resins and other unrecyclable materials. It required dogged determination and one-on-one educational efforts, but the work paid off. In an industry with a reputation for generating significant wastes, the company is now 99 percent "waste-free," meaning it throws out practically nothing. Says Art Frengel, Valley Plastics' president: "We wanted to show other businesses that you could provide medical insurance, recycle all your scrap, and make commitments toward your principles and still be okay. And sleep better at night."

• **Xerox Corporation** has launched a program called Asset Recycle Management, or ARM, to redesign its photocopiers, printers, facsimile machines, and other products so that their parts may be disassembled and reused. The idea is to create profit out of what had previously been deemed waste. The program's mission is "to maximize return on assets by increasing the velocity with which nonrevenue-producing assets are transformed to revenue-producing assets," according to company documents. Roughly translated, that means getting more use out of each product by designing them with parts that can easily be reused in other machines, or replaced with upgraded versions to keep current machines running longer. The result: Xerox's customers get more out of every Xerox product, with fewer machines going into premature retirement. An ARM team is working with each of the company's Product Architecture Teams to develop an Asset Recycle/Environmental Strategy. Among other things, that means standardizing parts for easy replacement, often using higher-quality (and more expensive) components that will have a longer life. This is a whole new approach to product design and manufacturing because it goes beyond the needs and desires of the initial buyer to those of any subsequent buyers. Already, Xerox reclaims about a million finished piece parts worldwide each year from existing machines, representing a total resale value of $200 million. That number is expected to grow considerably several years after its redesigned products enter the marketplace.

• **The Park Plaza Hotel & Towers,** a 977-room, family-operated hotel in Boston, Massachusetts, has become a showcase for environmentalism within the hospitality industry. The changes range from installing faucet aerators and low-flow showerheads in all guest rooms (saving more than 10 million gallons of water and 30,000 gallons of heating oil a year) to ridding guestrooms of individual soap, shampoo, conditioner, and mouthwash containers in favor of refillable dispensers (saving almost 2 million individual plastic containers a year). The owners have installed a water-filtration system in the hotel's laundry facility that annually saves 6.5 million out of 10 million gallons of water previously needed to wash linens and towels. The hotel's owners have dubbed their facility "Boston's Eco-Logical Travel Alternative" and have seen business boom: In 1993, the company attributed about $1.5 million in revenue to additional business from organizations that appreciate the earth-conscious accommodations.

A TALE OF TWO CIRCLES

Such efforts stem largely from these companies' leaders understanding that good environmental practices are good business, that waste and pollution represent things that a company makes or does that it cannot sell. These efforts also are the result of pressures by the public for companies to clean up their acts. For years, a succession of surveys and polls has established that Americans—along with citizens of most other industrialized nations—rank environmental protection high on their list of national priorities.

Polls that compare attitudes of consumers and business executives on environmental issues invariably find that the consumers perceive problems as more serious than the executives do. A 1993 poll, conducted by Opinion Research Corp. for Arthur D. Little, found that nearly three quarters of the public placed a high priority on cleaning up the environment, while fewer than half of 500 executives from the largest U.S. companies agreed. The poll also found that about two thirds of the public said they think the government is spending too little on environmental cleanup; only 45 percent of the executives agreed. Reviewing the results, J. Ladd Greeno, Arthur D. Little's senior vice president and managing director of its worldwide environmental practice, warned of an impending "collision course where everyone loses—including the environment."

One place where business may lose is in the regulatory environment, as public opinion, spurred by environmental activists, helps build pressure for increasingly restrictive and costly environmental laws. In 1993, U.S. companies spent $125 billion complying with environmental regulations, according to EPA, about 2.1 percent of the gross national product. By decade's end, that portion of GNP could rise to as high as 2.8 percent. Some federal and state regulations haven't yet had their full impact on business. The 1990 Clean Air Act amendments, for example, include provisions that won't kick in until after the turn of the century.

Business leaders should be especially worried about the stepped-up enforcement that seems to be regulators' response to increased public concern about companies' environmental practices. The problem isn't just the level of government oversight but rather the apparent disconnect between the environmental concerns of the public and those of the scientific community. For example, another 1993 survey, this one by Gerstman + Meyers, a New York–based "brand identity and design consultant," found that consumers ranked the "garbage crisis" as the number-one environmental issue, over air quality, water quality, ozone depletion, and deforestation. Moreover, concern over solid waste nearly doubled over the level five years earlier. In contrast, environmentalists and scientists rank such matters as climate change, species extinction, and overpopulation at the top of their lists, along with air, water, and ground pollution; solid waste ranks low. The implications should be obvious: If regulations track the public's concern, lawmakers and their enforcement agencies may spend an inordinate amount of time pressing companies to deal with the wrong environmental issues, perhaps ignoring those that have the greatest impact on reducing environmental degradation—and reducing corporate waste.

No doubt the public focus on solid waste results in part from an emphasis—some would say an overemphasis—on household recycling and source reduction as solutions to environmental problems. As effective as some recycling campaigns have been, they seem to be obscuring the real problems.

There's no better example of this than what might be called A Tale of Two Circles.

Just about anyone who has paid attention to environmental issues in recent years has seen a familiar-looking pie chart describing something called municipal solid waste. It shows the breakdown of the 180 million or so tons a year of wastes that go into landfills, based on data compiled by the Environmental Protection Agency. Roughly 40 percent of that waste is comprised of paper and cardboard. Another 18 percent or so comes from yard wastes—lawn clippings, raked leaves, and the like. Plastics, glass, metals, and food wastes make up another 7 or 8 percent each, with lesser amounts of rubber, leather, textiles, wool, and the rest of society's flotsam and jetsam.

That pie chart and its contents have been the prime focus of the solid waste issue and its accompanying debates—paper versus plastic bags, for example, or cloth versus disposable diapers. Manufacturers of one type of product or packaging refer to this circle to "prove" that their product's contribution to the so-called landfill crisis is infinitesimal—at least compared with that of their competitors.

But that pie chart doesn't even begin to tell the story of who's generating what kinds of waste. There's another pie chart, one rarely seen in public or even described by manufacturers, environmentalists, or regulators. This second pie—we'll call it the Gross National Trash, or GNT—represents the *entire* universe of waste. The GNT pie is over 70 times bigger than the first pie, comprising nearly 13 billion tons of waste generated mostly by industry, as reported to the EPA. GNT includes nonhazardous waste, hazardous waste, agricultural waste, mining waste, oil and gas waste, construction debris, and other refuse from the world of business and industry.

One tiny sliver of the GNT, representing only about 1.4 percent of the total, is municipal solid waste—that is, the entire first pie chart described above.

True, not much of the GNT goes into city dumps. Still, it goes *somewhere*—into what government bureaucrats variously refer to as landfills, waste piles, surface impoundments, and other "land disposal units." And while the bulk of it is classified as "nonhazardous," that doesn't mean it is harmless. For example, according to the EPA, some "nonhazardous waste" contains relatively high levels of heavy metals and organic constituents, including polychlorinated biphenyls, or PCBs, extremely toxic and persistent organic compounds that at high enough levels can cause severe liver damage and are suspected of causing cancer. Rinsed-out pesticide containers are also included among this "nonhazardous waste."

This little exercise in comparing pie charts is instructive. It points out that while public attention over the environment has focused on such things as Pampers, Pepsi bottles, and plastic bags, those items appear to be the least of the problem. The real action, it seems, has less to do with what we use at home than with what most of us use at work. A similarly disproportionate contribution would be evident if one were to calculate emissions of toxic materials into the air or water (although the impact of individuals' automobile use on air

Municipal Solid Waste
Total: 180 Million Tons per Year

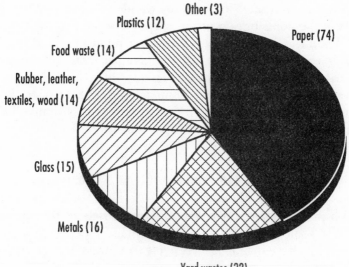

Other (3)

Plastics (12)

Food waste (14)

Rubber, leather, textiles, wood (14)

Glass (15)

Metals (16)

Yard wastes (32)

Paper (74)

Gross National Trash
Total: 12,915 Million Tons per Year

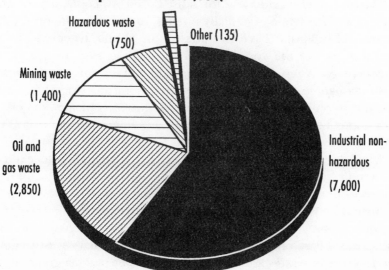

Municipal solid waste (180)

Hazardous waste (750)

Other (135)

Mining waste (1,400)

Oil and gas waste (2,850)

Industrial non-hazardous (7,600)

Numbers in parentheses represent millions of tons annually. © 1994, The Green Business Letter.

quality would mitigate the imbalance somewhat). Focusing on Pampers, Pepsi bottles, and plastic bags may be important, but it's far from the only issue companies should be concerned about.

As scrutiny continues to grow, the public will eventually come to recognize the contribution of the corporate sector to the Gross National Trash—as well as to air and water pollution—and the focus may shift from what's coming out of individuals' trash cans and drainpipes to what's coming from companies' dumpsters, smokestacks, and waste treatment facilities. Companies that can't offer credible evidence that they're doing their part to reduce these emissions may find themselves at a competitive disadvantage.

IN SEARCH OF "INDUSTRIAL SYMBIOSIS"

Later on in this chapter, we'll look more closely at the specific attributes of some of the most environmentally successful companies, and how they have managed effectively to address both environmental and bottom-line concerns. For now, what's key to understand is the need for companies to take a new look at the ecological impact of doing business—not just the waste and pollution created, but a much more systemic view that encompasses nearly every aspect of the design, production, distribution, and disposal of products and services.

This is a new world view for most business people, a view that recognizes that while practically no one *intends* to waste or pollute, waste and pollution have become a normal and accepted part of business, part of the cost of goods sold. Those costs have risen to unacceptable levels, both in financial and moral terms, leading many business people to rethink the way their companies operate. Often this means shifting from a linear view—in which money, materials, and goods flow in from one point to another—to a more cyclical view, where things operate in closed loops.

What does cyclicality look like? We're just beginning to explore the implications of what has become known as "industrial ecology," a system in which there is no waste in any part of the loop. These industrial ecosystems mimic nature by creating what the ecologist Harden Tibbs calls "complex food webs between companies and industries." Part of this thinking is the notion that "waste equals food"—that is, wastes are potential products or raw materials. "It's a landfill-less society," explains Paul Hawken, the co-founder of Smith

Flow Control

Veryfine Products, Inc., is in the business of turning fresh fruit into juice and related products. That requires a lot of water, and generates a lot of waste. Because that water comes from—and the waste goes back to—the groundwater system under the tiny town of Littleton, Massachusetts, where the company is headed, Veryfine worked closely with town officials and local residents to ensure local water quality that exceeded federal and state water-quality regulations.

To do that, the company built an $8.5 million water purification plant, using state-of-the-art techniques that returns to nature water that is sometimes purer than when it was taken from the ground. Out of respect for the treatment plant's location—close to a residential neighborhood—the building was specially designed to not look industrial; from the street, it appears to be just another brick office building.

Equally important, Veryfine has tried to reduce its waste consumption altogether. By installing cooling towers to service its can and bottle lines, the company reduced waste consumption by about 20 million gallons a year. "This project represented a $500,000 capital investment for which there is no corporate return on investment," says Samuel Rowse, Veryfine's president and grandson of the company's founder. "There is a great ROI for the environment, however, in that huge amounts of water are not pulled from the local aquifer.

"While acknowledging the problems is a positive start in the pursuit of achieving sound environmental solutions," Rowse adds, "manufacturing companies must do more than merely 'jump on the bandwagon' if we are to positively impact our children's future. Jumping on the green bandwagon implies letting someone else do the driving. My preference is to be in the driver's seat when it comes to the environmental future of our earth."

& Hawken—retailer of gardening and other products—and author of *The Ecology of Commerce.* "There's no place to put anything or to throw away anything at all. If we're going to have this sustainable industrial infrastructure, it has to imitate nature with respect to waste. Waste has to become a product."

This is no environmentalist's pipe dream. Already, there are examples of how a sustainable industrial infrastructure might work. Tibbs, a leading proponent of industrial ecology, describes the Danish town of Kalundborg, about 80 miles west of Copenhagen. Kalundborg has become a working model of what has been dubbed "industrial symbiosis," involving an electric power-generating plant, an oil refinery, a biotechnology production plant, a plasterboard factory, a sulfuric acid producer, cement producers, the local heating company, and local agricultural and horticultural interests. Asnaes, the largest coal-fired electricity-generating plant in Denmark, supplies process steam to the oil refinery and a pharmaceutical plant; previously, the power station had been condensing the steam and releasing it in a local fjord. Gyproc, the wallboard producer, buys surplus gas from the refinery, reducing the need to burn coal. The refinery removes excess sulfur from the gas to make it cleaner-burning; the removed sulfur is sold to the sulfuric acid plant. Asnaes has also desulfurized its smoke, using a process that yields calcium sulfate as a side product, which is sold as "industrial gypsum" to Gyproc. In addition, fly ash from the desulfurization process is used for cement making and road building.

There's more. Asnaes uses its surplus heat to warm its own seawater fish farm, which produces 200 tons of trout and turbot a year for the French market. Sludge from the fish farm is used as fertilizer by local farmers. Novo Nordisk, which runs the pharmaceutical plant, is also providing hundreds of thousands of tons of highly nutritious sludge, used as a liquid fertilizer by local farmers. Previously, the sludge had been disposed of as waste, but Novo Nordisk began adding chalk-lime and heating it to neutralize remaining microorganisms.

And so it goes in Kalundborg. Tibbs points out that none of these initiatives was required by law, and that each exchange or trade is negotiated independently. "The earliest deals were purely economic, but more recent initiatives have been made for largely environmental reasons and it has been found that these can be made to pay, too," he says.

Hawken and Tibbs's notion, that the unusable products of today become the raw materials and organic feedstocks of tomorrow, is beginning to transform companies—like Fetzer, for example, which recognized that by turning grape skins into fertilizer, it could eliminate waste and save money. But the notion extends far beyond agriculture. In products ranging from chemicals to computers to clothing, manufacturers are envisioning a near-term future in which they will take increasing responsibility for the waste products that result from the manufacture, use, and disposal of their products.

As the Kalundborg example shows, some of the impetus for what Hawken calls "this new cyclicality of thinking" is emanating from overseas—specifically from Europe, where laws are increasingly acknowledging the links between economic activity and environmental responsibility. In Germany, for example, so-called takeback laws have required companies to accept returns of their products' packaging from consumers. The law affects only a limited number of products—and has met with limited financial and logistical success—but its mere existence has had a powerful effect on companies worldwide, who see similar takeback laws potentially spreading to other products, throughout Europe as well as to North America and Asia.

The computer industry has been at the leading edge of these efforts, both in the United States and abroad. Although Germany has not yet passed takeback laws for electronic components, computer makers throughout the world are redesigning their products in anticipation of such a law. IBM has built a computer that literally snaps apart, meaning that at the end of its life, the owner has an opportunity to return the machine so that the manufacturer can easily disassemble it and sort the materials for recycling or reuse in other computers; the entire computer contains only seven screws. In 1993, IBM began identifying all plastic parts with a code showing the type of material and its manufacturer, to ease recycling. Compaq Computer Corporation, another industry leader, was the first to institute a nationwide takeback program for the rechargeable batteries that come with portable computers, and is working closely with customers to determine how best to integrate environmental considerations into future designs. "We have a firm belief that we're going to have a cradle-to-grave responsibility for our products," says Walter Rosenberg, Compaq's corporate environmental manager. "If you apply that principle to your products, you are not really selling products, you're renting them."

The idea is that whatever products a company makes, it potentially owns for life—that is, the lifetime of the product and its components. It may sell the product to a customer, who may then resell it to someone else. But eventually, when the product is no longer of use, it will become the responsibility of whoever made it in the first place. The concept extends even to a product's components, including chemicals. "If you make toxins, be careful, because they are also— like a car, a refrigerator, and a television—yours for life," warns Hawken of what he sees will be standard operating procedure in coming years. "So if I go into my well at my farm and find organo-chlorines, then I can send them to a county agent and say, 'Would you please look this up and see what the molecular marker is on it?' It's got a dogtag on it that says Royal Dutch Shell or Hooker Chemical, and each has a toll-free number I can call and say, 'There is something in my well that belongs to you. Please come and get it.'"

Whether such a system will come to pass remains to be seen. The point is that whether required or not, some companies view the manufacturer-as-owner protocol as a key component of a vision of corporate environmental—and social—responsibility.

You don't have to be an industry giant to engage in this sort of thinking. Crib Diaper Service, a million-dollar-a-year, family-owned enterprise located in a Minneapolis suburb, has seen the power of enthusiastic employees. Crib's thirty-five employees have tried to find ways to avoid throwing things out. For example, the company's laundry operations produce up to 600 cubic yards of diaper lint per year, which the company had to pay to dispose of. One Crib employee met an art instructor at a local junior college, who told her that diaper lint would be a valuable ingredient for making high-grade art paper. The company now gives away its lint to four local art schools. Crib's employees then began looking for other opportunities to keep materials out of landfills. Now, unusable diapers that used to be thrown away are sold as rags, used plastic bags are recycled, the containers in which water softener comes are reused for shipping goods, wooden shipping pallets are given to other companies that can use them. The company has received two local recycling awards for its efforts.

It's not earth-shattering stuff, admits company president Doug Flatz, and the dollar savings are minimal, but then again none of this was mandated by management. "It's all been sparked and grown and developed by employee involvement," says Flatz, who has tried to be supportive. Moreover, he says, the new employee attitude has spilled over into other aspects of their work. "They tend to increase their desire to be efficient in all materials that they handle."

Art students and ragmakers aren't the only beneficiaries of Crib's search for symbiosis. Along the way, Crib employees happened on a local casket maker, which was able to use its diaper lint in place of cotton batting in the lining of caskets.

From diapers to caskets. It may be the classic example of cradle-to-grave thinking.

THE SOLUTION TO POLLUTION

How do the most socially responsible companies reduce their environmental toll? And more important: Why do they go beyond regulatory compliance, and sometimes even bottom-line considerations, to involve employees, customers, and other stakeholders in their efforts?

The answers are as varied as the companies and the programs themselves. Some companies' actions involve relatively minor tweaks to their products, processes, or policies. Others require more significant changes in the way things are done and major investments in new technologies or processes. Still others demand new kinds of relationships between companies and their many stakeholders.

Diverse as the companies, goals, and visions may be, they share at least three things in common:

1. The companies designated someone high up to be in charge of the company's environmental performance, indicating that this is a priority of top management.
2. The companies issued a written policy statement detailing their environmental commitment, and set specific goals or benchmarks to back up those policies.
3. Everyone within the company was charged with being accountable to the policy and meeting the established goals. Sometimes pay and bonuses were linked to environmental performance. Whenever possible, those outside the company—specifically, suppliers and customers—were enlisted in the process.

This is hardly a revelation. It's a well-established fact of business life that any company striving for significant changes in the quality of its operation must involve the total organization—if necessary, re-engineering it (to borrow one currently popular buzzword) to create the culture of cooperation needed to engender excellence—as well as those outside the organization, including customers and suppliers. Top-management leadership is essential to the success of any major effort or cultural change. And the best results inevitably begin with an agreed-upon set of goals and objectives, with rewards for those that meet them and sanctions for those that don't.

But changing a company's operations, let alone its culture, is no simple thing, even for the most committed of companies. Practically speaking, most companies possess something less than total commitment to environmental change. The more immediate challenge is to inculcate company personnel (from top to bottom) with the understanding of the true environmental impact of their operations, focusing on the substantive issues as well as the symbolic ones. Without that perspective and sense of importance, corporate environmental efforts will be halfhearted at best, often focusing on a few "simple things." At worst, they can be costly and demoralizing exercises in organizational frustration, doomed by inertia and sabotage.

There are many barriers to change, most notably the natural resistance to most organizational change and the inability of companies to effectively communicate their environmental missions throughout their work force. One basic obstacle, say the experts, is the language of the environment in business. Most environmental matters are still seen as a matter of compliance—discussed in "parts per billion," "emissions per million units shipped," or some other technical statistic. Environmental managers in some companies are much more closely attuned to the government regulators with whom they must comply than with the CEO or CFO to whom they must report. As a result, many companies overlook viewing the environment as a strategic, bottom-line issue that can have implications far beyond the regulatory arena.

CEOs who articulate their commitment, and demand it of others, find that employees can be quick to respond. After all, a growing number of employees are recycling, insulating, and otherwise greening their personal lives, either because they want to or because they are being required to by state and local laws (or, in a surprising number of cases, by their spouses or kids). With the possible exception of recent nonsmokers, none are more self-righteous than newly converted environmentalists. They take pride in their deeds and the part they play in the future of their community, their nation, and their planet.

But then they go to work, where they see tremendous waste and inefficiency—in the front office, on the factory floor, on the loading dock, and just about everywhere else. The trash accumulated by employees may well dwarf the modest pile of newspapers they set out on the curb at home for pickup each week. The energy saved (and pollution prevented) by installing energy-efficient light bulbs at home may seem futile when compared to the endless banks of fluorescent lights at work, burning long after most people have gone home, controllable only by an inaccessible computer in the basement. It doesn't take a degree in the behavioral sciences to recognize the frustration and cynicism that can result. And those bad feelings can affect performance, commitment, quality, and pride.

The flip side is that when companies embrace an environmental ethic, they can tap into employees' natural enthusiasm. Often, environmental initiatives begin with line employees, bubbling up through the ranks until top management, like any astute leader, signs on to the program.

CHURCH & DWIGHT: PROFITING FROM EMPOWERMENT

One example of environmental empowerment is Church & Dwight, the company best known for its principal product, Arm & Hammer Baking Soda, which has turned the environment into a powerful employee empowerment and productivity-enhancing tool. Over the years, the company has managed to transform its decidedly unsexy product—sodium bicarbonate, derived from a naturally occurring mineral left behind after evaporation of an inland lake in Wyoming 50 million years ago—into an environmental miracleworker. No longer confined to being a dentifrice, or to keeping refrigerators smelling fresh, baking soda–based products are now being used as a substitute for ozone-depleting chlorofluorocarbons in cleaning electronic circuit boards, as smokestack scrubbers to reduce acid rain–producing sulfur dioxide emissions, as nontoxic alternatives to solvent-based industrial cleaners, and as a benign means for cleaning graffiti off everything from brick walls to trees. Add to this the product's increased reputation as an effective and environmentally safe household cleaner, and it's no surprise that Church & Dwight's sales have grown handsomely in recent years.

Clearly, environmentalism has been a highly successful marketing vehicle for Church & Dwight. According to one internal company estimate, about $75 million of the company's $500 million annual sales can be attributed to CEO Dwight Minton's strategic focus on the environment as a corporate issue. Over the years, the company has formed partnerships with a wide range of stakeholder groups. Besides communicating environmental messages to employees around the world, the company introduced the "Environmentors" project in the Princeton area, matching inner-city kids with mentors to develop environmentally oriented projects that address the needs of local community service organizations. Church & Dwight has co-sponsored a program with the EPA that awards a trophy and cash grants to children who have shown environmental leadership in each of the EPA's ten regions, and has introduced a program to provide training and capital for inner-city homeless people to start their own businesses, removing graffiti with baking soda blasters. The company has created school curricula that use baking soda to demonstrate aspects of environmental science to those in grades four through six, and has sponsored many conferences on factoring the environmental ethic into business decisions. Church & Dwight is also a financial benefactor of Earth Day USA, Renew America, the National Fish & Wildlife Foundation, American Rivers, Clean Water Action, and other groups.

Its investment in donations, educational campaigns, and joint ventures has yielded handsome returns, according to Bryan M. Thomlison, the company's director of public affairs and environmental management. He offers calculations showing that every dollar spent by Church & Dwight on these collaborative efforts has yielded ten dollars in increased sales, a ten-to-one return on investment. "If more companies realized the power of this model, there would be less money wasted on conventional marketing and more money invested in addressing social issues," he says.

But increased product sales are only part of the equation that has led to the company's financial success. With each new enhancement of the company's reputation, top management feeds the success story back to its employees, which further drives them to work hard and smart. "We want to make sure we deserve the reputation we get," says Thomlison. "So it's like a closed loop: We drive our reputation outside, which spurs further efforts inside, which furthers our reputation outside. It's an energizing and empowering mechanism internally. When we win an award, or we get favorable newspaper copy, all of us feel more proud and we are more vigilant internally for actions we can undertake that reduce environmental impacts of our products, processes, and individual actions."

Closing the Loop

Herman Miller has found many ways to minimize waste and maximize resources. Perhaps the most intriguing notion involves a partnership between the furniture maker and a local tannery that supplies leather for the company's upscale furniture. It goes something like this: In the tanning process, machines remove hair, bits of meat, and other organic matter from the cow hides. This waste was then flushed into the sewer system at a cost to the tanner. But that organic material is rich in nutrients that could potentially be used as fertilizer. Unfortunately, it is too soupy for use on farmland, so the tanner has developed a process that mixes the animal sludge with Herman Miller's sawdust waste. If all goes according to plan, the fertilizer will be used on 1,600 acres of farmland to grow corn. The corn, in turn, will be fed to the cows, whose hides will eventually become part of Herman Miller's furniture.

In the end, it's one of those classic closed-loop deals in which everybody comes out ahead. Except the cows, that is.

The proof is in the productivity. The financial returns for Church & Dwight's environmental initiatives bode well for other companies' efforts to use environmental responsibility as a strategic focus. Thomlison says that for most of the past decade, Church & Dwight's sales per employee were two to three times the average for *Fortune* 500 companies. "That's a very startling number," he says. "It shows that we're very productive. It also means that each of us has to work hard because we all have so much responsibility."

In the end, Thomlison argues that employee empowerment gives his company a huge competitive advantage in its environmental success. "It isn't the formal models of pollution prevention and the reporting systems that will get you from here to there. In fact, you don't even need the formal structure if you just have people motivated to act because they feel good about the company and they want to protect its image."

QUAD/GRAPHICS MAKES A GOOD IMPRESSION

Harry Quadracci would probably agree. As president and principal owner of Quad/Graphics, he has fostered an atmosphere in which employees are encouraged to innovate. When it comes to the environment, Quadracci admits, "I don't know whether I led or followed. I think that taking better care of ourself and our world is good business. I think it is all a matter of establishing values."

Much like those at Church & Dwight, the impressive array of environmental initiatives undertaken at Quad over the years has benefited from the company's existing culture of empowerment. Quad employees are encouraged to communicate with one another, and with Quadracci himself, using the company's electronic-mail system. "Harry's the force behind the company," says John Imes, Quad/Graphic's environmental manager. "He's the one that makes it fun." When asked about the number of salespeople employed in the 6,800-person company, Quadracci is quick to respond: "Sixty-eight hundred." Imes answers similarly when asked about the number of environmental professionals at Quad.

Quadracci doesn't motivate all of these employees by himself. He has help—from a 90-pound Angora goat named Gruff, who lives at Quadracci's house, grazing on his acreage. An employee once suggested that Gruff get involved with environmental activities by becoming a mascot for recycling—which is a large part of what goats do all day. Someone came up with a slogan: "Be a Gruff ... Recycle Stuff"—and the goat's image was soon emblazoned on mugs, posters, and brochures. Gruff has his own electronic-mail address within the company, and employees send questions and comments about recycling and the environment, which are "personally" answered by a Gruff ghost.

Gruff's role as a conduit for employee participation is just one part of environmental efforts that have made Quad/Graphics a leader in the printing industry. The company's ink-manufacturing division, Chemical Research/Technology, has reformulated ink for web offset printing to create a new generation of Enviro/Tech inks. Enviro/Tech lowers emissions of air-polluting volatile organic compounds (which contribute to ground-level smog) by an average of 15 percent, compared with traditional inks. Even low-tech solutions to environmental problems seem innovative: A master carpenter on staff, who "can't stand to see good wood go to waste," as Imes puts it, developed a highly efficient team that repairs more than 150,000 wooden shipping pallets a year. When pallets are beyond repair, they are turned into landscaping mulch, which the company uses on its grounds, gives to employees to take home, and sells to a company that colors and repackages it for retail sale. The pallet-repair shop offers its services to other businesses in the area that generate wood as a by-product.

The ability to turn problems into profits has helped make Quad/Graphics one of the most financially successful printing companies in the nation, with an annual rate of growth that has averaged over 40 percent since 1980. The company's environmental commitment has attracted the printing business of many environmental and outdoor magazines such as *Audubon, Sierra, Outside,* and publications of the Cousteau Society and the National Wildlife Federation. They join *Time, Newsweek, U.S. News & World Report, Playboy, Mother Jones, The Atlantic, Harper's,* and some ninety other magazines as Quad customers. Quad/Graphics has added more employees since 1980 than any other private company in Wisconsin.

For Quadracci, caring for the environment is part of a mind-set that includes other socially responsible goals. "It really is sort of a seamless concern," he says, "taking care of the environment, taking care of our families, our minds, our bodies. Just a totality of good business practice. Good air and good business. We breathe the air that our plants are in. If we have bad air, our medical costs are going to go up and our employees are going to be unhealthy."

And it works. Quad/Graphics employees are paid well, work in clean and safe conditions, are given excellent benefits, and toil for a company with an excellent reputation in local communities. In a variety of ways, they are shown by their employer that they are important to the company. And their satisfaction and pride translate into a willingness to care for their employer, to go the extra mile to support their company's environmental commitment.

Quadracci admits that his company spends more than required by law on environmental initiatives, and that sometimes the paybacks take years. But, he says, "We could demonstrate in almost any area that environmentalism is very cost effective. We generally spend much more money than the cost of compliance. On a short-term basis, that could be viewed as a competitive disadvantage. But it has worked out because of the efficiencies and the savings we have gotten as a by-product of our environmental efforts."

A few years ago, when press operators began to examine the amount of waste ink being discarded from the pressroom of its main plant in Pewaukee, Wisconsin, they were taken aback by what they found: more than seventeen fifty-five-gallon drums of ink—a hazardous material—were being wasted every month at the plant. Besides the cost of the ink itself, there were additional costs inherent in this toxic waste, including those needed to handle, label, and transport the ink-filled drums to their proper disposal at hazardous waste sites. Recognizing the financial and environmental toll of this waste, the press team set up recyclable ink stations and implemented other simple changes in habits. With no additional costs or technology, Imes and his colleagues reduced their production of waste ink from seventeen drums a month to only eight a year—a 96 percent reduction. The half-million dollars or so in annual savings is not insignificant to employees in a company with an approximately $4 million annual profit-sharing plan.

"The reason we've been successful in the environmental arena is that we've linked it to business on a very crass bottom-line standpoint," says Imes. "We can bring the profit and loss statement down to each press, so the pressmen on that press are a small business. It gets us ownership. It gives the employees ownership and the ability to solve problems at the lowest level possible. Our corporate philosophies are to find the best way to do things and take responsibility for what you do. Each press manager, each department head is responsible for his own bottom line and for contributing to the company and finding the best way to do things. Cutting ink waste, cutting our potential to emit—all that has potential business ramifications. We're a fast-growing company. If we don't continue to reduce our environmental impact, it's going to be more difficult to grow. And growth means jobs, and greater opportunities for all of our employees.

"Harry has said this quite a bit: Business is about taking better care of your employees and your clients," Imes continues. "And I think we are doing that with our environmental program in terms of reducing the environmental impact in the communities where we're located, and our employees live in those communities. They breathe the same air that we put out. And we want to put out clean air. In terms of our clients, we're there to help anticipate environmental issues, so we can reduce the overall environmental impact of the industry in a way that's technologically viable and economically sound. We also believe in taking better care of our communities and taking better care of our world. That's truly what the business is all about."

THE GREENING OF THE GAP

Not all CEOs cotton to environmental issues as naturally as do Harry Quadracci and Dwight Minton. More often, the greening of the boss—and everyone below the boss—is an incremental, time-consuming affair.

Consider The Gap, the trendy, fast-growing San Francisco–based clothing retailer with 1,300 stores and annual sales of $3.3 billion in 1993. Despite its youthful image and its progressive stance on some social issues—the company has featured AIDS activists in its well-regarded series of black-and-white advertisements—The Gap arrived relatively slowly at a corporate environmental consciousness. As such, it is a good example of a large company that has had to grow into its environmental commitment in recent years. Much like buying a new pair of jeans, making environmentalism "fit" with a mature corporate body isn't always natural, requiring a few tugs and an occasional stretch to reach an appropriate level of comfort.

The company's environmental responsibility rests on the shoulders of Robert Fisher, executive vice president and chief financial officer and son of Gap CEO Donald Fisher. Born in 1954 in San Francisco, he didn't develop an affinity for environmental issues until long after the city's countercultural heyday. "I played tennis as a kid and spent most of my life on asphalt," he says. "I led a fairly isolated life. When I graduated from college and stopped playing tennis, I had no hobbies, no outside interests."

Then Fisher's wife gave him a fly-fishing rod as a gift. As he began fishing, he gained his first exposure to the outdoors. "When you are down in a river, seeing the bugs, seeing the fish, you have a very different view of the world than you do when you're not wading the stream," he says. Fisher became a passionate fly-fisherman, making regular pilgrimages to fish the streams of Montana and northern California. About that same time, Fisher and his wife had the first of three children. "When you have just yourself and your wife, you're not as concerned about the world that you're going to leave as you are when you have kids," says Fisher. "All of a sudden things started to feed on one other. Kids start to bring back things from school about recycling and start asking you why you're not recycling at home. And I started to hear about it from employees and friends."

When he became responsible for The Gap's management information systems, distribution, sourcing, human resources, and finance, Fisher began to see the environment register with greater frequency on his radar screen. "I saw a lot of things changing at the grass-roots level, both within our organization and within the country as a whole. We are an organization that's got a lot of receptors out there, and when your receptors are heightened and all of a sudden you start hearing about the environment from ten different angles, all of a sudden everybody starts to think it's an issue. We were hearing from a lot of people in the stores: Why were we producing stone-washed jeans? [Mining the chemicals used for stonewashing is considered environmentally harmful.] Why weren't our paper bags made of recycled material? How could we be giving customers plastic bags? People wanted to learn more about what we were doing for the environment as a company."

Fisher encountered the challenge faced by a lot of executives who embark on environmental initiatives. On the one hand, a growing number of employees and customers were expressing environmental concern. On the other, the feelings weren't universal among the company's 44,000 employees nationwide, and it would require an effective communications and education strategy to bring everyone up to speed and to arrive at common environmental goals. Some people didn't care; others saw it as a burden or even as a threat to their jobs.

Fisher began by setting up a "green team," a committee of fifteen people that he knew to be interested in the environment: "One of the key things was to take people at a level where they were interested and willing to devote their time. They weren't at such a senior level that they may have had a lot of conflict with trying to do their job and do their environmental thing. And these were people who were able to effect change within their own organization." One employee assumed responsibility for purchasing paper shopping bags used in Gap stores, for instance. "She became very interested in the project and set out on a personal mission to improve the quality of the recycled content of the paper in our bags."

The group eventually took on a name—Gap Environmental Organization, or GEO—and created an environmental mission statement and a set of guidelines. The mission statement is simple, but it speaks volumes about the company's commitment:

> We believe that actively promoting a healthy global environment is both a corporate and individual responsibility. It is also simply good business. We are committed to operating with respect and sensitivity to the environment, locally and on a global scale, but with a particular attention to those areas in which we do business. We will encourage our employees to take steps as individuals to protect the environment,

as well as empower them to ensure that all corporate actions are in compliance with our environmental policies.

Turning that mission into action has not been easy. Fisher acknowledges that while GEO continues to meet and innovate, making companywide change—even with a youthful corporate culture—is slow and sometimes frustrating. "I have personally been trying to push us a little bit faster," says Fisher. "Sometimes that works and sometimes it doesn't. Sometimes people go along with you and sometimes they don't. When you are a high-growth business and a business that has been as visible as we are and has had the rate of growth we've had, it's easy to not place social concerns as high as perhaps they should be. What we're trying to do now is move in a social direction at the same pace as our growth pace."

Growing pains notwithstanding, there is progress. The company has managed to increase the amount of post-consumer waste contained in the recycled packaging it uses. Eschewing printed memos and reports whenever possible, the company estimates it uses only a tenth the office paper used by other companies its size. The Gap is beginning to work with vendors to improve the environmental quality of the products it buys, and is trying to integrate environmental and energy conservation measures in the design of Gap stores. Fisher recognizes that the changes may seem modest compared with those of some other companies, but they represent what he believes is a genuine effort to inculcate environmental thinking throughout the organization.

"A lot comes through education," says Fisher. "That's something that takes a lot of time. The more people know what it is they're doing and how it impacts the environment and the workplace, I think the more concerned they become and the more they want to change. We have done some seminars, tried to educate our purchasing people. We're in the process of educating our merchandising people to the effects of what it is that they're doing. It takes time."

Slowly but surely, the environment is finding a fit at The Gap. The company's transformation shows that even companies without a long-held commitment to environmental issues can develop a green corporate culture.

THE POWER OF REWARD AND RECOGNITION

Of course, getting an environmental policy off the ground is one matter; making sure that employees sustain it is another. That requires changing people's behavior and instilling a mind-set that everyone's job has the potential to innovate, save the company money, improve its reputation, and reduce the company's environmental impact. The key here is that when employees do succeed at doing these things, they receive appropriate recognition and rewards.

It's a well-established fact of business that most people don't get sufficient credit for what they do. Business tomes urge managers to proffer "one-minute praisings" and other pats on the back to employees for a job well done, but a mere "thank you" isn't often enough to engender long-term changes. When it comes to getting employees to think green—tuning in to waste reduction, recycling, pollution prevention, and other environmental initiatives—giving credit where it is due can yield rich rewards for employees and companies alike. A few well-placed acknowledgments and incentives can encourage everyone to find waste- and cost-cutting ways of doing things.

"I think that you've got to assist at all levels of change in order to get environmental, health, and safety programs geared up to where they're aggressive and positive," says Robert D. Shelton, director of environmental, health, and safety management for Arthur D. Little. "Let's face it: these employees have been doing things a certain way for a long time. To cause them to change is not easy. It's going to take a bit of positive reinforcement." But how you reinforce employee behavior is important, says Shelton. It requires some considerations of which carrots will motivate which workers, the criteria you use in choosing winners, and whether your rewards program may frustrate or discourage those who don't get recognized.

The most successful programs are those that establish definite goals and criteria. Indeed, reward and recognition simply cannot work effectively without clearcut goals. "I would recommend that any reward be based on measurable criteria," says Chuck Davison, corporate manager for environmental affairs at Baxter Healthcare, which has five different environmental awards programs. He recommends a point system, with nominations based on some preset scoring system. "We get questions all the time about 'Why did this facility win and this one didn't?' And we can go back to the criteria and show exactly how it was done."

One problem is that the departments and facilities that have come a long way often get penalized, because the subsequent improvements they make aren't as dramatic. Rob Shelton counsels that worker-management teams develop their own criteria for reward and recognition. "That kind of collaborative activity is educational because it causes people to stop and consider, 'What is it that really

Ben & Jerry's Environmental Challenges

While Ben & Jerry's is often viewed by the public and the media as an environmentally exemplary company, it is far from perfect, as company officials are quick to attest. Even its own audit, published in its annual report, points up problems.

One ongoing dilemma has to do with the company's firm commitment to using only Vermont dairy products, part of Ben & Jerry's longtime commitment and strong bond with the state's farmers. An audit in the company's 1992 annual report questioned the environmental efficacy of that policy in a company whose sales roughly tripled in five years to $140 million in 1993, and whose net profit more than quadrupled during the same period to more than $7 million. "Now that the company is growing to increasing proportions, it finds that it is shipping frozen ice cream three thousand miles across a hot country in refrigerated trucks to its national markets," the audit said. "This is highly energy inefficient, and it raises the question whether at some time, the company may have to reconsider its Vermont-only policy." The company has vowed that when it further expands its ice cream–making capacity, it will likely do so by opening a plant on the West Coast.

The company also grapples with such issues as overloading the waste-water treatment capacity in the tiny Vermont towns where it has plants. And the company sometimes finds itself faced with quandaries over the problems that arise despite its efforts to "do good." For example, when the company needed to build a third production plant, one of the obvious choices was to place it in St. Albans, Vermont, the location of the 550-dairy cooperative that provides the 18,000 gallons of milk and cream that Ben & Jerry's uses every production day. But the site was on St. Albans Bay, one of the most environmentally fragile parts of Lake Champlain. That required a more sophisticated and far more costly technology for treating waste water than might otherwise be used.

Ben & Jerry's Environmental Challenges (continued)

Still, the company has initiated a variety of innovative technologies to minimize its energy use and effluents. It developed a pilot "solar aquatics greenhouse" to evaluate the suitability of technologies to treat raw ice cream waste, created any time a production line is started up or shut down. Another technology, called dissolved air flotation, is in use at one Ben & Jerry's manufacturing plant to minimize the volume of waste that is ultimately discharged into the sewage system.

One low-tech waste treatment program involves sending ice cream waste to a pig farmer a few miles away, who feeds it to what may be the 700 happiest pigs in North America. The pigs' favorite flavor is said to be Cherry Garcia. One wag dubbed the sated swine "The Grateful Pigs."

---

needs to be done?' Such collaboration inevitably results in greater employee buy-in of the program." Equally important is that the rewards reflect the company's environmental goals. "Management has to make sure that rewards are properly linked to the change that needs to occur," says Shelton. "There's simply no sense in rewarding people for attending training sessions if what's really required is pollution prevention or zero-compliance problems."

It would seem logical that the ultimate employee reward be cold, hard cash: money talks. Bonuses for Inter-Continental Hotels' North American hotel managers are tied to how well their hotels measure up on a six-page, 134-item environmental checklist. As part of its efforts, the chain's management published a 200-page environmental manual specifying measures for waste reduction, purchasing, air emissions, noise control, energy and water conservation, asbestos elimination, laundry and dry-cleaning operations, and other aspects of hotel operation. Those efforts have helped the chain to make dramatic reductions in waste and dramatic gains in recycling.

Some companies' incentive programs offer cash bounties well into the thousands of dollars. Whatever the reward, though, what's key is to tailor it to specific deeds. That's what 3M has been doing for years with its well-regarded Pollution Prevention Pays (3P) program. At its simplest, 3P is a glorified employee suggestion box. But the suggestions, in this case, have to do with projects the company could undertake that would have a demonstrable effect on reducing emissions of toxic materials. To qualify for an award, a 3P project must actually prevent pollution, not just control it. It must result in cost savings to 3M and meet an acceptable return on investment. And it must involve a technical accomplishment, innovative approach, or unique design. For their ideas, employees can receive $500 gift certificates. Since 1975, when the 3P program began, 3M estimates that it has saved the company more than $600 million and reduced the company's pollution by half.

There is a continuum of approaches. At Baxter, for example, Chuck Davison says that monetary awards "are too difficult to manage. We want the awards to be fun. But if you start putting price tags on things, it can get too competitive." Davison suggests that monetary incentives work better on a smaller scale—at individual plants, for instance. In many cases, a memento—typically a plaque, certificate, or trophy—will suffice. The Saunders Hotel Group, which operates three hotels in Boston, hands out annual employee environmental awards: a glass globe and a recognition plaque. Rewards needn't be so formal. Special privileges—prime parking spaces, coupons redeemable at a company store or cafeteria, or a party, outing, or other special event for the winning office or department—can also be effective. Some rewards serve double duty. To thank employees for their efforts to conserve water at the Boston Park Plaza Hotel, the Saunders Hotel Group handed out low-flow showerheads for employees to use at home. The company also played up the benefits of its gifts: the 820 employees are told that if everyone installed the showerheads, they could collectively save 10 million gallons of water a year.

Sometimes, a simple "thank you" offered by a supervisor, division head, or other higher-up does work. Or it could be in the form of a more public effort—a publicity campaign highlighting employee achievements, targeting company, community, and trade publications. At Arthur D. Little's headquarters in Cambridge, Massachusetts, a "Green Acorn" awareness campaign nearly doubled the practice of two-sided photocopying. Framed certificates near the company's copiers testify to the fact that this change in employee habits saved 6 million sheets of paper in one year—the equivalent in height of a 217-story office building.

Peer recognition also is key. Winners of Baxter Healthcare's environmental awards are asked to give presentations on their efforts at an annual company conference. 3M runs internal seminars where technical papers are presented; if the information is not considered proprietary, it also may be presented to other companies as well. "Play it up wherever you can," counsels Baxter's Davison. "Bulletin boards, publications, whatever. That goes a long way to giving people a boost."

Those little boosts add up. As executives at many other companies have learned, employees genuinely want to feel good about their jobs and their employers, including knowing that what they do and the organization they work for are making a positive contribution to the environment, both locally and globally. And as companies are finding, employees are willing to work hard for environmental change—if they are made partners in the process, and if they can share in the success.

THE SYNERGY OF PARTNERSHIPS

Many of the most impressive environmental initiatives have resulted from partnerships between companies and others: government agencies, competitors, even environmentalists. The synergies created when these seemingly competitive or antagonistic entities team up can be powerful indeed.

These new partnerships are by no means easy; often, old adversaries must break down decades of mistrust or competition to find mutually satisfactory solutions. In most cases, the relationships are double-edged: environmentalists and executives working jointly while one is watchdogging the other's performance; competitors sharing information and technologies while trying to gain advantages over one another; companies pushing their customers to accept environmental changes to their products, while at the same time trying to retain their loyalty. And when environmentalists and corporations get too cozy, it raises more than a few eyebrows among members, supporters, stockholders, media, lawyers, and competitors.

The joint task force formed by McDonald's and the Environmental Defense Fund (EDF) to find ways to reduce McDonald's solid waste is one highly successful example of the synergy of partnerships. The task force was formed in the early 1990s after months of discussion and trust building between the two organizations. Although both parties were genuinely interested in finding ways to reduce the considerable trash output of McDonald's nine thousand U.S. restaurants, they had reservations about how their relationship would fare.

Originally, EDF hoped the task force would develop a set of options for waste reduction, which McDonald's management would then consider. The company would be free to do whatever it wanted with those recommendations. EDF, for its part, could say whatever it wanted about the recommendations and the degree to which they were implemented. But the task force became much more substantive and action-oriented than anyone would have imagined. Says Robert Langert, director of environmental affairs at McDonald's: "We just got excited about all the different aspects of reducing, reusing, and recycling. The momentum quickly shifted from 'These aren't just things that we should be thinking about. We're going to do these things.' "

EDF's initial proposal quickly turned into a set of actions to which McDonald's management would commit as part of the task force's final product. The new corporate waste reduction action plan that was ultimately drafted by the task force was accepted with virtually no modifications by McDonald's management, according to EDF senior scientist Richard Denison. And to back that policy up, McDonald's committed itself to implementing forty-two discrete actions of a Waste Reduction Action Plan over two years. By the end of the first year, the company had added twenty of its own initiatives. By mid-1994, the number of waste reduction initiatives had grown to more than one hundred and McDonald's had reduced its solid waste output by seventy-five hundred tons of packaging annually over three years.

Another successful synergy involves New England Electric System (NEES), a public utility holding company headquartered in Westborough, Massachusetts, serving more than 1.2 million homes and businesses in three states. In 1993, NEES unveiled something termed NEESPLAN 4, what it calls "a comprehensive approach to delivering environmentally sustainable, low-cost electricity to customers" that "goes beyond traditional utility thinking."

NEESPLAN 4 resulted from a unique partnership between NEES and the Conservation Law Foundation (CLF), a nonprofit environmental advocacy group based in Boston. Since the 1970s, CLF had been battling NEES, opposing nearly every construction project the utility proposed, urging it to focus on conservation rather than construction as a means of balancing its customers' electricity needs with the available supply. But NEES wasn't buying into conservation for one simple reason: given the regulatory structure at the time, it did not make financial sense. By helping customers to reduce energy use, utilities stood to lose business.

Doug Foy, CLF's executive director, had known John Rowe, NEES's president and CEO, for years, back when Rowe headed a utility in Maine. Over a period of several months they discussed how to provide incentives for NEES to promote energy conservation. Some pieces of the puzzle already had been solved. In California, for example, the public utility commission already had allowed the state's utilities to recoup the cost of conservation investments—the cost of energy-efficient light bulbs installed in customers' facilities, for example. Some utilities also had been permitted to raise rates to cover the cost of lost revenue from customer efficiency measures. Those initiatives helped utilities avoid losing money from conservation, but there was still a missing link: How to turn energy conservation into a profit center for utilities.

Foy and Rowe hammered out a plan to do just that, which they subsequently pushed through the public service commission in Rhode Island, followed by Massachusetts and New Hampshire. The ambitious plan permitted NEES to recover the cost of its investments in energy efficiency, changed the ratemaking structure to allow NEES to earn a reasonable rate of return to compensate for the lost revenue resulting from its customers' conservation, and provided other incentives for the utility to push conservation over consumption. The effort, the first of its kind, has since been copied by utilities throughout the United States.

Encouraging customer efficiency is only one part of NEESPLAN 4. It calls for NEES to develop approaches "to provide electric service in a more environmentally sustainable way" through such means as renewable energy projects, stabilizing greenhouse gas emissions, and reducing other pollutants and wastes. It also calls for a new kind of flexibility, in which NEES will provide energy solutions tailored to individual customers' energy and environmental needs, whether from renewable sources, like solar and wind energy, or nonrenewables, such as coal, oil, and natural gas.

Energy conservation has provided a financial edge for NEES. In 1993, for example, 7 cents out of $2.93 in earnings per share were directly attributable to conservation. That may not seem a windfall until you understand the financial realities of the utility business. "Most of the time, you don't have a huge range of profit and loss," explains John Rowe. "For us, success isn't 20 percent on equity; it's

13 percent. And mediocrity may not be 5 percent on equity, it's 11 percent. And so when you put it in that context, those extra pennies make a big difference between being one of the better utilities and one of the more mediocre ones." In the case of NEES, those "extra pennies" amounted to around $5 million of additional profit annually.

Aside from NEES's improved relationship with CLF and the increased profits generated by conservation, Rowe says NEESPLAN has revived his employees' spirits. "Five years ago, most employees still felt that the environmental issues were a bunch of nasty standards that had to be met and then they would go away," he says. "We have gotten most people to understand that a curve of continuous improvement must be found with respect to all sorts of pollutants. Just as we get better and smarter in service every day, so should we get better and smarter at getting greener. It doesn't get one to sustainable development, but it at least puts one on the right road."

The partnership forged by CLF and NEES is significant beyond the utility's customers, or even beyond New England's environment. It represents a new way of doing business, the recognition that there are power and profits to be had by creating win/win relationships. The NEES-CLF partnership represents the kind of voluntary, private-sector initiatives that the current political administration is encouraging, in which government, private industry, and activists spend less time in court and more time involved with fomenting real environmental change to the advantage of the company and the public.

SAVING ENERGY, SAVING JOBS

The benefits of this new mind-set among Rowe and some other utility executives extend beyond mere energy efficiency. That's particularly true in the manufacturing sector, where older, inefficient plants simply can't compete with newer facilities that may use only a fraction as much energy to produce identical goods. For companies with excess manufacturing capacity, there may appear to be little choice but to close the older plant and shift production to the newer one, with all the concomitant impact of job loss on employees and communities. But there are often better solutions.

Consider the case of a Framingham, Massachusetts, factory that makes ice cream under the Sealtest, Breyers, Light n' Lively, Frusen Gladje, and Good Humor brands. Up to October 1993, the plant was known as KGF Framingham, reflecting its ownership by Kraft General

Foods; that fall it was sold to Unilever and renamed the Good Humor–Breyers Plant. (Because most of the story took place under its previous ownership, we'll refer to it as KGF Framingham.)

KGF Framingham, built in 1963, produces some 20 million gallons of ice cream a year in its 120,000-square-foot plant. Though considered state of the art when originally built, the facility over time came to be considered inefficient. By 1988, KGF Framingham's situation was critical. The plant's production costs were not competitive with other manufacturing facilities in its division and company officials were considering closing the plant and laying off its 200 employees. One big problem was that increased electricity costs had been causing overall budget problems at KGF Framingham since the late 1970s. Joe Crowley, the plant's operations manager, had reviewed and analyzed various options to reduce energy consumption, but nothing seemed viable.

During the late 1980s, KGF Framingham's electric utility, Boston Edison, joined with other utility companies throughout the United States in offering a series of energy conservation programs known generally as demand-side management, or DSM. The idea behind DSM is as simple as it is synergistic: By helping companies reduce their energy consumption through efficiency measures, utilities can help their customers cope with economic and environmental competitive challenges. In the process, utilities maintain their customer base in a way that maximizes their current investments in generating capacity. A 1993 survey by the Electric Power Research Institute (EPRI), which conducts research and development on behalf of the electric utility industry, found more than 2,300 DSM programs being offered by 666 U.S. utility companies. EPRI estimates they reduced annual electricity sales by about 23 billion kilowatt-hours (kWh) in 1990, just under 1 percent reduction. That's the equivalent of nearly 14 million barrels of oil. EPRI estimated that DSM-based savings by the year 2000 will be about 4.3 percent, or 141 billion kWh, and 233 billion kWh (6 percent of sales) by 2010.

KGF Framingham qualified under one of Boston Edison's DSM programs targeted at large commercial and industrial customers, in which the utility company offered free energy audits. For the ice cream plant, that consisted of a sixteen-day on-site evaluation of the energy used for cooling, storage, manufacturing, packaging, sanitation, and all other aspects of its operation. The findings of the 1990 audit incorporated several recommendations, including replacing a 1,700-ton freon refrigeration system with a 2,000-ton ammonia system that has an automated system for centralized refrigeration control; freon is undesirable because it depletes stratospheric ozone. It also called for replacing the air-handling equipment in the ice cream hardener and freezer, as well as installing a new lighting system, high-efficiency motors for homogenizing and pasteurizing equipment, and a new heat recovery system to capture and use exhaust heat from manufacturing processes. The auditors estimated that by adopting these measures, KGF Framingham would save more than 6 million kWh of electricity a year—roughly the amount needed annually to power 1,000 Boston-area homes. Moreover, the improvements would reduce KGF Framingham's energy costs by a third, nearly a half-million-dollar annual savings.

The cost of these conservation measures wasn't cheap—around $3.3 million. KGF, the parent company, wasn't prepared to foot the bill, so another funding source was needed. That came from the Energy Efficiency Partnership, a previously untested Boston Edison DSM program under which KGF could recover most of its improvement costs through an incentive program based on actual efficiency improvements. After intense negotiations over the renovation details, the seven-month construction process began in September 1990. After its completion, the energy-efficiency improvements met or exceeded their original expectations.

The changes have had a tremendous impact on KGF Framingham. For starters, the plant's electricity costs have dropped two cents per gallon of ice cream. That may seem a pittance compared to ice cream's per-gallon retail cost, but it represents a significant reduction in overhead production costs. That two cents, multiplied times 20 million gallons, represents $400,000 a year to the plant's bottom line—"a lot of money when you're looking to stay open or close," says plant manager Joe Crowley. The plant now consistently ranks number one or two in efficiency among its division.

But that's just the beginning. Because KGF employees had a major role in designing and implementing the efficiency measures, their motivation and commitment improved dramatically. "From the day that we started up after installation, employee ownership has gone a complete circle," says Crowley. "Efficiency has improved by over 10 percent across the board in all departments. Employee ownership is there, day in and day out, where it might have been questionable before. There is pride in what they do, pride in the installation, pride in what they've accomplished for the environment. It has had far-reaching implications for our company. It's almost like we were an old dinosaur and now we're a young tiger, ready for the future."

*　　*　　*

The Boston Edison–KGF Framingham partnership is just the tip of the DSM iceberg. As the success of this and other efforts have gained recognition, several forward-thinking utilities have gone even further to help companies become efficient—and, in the process, remain good customers for the utilities. At Southern California Edison, for example, a Customer Technology Applications Center (CTAC) features showrooms demonstrating energy-efficient lighting systems, heating and air-conditioning systems, and electric motors. CTAC also brings in retired engineers from the region to work with companies struggling to meet strict clean air laws. For example, auto-body and metal-finishing shops are shown how to spray coatings in a way that minimizes release of smog-producing volatile organic compounds (VOCs). Other utilities, including Georgia Power, Pacific Gas & Electric (PG&E), and Seattle City Light, have made similar use of such research centers.

What do auto painting and metal finishing have to do with an electric utility? Not much—at least until you look more closely.

Keeping commercial and industrial customers in business, or preventing them from fleeing the area to places with fewer environmental restrictions, helps utilities maintain their customer base, increasing efficiencies and profits. "They don't want to see any more industry go offshore," explains Myron Jones, project manager for environment and energy management at EPRI. "If you lose an industrial customer, you also lose commercial and residential customers." This domino effect, he says, leads to the wholesale abandonment of communities, what Jones calls the "Rust Belt syndrome." So, by helping to stabilize the job base through environmental initiatives, utilities can help stabilize their bottom lines.

The future of utility partnerships with business may be seen in California, where in 1993, PG&E teamed up with local government agencies and businesses to create job opportunities for its service area. Specifically targeted was hard-hit Silicon Valley, home to a large pool of skilled workers and idle facilities. In 1994, PG&E helped fund "Joint Venture: Silicon Valley," an environmental business "incubator," to spawn a dozen or more companies in the environmental sector. That could help improve northern California's environment along with its job base.

All of these conservation partnerships between companies and utilities will yield dividends for both parties for a long time to come. Utilities will find themselves more able to compete in the fast-approaching era of utility competition, in which state and other boundaries will be lifted and energy rates deregulated, resulting in true competition. Utilities like NEES and PG&E, innovative and flexible, will be better suited to compete in that business environment. Their customers will become more competitive, too, as they reap the benefits of the new efficiencies and opportunities generated by working with their utilities. It is an exemplary case of synergy between business and socially responsible interests, with everyone coming out winners.

GREENING THE SUPPLY CHAIN

Another type of environmental partnership takes place between companies and their suppliers. That relationship is changing, too, as a growing number of companies—as well as government agencies—now give preference to greener products, those that are made from recyclable materials, are more recyclable themselves, or are manufactured with fewer problematic ingredients. Some of these companies and agencies give price preferences as well, agreeing to pay a small premium for these environmental benefits. That, in turn, is having a ripple effect throughout the economy, as suppliers to all these companies and agencies revamp their products, or lean on *their* suppliers to do likewise.

Consider the impact of a policy at General Motors' North American Operations, which runs twenty-five assembly plants. Like Valley Plastics, the company has set an ambitious goal of being landfill-free—generating no solid waste. To do that, it is getting a lot of help from the 10,000 or so suppliers that ship parts to General Motors.

To meet its goal, G.M. sent its suppliers detailed instructions on how to package and ship parts. For example, suppliers must use corrugated cardboard shipping pallets instead of ones made of wood. Some G.M. plants had received up to 2,000 unrecyclable wooden pallets per day. In addition, G.M. will no longer accept any shipment that uses wood corner supports, foam, or other materials stapled or glued to cardboard boxes. Such "foreign" materials can hinder cardboard recycling. Similarly, needless wrapping, bagging, and taping are *verboten*: only strapping made of polyester and polypropylene is accepted. And don't even think about polystyrene peanuts and polyethylene shrink-wrap.

It doesn't take much imagination to see the trickle-down effect such a policy has throughout G.M.'s supply line. Its suppliers will

Purchase Order

Below are excerpts from a letter sent to suppliers by Fred G. Peelen, executive vice president, North America, for Inter-Continental Hotels, and David Thorn, the environmental chairperson, North America, for the 100-hotel chain. Attached to the letter was a supplier questionnaire and a copy of the company's Environmental Purchasing Specifications.

... Over the months, our hotels have made great strides in substituting products manufactured and packaged from non-environmentally responsible to those more proactive to this concern.

As a supplier and an important element to this critical issue we ask that you take careful note of our Environmental Purchasing Specifications attached, appreciating that environmental merit of a product will be weighed equally with Price, Quality, and Availability in the purchasing decision. While "perfectly green" products may not be achievable in all aspects, it is our aim that each and every purchase have the least negative impact on the environment.

Preferential treatment may be offered to companies which actively source and offer ecologically sensitive product lines, are responsive to our requests, and practice good environmental stewardship. Conversely, hotels reserve the right to reduce the size of orders given to, or eliminate from the bidding process entirely, any company which fails to address these concerns.

Claims such as "Green," "Biodegradable," "Natural," "Organic," "Environmentally Friendly," "Recyclable," and "Recycled" need to be substantiated with the initial bid. ...

have to change the way they do business with the auto maker, or risk losing its business. By the way, G.M. will save carloads of cash by reducing, perhaps eliminating, the number of trash dumpsters, as well as the hauling and tipping fees associated with getting trash from the loading dock into the local landfill.

Whatever the cash savings—G.M. won't disclose them—the trash savings are impressive. When the company started measuring its solid waste output in 1991, its assembly plants were generating an average of 88 pounds of trash for every vehicle made. Within six months of beginning the program, that number dropped nearly two thirds, to 31 pounds per vehicle. Two years later, in March 1994, the number had been cut in half, to a mere 15 pounds. A few plants had even more dramatic results: one in Fairfax, Kansas, which builds Chevrolet Grand Prix cars, has reduced its output to less than one pound per car; a truck plant in Fort Wayne, Indiana, generates just over two pounds. Those savings add up. When you consider that General Motors manufacturers roughly 15,000 vehicles a day, 240 days a year, the average savings of 67 pounds per car amounts to more than 120,000 tons of trash a year. Assuming a typical dumping fee of $55 dollars per ton, that's roughly $6.6 million dollars in reduced dumping fees alone—with no initial company investment.

What happened to the original zero-landfill goal? "We didn't quite make it," admits Kenneth J. Horvath, a G.M. senior project engineer who has overseen the effort. Still, he says, "we haven't given up. In fact, we're getting even stronger. We like the term 'aggressive achievable goal.' We're going to shoot for zero, but what if we only get to seven? That's still impressive. We're going for the toughest thing we can go for."

Horvath is encouraged by the results of G.M.'s semi-annual measurement and internally published ratings, which have created competition among plants. In 1993, for example, a Chevy S-10 truck plant in Shreveport, Louisiana, showed up at the bottom of the list, generating 157 pounds of trash per vehicle. Six months later, its per vehicle number had dropped to a mere 17 pounds. "The plant manager just didn't want to be at the bottom of the list any more," says Horvath. "He started getting clean and green just because somebody was measuring and rating. The good guys are at the top and the bad guys at the bottom, and no one wants to be at the bottom."

General Motors' purchasing policy won't mitigate the company's many environmental problems. It still emits high volumes of toxic materials into the air, land, and water. And the company has been criticized by environmentalists and some politicians for fighting clean air laws, improved fuel efficiency, and some states' requirements that G.M. and other auto makers produce zero-emission vehicles, such as electric cars. The company's zero-solid-waste goal doesn't address these issues. Still, by wielding the power of the purse to encourage suppliers to be more environmentally responsible, G.M. is leveraging its own actions to affect the environmental policies of thousands of other companies.

As General Motors has found, companies around the world are beginning to recognize the tremendous power they wield to effect environmental and social change through their purchases. So have federal, state, and local government agencies, many of which have established purchasing policies that give preference to recycled products. In 1994, for example, the federal government mandated that the office paper it purchases contain at least 20 percent post-consumer recycled material by 1995, and 30 percent by 1998. (Environmentalists were critical of this policy, charging that the technology already exists to produce sufficient quantities of paper containing 30 percent or more recycled content. But the paper industry successfully lobbied for lower levels.) Even though Uncle Sam represents only about 2 percent of paper purchases, its buying policy is expected to have a major impact on the paper market, if only because state and local agencies will likely follow the federal government's lead. All who do are helping effect a fundamental change in the way paper is produced.

Another leader is McDonald's Corporation, which has been one of the largest private-sector purchasers of recycled goods for its restaurants, from the napkins and bags given its customers with their orders to the recycled plastic building materials it uses in construction. When introduced in 1990, its "McRecycle USA" campaign committed the company to buying $100 million a year of these greener goods. So enthusiastic were the company's suppliers that McDonald's purchases of goods made from recycled materials totaled $900 million during the first four years of the program.

Still another leader is S. C. Johnson & Son, better known as the Johnson's Wax people. In 1992, it held an International Suppliers' Day Environmental Symposium at its Racine, Wisconsin, headquarters for representatives from fifty-seven of Johnson's top seventy supplier organizations worldwide. The two-day meeting featured both general and specific presentations from in-house and outside speakers, including Johnson president and CEO Richard M. Carpenter, National Wildlife Federation president Jay D. Hair, former U.S. senator Gaylord Nelson, and representatives from the President's Council on Environmental Quality and the International Chamber of Commerce. Afternoon breakout sessions focused on such topics as biodegradation of products and packaging, source reduction and recycling of products and manufacturing processes, improved communication between suppliers and S. C. Johnson, and the need to reduce volatile organic compounds in the company's aerosol products.

The symposium wasn't the end of the communication efforts between Johnson's Wax and its suppliers. A summary booklet was mailed to all participants, and a newsletter, *Partners*, continues to keep suppliers and other interested parties up to speed on the company's environmental goals and progress. As Edward C. Furey, Johnson's director of U.S. strategic purchasing, put it in the premiere issue: "From the raw materials and components you supply us to the containers in which they are packaged, your commitment to helping S. C. Johnson attain these objectives is critical.... Partnering together, we can and will have a measurable impact on improving the condition of the environment."

Individually and collectively, these and other manufacturing and service companies control vast sums, used to acquire everything from simple office supplies to raw materials for manufacturing to an endless list of big-ticket items. By favoring vendors with environmentally and socially responsible records, products made with recycled or less toxic materials or with environmentally improved technology, or services performed in environmentally beneficial ways, a relatively small number of businesses literally can move markets, becoming powerful agents in the greening of businesses around the world. Transforming the markets for products ranging from auto parts to computer chips will not only result in environmental improvements, but will also help reduce the cost and increase the availability of "green" supplies in the market.

Working with Suppliers

Even for the most environmentally savvy corporations, though, greening the supply chain can be difficult. Ace Hardware Corporation, the 1,200-store chain based in Oak Brook, Illinois, has had mixed success with its green vendor program. In 1991, Thomas J. Daly, general manager of the company's paint division, sent a letter to vendors, accompanied by a sixteen-page questionnaire and an environmental policy statement. "The Paint Division will begin conducting audits of all our vendors during 1992—with special emphasis on safety and environmental issues," the statement read. "We reserve the right to immediately cancel any business awarded to a vendor

A Small Company's Big Success

Conventional wisdom has it that big companies have an advantage over small companies in reducing emissions and waste because of the economies of scale they enjoy. But small companies are equally capable of improving their operations. At Valley Plastics, for example, owner Art Frengel has set the ambitious goal of being 100 percent waste-free—recycling or reusing whatever waste his company generates.

Valley Plastics buys premanufactured plastic and fashions it into precision components for the electronic industry and other clients—items that must be manufactured to highly controlled specifications, including holes drilled to tolerances no bigger than the width of a human hair.

To reach his waste-free goal, Frengel sought out plastics he could readily recycle near his northern California facility. He pressed suppliers to produce more recyclable materials and worked with customers to re-engineer their products. He provided prototype parts at his own expense to show customers how to eliminate nonrecyclable materials from their orders.

Frengel wanted to do still more. He recognized that some percentage of what he produced for customers never got used; it was damaged by the customer, perhaps, or simply became obsolete. So he established a take-back policy, which became one part of his company's "Guidelines for Good Stewardship." Frengel sent the guidelines to all his customers, detailing his company policies on the environment as well as on the workplace, the community, and the marketplace.

Recycling plastics costs Frengel more than throwing them out. He estimates Valley Plastics loses about $400 a month on recycling, compared to what it would cost to throw waste plastic out.

But Frengel believes the costs come back in customer loyalty: "Some of our customers say, 'I received a copy of your Guidelines for Good Stewardship and we just wanted to tell you that because of your commitment to the environment and your take-back policy, we're going to use you exclusively.'"

found to be in noncompliance with any applicable federal, state, or local regulations, or who ... shows blatant disregard for the best interest of our environment...."

Not everyone complied; some vendors did not want to disclose proprietary information or didn't want to make the effort. A few refused to respond altogether. Daly dropped a few suppliers in the process and admits that "the communications could have been a little better." But "a lot of the suppliers were more than willing to provide the information and were surprised that anyone was doing this sort of thing. There aren't a lot of people who are spending the time to look at their vendors."

For a company to persuade others to turn their products, processes, and policies topsy-turvy in order to adhere to a set of corporate environmental philosophies is no mean feat. Vendors—who often feel besieged by the demands of several companies' seemingly conflicting purchasing policies, as well as traditional competitive pressures—may stall, stonewall, or simply ignore such mandates. Even General Motors reports that some vendors, especially those that are the sole source for a certain key product or raw material, may simply rebel against customer purchasing policies, knowing full well that their customers have nowhere else to turn.

That means any company wishing to impose "green screens" on its suppliers ought to consider carefully the type and amount of information it wants suppliers to disclose—how much proof, how much certification, how much disclosure of proprietary information. Some or all of these may be appropriate. As the questions probe deeper into company operations, however, there is a natural reluctance for suppliers to respond as fully as their questioners might like. The challenge is to strike a balance between information that is needed to determine a supplier's compliance with company policy and information that will lead to stonewalling and subterfuge on the supplier's part. Unfortunately, it's not often an easy balance to achieve.

And then there's the matter of communications: A lot of it is needed to get buyers and suppliers to cooperate with a green purchasing policy. If procurement is not centralized, each buyer will have to work directly with his or her own network of suppliers in switching to environmentally preferred goods and services. Keeping all these disparate purchasing people apprised of evolving green-purchasing data must be an ongoing effort for a program to be effective over the long term.

Ultimately, greening suppliers involves a delicate dance between buyer and seller. Like most dances, this one requires that each party adapt to the other's stance, know when to lead and when to follow, and adapt to constantly changing conditions, lest they step on each other's toes. And most companies "dance" with dozens, hundreds, or even thousands of supplier "partners," each of which brings to the relationship a different personality and style. So, companies seeking to integrate environmental considerations into their procurement policies and vendor relationships must be light on their feet, metaphorically speaking. In practical terms that means buyers must work closely with sellers, communicating openly, being flexible, and, most important, being patient.

Still, some companies are finding environmentally responsible suppliers, and are discovering that these suppliers' products are often superior in price and performance. Moreover, products that feature less disposable packaging and fewer problematic ingredients can in turn reduce their own disposal costs and their release of hazardous materials into the air, water, or land, lowering costs and liability.

But the process is usually neither quick nor easy. The challenges are both internal—developing standards, communicating them companywide, identifying alternate materials, changing old habits—and external—getting suppliers to pay attention and make changes in a way that doesn't compromise quality or price. That's a tall order, but not an impossible one.

A common refrain among companies that have made the effort is the need for a new kind of relationship with trading partners. "You need to be a partner with those you work with," says Arthur Toopmas, corporate environmental manager at Cone Mills Corporation, a Greensboro, North Carolina–based maker of denim for the cut-and-sew garment industry. "We have some suppliers that we feel are very important and we want them to be long-term suppliers. We want them to make a reasonable profit. But we want to stay in business while we help them stay in business. So we have to make sure the situation is equitable."

Committing time and personnel resources is another challenge. Many companies find themselves in the role of teaching suppliers some basic environmental concepts. Quad/Graphics, for example, distributes a two-page "Gruff's Purchasing Guide," named for its mascot goat, listing questions for their staff to ask vendors about the environmental nature of their goods. At the Hotel Inter-Continental in New Orleans, project coordinator Brenda C. Kelt researched part time for over a year to come up with a set of Environmental Purchasing Specifications, or EPS. But she found that sales reps calling on her company didn't understand them. "So we set up appointments with all of our reps and went over the specific sections that applied," says Kelt. "They at least understand the difference between 'post-consumer' and 'post-industrial' [waste] now." Not all of her counterparts at other Inter-Continental hotels bothered to do this. "They didn't take the time to go over the EPS with suppliers. They just assumed that they could decipher it." Sometimes that worked. But many vendors either ignored the EPS or came back with "a lot of mixed propaganda" about their so-called green products, says Kelt. In addition to the EPS, Inter-Continental also sends out a standardized questionnaire to prospective vendors, asking about types of packaging used, as well as the ingredients used in cleaning products, and whether the vendor has a means of collecting disposable parts of their products for recycling. Putting this questionnaire together was an education in itself, says Kelt, requiring her to consult with others in the company as well as outside experts. And, she says, the questionnaire has been continually revised, based on new information and vendors' comments. Such revisions are inevitable in a world where the state of the art can change quarterly, or even faster. That means any set of criteria—for products or the suppliers themselves—must be fluid.

Executives at General Motors took a look around and found that "we had never told our supply base what to send us. We just tried to deal with what they gave us," says Ken Horvath. The company set ambitious goals to get its thousands of vendors to change the way they ship parts to its North American assembly plants. Horvath put together a ten-page booklet listing packaging requirements, along with suggestions for substitute products. For example, rather than using shrink-wrap to hold boxes together on a shipping pallet, Horvath suggested an adhesive product such as Lock 'n' Pop, which adheres cartons to one another but doesn't hinder cardboard recycling. "I got feedback from suppliers saying, 'Thanks for giving us choices, not telling us what we had to do,'" says Horvath.

One problem was getting the information in the right hands. "Some of the material never got to the person it was intended for," says Horvath. "We didn't know if we should send it to the general manager, sales manager, or packaging engineer." Horvath says G.M.'s suppliers were generally enthusiastic. "There is 10 percent who can't wait to help you. There's 10 percent that are going to fight you tooth and nail. And there is 80 percent that you have to educate, cajole, and hold their hand." Even the resisters were worth working with, he says. "We would rather work with them than shoot them. You can't gain anything by starting a war. The ones that don't comply need a different tack. You have to find the right person, or find their soft spot. You just have to work harder."

Sometimes, working with suppliers can bring profitable results to both buyers and sellers. That's something the computer industry found when it pushed suppliers to eliminate ozone-depleting chlorofluorocarbons from their manufacturing processes. "Back in 1988 we indicated our goal to eliminate [ozone-depleting] chlorofluorocarbons to our suppliers," says Walter Rosenberg of Compaq Computer Corp. "We indicated to them in a very soft-sell type of way that this was our plan and that we believe if you're going to be a long-term player with us, then you'd better adopt a similar approach." To date, 90 percent of Compaq's suppliers have found alternatives to CFCs, and the rest are in the process of changing. That move helped the computer industry meet or beat international deadlines phasing out CFCs, while enabling component manufacturers to develop new, profitable technologies.

The possibilities for such collaborations are endless. At Mattel, the toy company, officials are talking with a supplier "about taking waste from theme parks and stadiums and turning it into a by-product that can be used in our products or packaging," according to spokesperson Donna Gibbs. The idea is currently in the development stage. Officials at Mary Kay Cosmetics decided not to set procurement goals that they perceived could restrict creativity; instead, the company offers itself as a testing ground for vendors' environmentally improved packaging designs, says Randall L. Boeller, manager of global package development. "We test what they've done and then we give them feedback." That cuts the company's R&D costs and still gives them access to environmental innovations.

It's all a matter of give and take. "Companies and their vendors are always negotiating all the time about different things," says Mike Collins, spokesperson for Recreational Equipment Inc. (REI), a national retailer of outdoor gear that has worked hard to reduce packaging. "I think it is most successful when both sides recognize the importance and benefits that can come." Its spirit of cooperation notwithstanding, REI sometimes must flat out tell a supplier that "some things are just not acceptable."

*   *   *

All of these efforts—waste reduction, recycling, procurement policies, employee reward and recognition, and many others—are destined to become a way of life at environmentally successful companies. Spurred by the growing demand from stakeholders for signs of serious environmental commitment, companies will be looking for ways to demonstrate their responsiveness.

Some will no doubt look for guidance to the CERES Principles— the set of ten goals for corporate environmental excellence mentioned in chapter 4. Among other things, the principles ask companies to commit to protection of the biosphere by minimizing the release of any pollutant that may damage the air, water, or earth; to a sustainable use of natural resources; to reduction and disposal of waste; to damage compensation for environmental harm; and to annual audits and public disclosures of environmental performance.

The principles were first embraced by smaller companies like Stonyfield Farm and Aveda, which were already living many of the goals. But in 1993, the Sun Company, a refiner and marketer of petroleum products, became the first *Fortune* 500 company to endorse the CERES Principles. Then came H. B. Fuller, the adhesive and sealant maker. In 1994, CERES landed an even bigger fish, General Motors, after several years of shareholder resolutions asking company management to endorse the principles. At other companies, similar shareholder actions had resulted in a compromise in which the company agreed to issue an annual environmental report (one of the principles' mandates) in exchange for withdrawal of the resolution. But in 1993, G.M. management decided it wanted to go further and entered into discussions with CERES leaders "to see if there was a circumstance where we could endorse the principles," according to Dennis Minano, G.M.'s vice president for the Environmental and Energy Staff, who represented the auto maker in the talks. Minano says he had been impressed with the changes made by CERES's organizers over the years. The principles had shifted in his perception from one of "a binding, legal, restrictive contract" to one "committed to continuous improvement and financially responsible environmental progress."

Some activists were unsettled to find General Motors in the same league with companies like Aveda, an environmentally conscious maker of personal care products. But other activists had seen a sea change in the auto maker. The Council on Economic Priorities (CEP), which in 1992 listed G.M. among the worst environmental actors as part of its Campaign for Cleaner Corporations, "de-listed"

G.M. a year later because of improvements it had made. "I think you see some genuine effort at turnaround at G.M.," Alice Tepper Marlin, CEP's executive director, said at the time. After the council gave G.M. the initial thumbs-down, the company invited CEP staffers to its Manhattan offices, where "twelve people spent four or five hours and presented stacks of information," says Marlin. "They had made some genuine improvements and were enormously open to discussing with us, exchanging information, and answering questions."

It's that level of openness and disclosure that General Motors brought to CERES, and it made a statement about more than just the auto maker. It demonstrated that even large companies with significant environmental impacts could enter into a dialogue with environmentalists and socially responsible investors, and that such a dialogue could lead to a significant environmental commitment.

General Motors' endorsement of CERES isn't just symbolic. By doing so, the company committed itself, along with CERES's other signatories, to release an annual CERES Report, disclosing a great deal of information about its environmental policies and performance. That will put G.M.'s record in the public spotlight on an ongoing basis. And while that alone won't reduce the company's substantial emissions of waste from its operations, it will help set a new standard for openness and collaboration.

When it comes to socially responsible environmental practices, the old saw may be right: What's good for General Motors truly might be good for the country.

Chapter Seven

The Workable Workplace

"You deal with the fact that these are people, they are not merely an extension of a machine. And the minute you say that you then establish all of the human reactions to all situations, both tangible and intangible."

—ELLIOT LEHMAN,
chairman emeritus, Fel-Pro

Robert Frey is nothing if not an optimist. In 1984, he and a partner took over a small company in Cincinnati that was hemorrhaging financially. The company had been plagued for years by poor labor relations, rigid job descriptions, and high labor costs. The company's product line—mailing tubes and other paper containers with metal ends—hadn't changed in two decades. The company was losing about $30,000 a month.

Today, Frey's company is prospering, despite the fact that its employees haven't had a raise in their contract wages in nearly a decade. Productivity is up, labor relations are good, and the company has launched two new subsidiaries—without adding any new personnel.

What happened? Nothing short of a revolution. Frey recognized that to survive he had to tap into the unfulfilled potential of his work force, inspiring, exciting, and motivating them to achieve the potential he knew existed. So Frey empowered his workers to think and act like owners, and rewarded them for doing so. And everyone involved has reaped the financial rewards. Frey's company has grown fivefold in five years. Its profitability is fifteen times the industry average.

His modest, forty-one-employee company, Cin-Made Corporation, is a shining example of what can happen when employers embrace their employees as partners, treating them as adults rather than children, as assets to be nurtured rather than costs to be eliminated, empowering them rather than managing them. As Frey has learned, employees more often than not rise to the challenge, bringing their best efforts to work each day in support of their company.

What exactly is the social responsibility of companies within the workplace? The specific strategies and practices vary from company to company, but there are common approaches for companies of all sizes and sectors: respecting employees' roles as both workers and family members; integrating their diverse backgrounds, lifestyles, and beliefs into company culture; empowering them to have a say in the work they do; honoring their need to grow and flourish and prosper in their jobs; accommodating their desire to have meaningful lives outside of work; and recognizing their need for a helping hand when times are tough, including when employers can no longer afford to employ them.

The workplace issues facing socially responsible companies are many and varied, and usually quite complex: fair wage and salary levels, equitable distribution of benefits, improving labor relations, ensuring a diversity of employees at all levels of the company, ensuring occupational safety and health, providing training and career enhancement opportunities for all employees, and generally creating a fair and trusting work environment. Beyond that are such programs as employee scholarships, adoption assistance, wellness programs, and domestic partner benefits, each of which has its own costs and benefits. Addressing all these issues demands innovation and creativity, particularly during an era when companies are striving to create high-performance environments that maximize productivity, minimize bureaucracies and mid-level managers, and squeeze budgets to become more competitive. This push for high productivity has put additional pressure on companies to conduct themselves in ways that on their face appear to go against socially responsible thinking: reducing personnel, paring benefits, delaying raises, cutting frills.

But a socially responsible, high-performance workplace need not be a contradiction in terms. As we'll see throughout this chapter, socially responsible policies and practices can increase company prosperity along with employees' motivation, loyalty, and commitment. Even in bad times a company may need to focus on preserving jobs while remaining competitive, as opposed to laying off workers and closing plants in response to shifting markets and increased competitive pressures. And when it has no choice but to close facilities or reduce the work force, still more issues may emerge in ensuring that these things are done as equitably and as fairly as possible for the employees and the community, as well as for the company.

"The dual goals of social responsibility and a high-performance workplace aren't at odds," says Alan G. Hassenfeld, chairman and CEO of Hasbro, Inc., the $2.5 billion, Rhode Island–based manufacturer of toys, games, and infant-care products. "In fact, they are synergistic, with each enhancing the other. Ultimately, both employees and companies come out ahead."

Socially responsible leaders like Hassenfeld understand that the needs of the people who work for them—who bring their bodies and minds, if not their spirits, to work each day—are not necessarily in conflict with a company's bottom-line needs. They recognize that confronting these matters in a socially responsible way can actually enhance a company's performance and competitiveness. Socially responsible companies are geared to meet both the employers' and the employees' needs, at the expense of neither.

THE WORKPLACE AS WINNING EDGE

Creating a vibrant, committed work force is vitally necessary for nations as well as companies in today's highly competitive global environment. Lester Thurow, the Massachusetts Institute of Technology economist, points out that in previous decades, national competitive advantage stemmed from access to natural resources, raw materials, machinery, or technology. Now, such access is far more widespread and attainable. The winning edge, he says, can only come from educated and motivated workers. And, he might have added, what's true for countries is equally true for companies.

Former Stride Rite CEO Arnold Hiatt agrees. "One way of looking at it is to say, 'I am not going to be able to compete with low-wage countries on salaries,' " he says. " 'I'm going to have to focus more on productivity.' And if I am going to focus on productivity and high performance, I've got to have good people who are deeply committed and skilled to carry out that mission. Not everybody is going to be as productive as everybody else. If I am responsive to the needs of those employees or perceived as caring, I'm going to attract better people and retain those people."

"Organizations of the future are networks of relationships," is how Healthy Companies' Robert Rosen puts it. "And the relationships are what glue people together. We are really running human communities or human enterprises. The question is, how do we focus their energy, leverage the talent in there, toward a common goal? That is one of the great challenges of tomorrow's leaders. It's very different from running organizations in the past. Yes, product is important, and land and capital are important, but it's the people who create and innovate and service the customer, and who come up with new ideas and learn and develop on the job."

Companies' workplace strategies are being given increasing weight by potential employees, the media, and the public, as a range of publications and organizations attempts to rate companies as "best places to work"—in general and for Hispanics, blacks, women, mothers, fathers, and working parents. In compiling their rankings, all of these listmakers rely heavily on assessing companies' wage, benefit, and retirement policies, as well as their approaches to hiring, promotions, and the overall workplace environment.

We won't attempt to cover all the possible workplace issues in this chapter; many warrant entire chapters or even books of their own. Rather, we will focus on a handful of issues: employee empower-

> Create a family atmosphere in the workplace, make the workplace a congenial, pleasant place to spend time. Communicate a sense of concern to your employees for their well-being. Create a sense of involvement in your company's fate within the work force. To the extent that an employer can accomplish these things, the company will be more than repaid with employee loyalty, creativity, hard work, and concern for high quality.
>
> —KEN LEHMAN,
> *president, sales and marketing, Fel-Pro Inc.*

ment, benefits enhancements, work versus family issues, employee profit participation, family leave and day care, workplace diversity, job preservation, and fair and responsible layoffs. In each case, we'll attempt to show how a variety of companies have approached these areas with enlightened visions and strategies, ones that respect and value employees as they bring bottom-line benefits to the companies involved, or at least offset their costs and liabilities.

THE TRANSFORMING POTENTIAL OF GAIN SHARING AND EMPOWERMENT

Bob Frey didn't have a socially responsible game plan when he took over Cin-Made. "I can't say that I had a total master plan," he says in retrospect. "I had sort of a dream and a vision of what we could be." But after a few months he realized his vision wasn't coming into focus. "I didn't understand all the dynamics. I didn't understand how long it was going to take and how difficult it was going to be to change the many people involved. I was working under the horrible handicap of having a bunch of people very set in their ways who had done things for twenty years or more in a diametrically opposite way to what I was envisioning. There was literally no change occurring in the system."

His employees were not any happier. "The change in ownership came as kind of a shock at first," recalls Dorothy Wesley, who at the time worked at cutting the long tubes of cardboard into their proper lengths. Only weeks before, Wesley and her colleagues had been on strike because their contract had expired and not been renegotiated, and they were leery of new management. "Bob had a lot of different ideas than we did. We had been working in a certain way for the same employer and had gotten set in our ways. At first it was a conflict."

However unhappy his employees may have been, Frey felt alone in his struggles to make things work better. "Why am I the only person feeling so darn bad in this organization?" Frey found himself wondering. "I'm worried that we are going to go belly up, I'm worried about the cash drains, I'm worried about the lack of profitability. I worry, worry, worry from the moment I wake up until sometimes when I'm laying in bed. I worry seven days a week and it seems like twenty-four hours a day. I've got a few people I have working for me who worry a little bit while they are here, but not too many of them.

Then they go home to a happy family, and that's the end of it for them.

"And I said, 'What is the way in which I can create this same sense of deep concern within the company?' If we could utilize the power of mass worry and mass focus and pulling together the solutions, we'd have many, many different people with all their horsepower joining with my horsepower. And we could be a powerful force."

The answer, he decided, was profit sharing—giving employees a piece of the profits they helped to generate for the company. It was a dubious proposition at first: Cin-Made had no profits. Nonetheless, Frey spent several weeks studying profit-sharing systems. "I really didn't find anything that I liked. They didn't meet my criteria. They were far too complicated and had minimum threshold limits and maximum payout limits and they were based on a bunch of formulas—X percent over the normal rate-of-return investment. And the numbers were most of the time arbitrarily set and announced by some mysterious board of directors, and they weren't known along the way during the year."

So, Frey designed his own system and took it to his workers, who were represented by United Paperworkers International. "I went to the union group and said to them, 'This is really a struggle. What we need to do is figure out how we are going to turn this company around. And I promise you if I turn this company around that you will do well with me.' I told them how I proposed to do it. I basically promised them that they wouldn't get a raise until the sands of time ran out. The way they looked at it was they had no choice because they weren't going to get a raise, so why not take a profit-sharing plan even though they didn't understand it all and weren't sure how it was going to work."

There was some immediate effect. The financial hemorrhaging stopped and the company began earning what was average for packaging companies—roughly 2 or 3 percent on sales. "But that wasn't my idea of why I was in business and that wasn't my idea of what we could become," says Frey. "I knew that the company would never succeed, perhaps not even survive, unless we gave it the same total commitment," Frey wrote years later in the *Harvard Business Review*. "But the workers didn't see Cin-Made as their company; they saw it as the owners' company. That had to change. I didn't want to be their worthy adversary; I wanted to be their worthy partner."

Frey made two pronouncements to employees, things that "I'd been thinking about for months." First, he said, "I do not choose to own a company that has an adversarial relationship with its employees." He also announced that "employee participation will play an essential role in management."

As Frey's partners, the employees got 30 percent of before-tax profits; the percentage eventually has since grown to 35 percent. He began holding monthly state-of-the-business meetings with employees to tell them how things were going. At those meetings he shares month-to-date sales, year-to-date sales, and monthly and year-to-date profits. Today, he also shares such things as profit projections, materials price changes, and operation efficiencies.

"Owners typically believe that information is power," says Frey. "And that there have to be secrets in every company—financial secrets, especially—from their employees. And they want to hold on to the power. They don't want to have a true information open-door policy. We go out of our way not to lock our information up. It turns out that I don't see many people browsing through my desk or anything, but I make it a point that if they want to browse, there it is. What's the big deal?"

Little by little, the phrase "It's not my job" faded away at Cin-Made, as employees took on increasing responsibilities: allocating overtime, scheduling layoffs, deciding when to take on temporary workers and when to let them go. Today, there are no authorization limits for signing purchase orders at Cin-Made. "Our people commonly buy $100,000 to $200,000 worth of material a year each, depending who they are and where they are, but that is not uncommon. They proceed with projects without asking anybody. The only guidelines are that when making a decision, you ought to make sure you get all the best advice possible, and if you think you need the advice of the few managers there are in the system, you ought to go and ask them. And if you think you need some advice from me, my door is always open. But it is your decision. And if you think you are going to bet the farm for the company, then you ought to for sure ask me. But that is about it. It works surprisingly well."

Dorothy Wesley thinks so. "Everyone knows they have to do their share," she says. "Everyone works together more, helping each other out." She describes the cross-training Frey implemented, which she and others are going through to learn one another's jobs. "I feel like I am more a part of everything. The better the company does and the more effort you put in, the more the company makes and the more you make. I think it works well for everyone. I know if I don't get the job out, it is money out of my pocket, too."

We encourage all of our pressmen to run the press the way they want to. Just as each lawyer is a partner and runs his own part of the business, I said each pressman is going to run his own press. Other managers objected. "You can't do that," said one. "You'll fragment management." I said, "I think that sounds like a good idea. Let's fragment management."

—HARRY V. QUADRACCI,·
president, Quad/Graphics Inc.

It's important to note that all of these changes came in a unionized shop. Traditionally, labor unions have been seen as an impediment to such dramatic shifts of responsibility—at times, quite accurately. In this case, the union's local leadership got behind Frey's proposals and played a key role in helping the initially skeptical rank and file understand the changes that were required to be more successful in the future, and how everyone would benefit from those changes. The local union faced considerable skepticism from international headquarters, which brought in its experts in the hopes that they would find fault with Frey's proposals. Instead, they strongly supported them. In the end, the international went along with the plan.

Today, Cin-Made is thriving. Profitability has grown fivefold over five years to a level four times the industry average. Productivity is up 30 percent. Turnover is virtually nil, says Frey. Grievances to the union number only one or two a year. Except for merit raises, wages have been fixed since 1984. Three times a year, every hourly worker gets a check for his or her equal share of the pre-tax profits from the previous fiscal year. Those profits were modest at first, but in recent years have averaged $2.62 an hour—36 percent over the average base salary. In addition, Cin-Made has created two subsidiary companies, DOR PAK and Molded Pulp Products, making specialized packaging out of recycled materials. Remarkably, Cin-Made was able to launch both companies using only the existing work force, at least initially.

Frey's belief that "information is power" has forced empowered employees to keep a close eye on both income and expenses. "There's a real interesting reason for keeping the number employed here down," says Frey. And they realized that fewer employees meant a larger share of the profits for each of them—"more jingle in their pockets," as Frey puts it. DOR PAK and Molded Pulp Products managed the first year of startup with only existing personnel. It wasn't until 1994, as the two spin-off companies geared up production, that Cin-Made employees decided it was time to begin hiring new staff.

Frey is justifiably proud of how far things have come in the past decade. "I think we have done something reasonably extraordinary and not many people in their lifetime get the opportunity to do something like that." He is swamped by invitations to give speeches and presentations to other companies. He often sends employees in his place to preach the gospel of empowerment, and of sharing information and profits. For him, Cin-Made's accomplishments are his statement about what companies can and should be doing to be a positive and profitable force for change. "For this company, social responsibility starts at home," he says.

BUILDING GOOD PEOPLE AT SPRINGFIELD REMANUFACTURING

Cin-Made was certainly not the first company to use one of the many forms of gain sharing—in this case, employee ownership—as a survival tactic. Nor is it the first to share information with employees, or to embrace empowerment as a means for getting employees to think and act like owners. It is part of a new breed of company whose leaders have come to recognize the potential power of gain sharing to create a high-performance workplace. As Jack Stack puts it: "If you make good people, they'll make you a good organization."

Stack, you'll recall from chapter 3, is president of Springfield Re-Manufacturing Corporation (SRC), the highly successful automobile engine rebuilding company with the open-book policy. Stack isn't kidding when he talks about "making good people." "A lot of our systems are designed to focus on the product," he says. "Whether it's statistical process control or total quality management, what we're concerned about is the product and its relationship to the customer in terms of good service and things of that nature. Well, what if you said, 'I'd like to take all the things that you have learned, and instead of making a good product, I'd like to make a good company'? Okay, so what makes up a good company? A good company is good people. So, let's focus on making good people.

"When I look at a product from some other company," he continues, "I always ask myself, 'What's going on with the people inside that company? Are we making good people? Are we making good contributors to society? Are we taking our work environments and building self-esteem and creating wins?' When we create wins and create security, that overflows into society. That means the real tools we have in terms of making things better are right under our very nose."

One of the principal tools Stack has used to help his employees build a good company is financial literacy—the ability to read balance sheets, spreadsheets, profit and loss statements, and other instruments commonly used by those in the finance office and management suites. By giving them the tools to understand the bottom-line implications of everything they did, week in and week out, Stack made his employees dedicated allies, working toward a common cause.

"If you teach people how to build a good balance sheet, like you'd teach them how to build a good car, they'll build you a good balance sheet," says Stack. "The common sense in all this is that we never assume that they can understand these things. But when you start teaching people this whole aspect about how the business works and you find out that the only way that you can beat this game is by performance, magical things happen."

Granted, teaching the average American the arcane world of stock splits and liabilities-to-equity ratios is no mean feat. Stack has found that using a real-life case study—their own company—helps break through learning barriers. But there are limits. "In the elementary levels, it goes relatively quickly," he says. "And in the middle, it's pretty satisfying. But when you get up to a higher level, where we are right now, we're constantly walking on ground that we haven't been on before. When you get a community of people who are always learning and really hungry for knowledge, and they're also rewarded for that knowledge—they're rewarded by a higher standard of living and a better community—they keep wanting more information. They keep wanting to be fed. And for us to feed them as the teachers, we have to keep learning ourselves. There's really not books about this. And there's not too much data where we can get help that say, 'When you're at this particular level, here's what to do.' "

Stack says he finds himself tickled from time to time by the kind of discussions that take place among his company's employees, based on their knowledge of financial matters and their eternal interest in boosting the company's value—and their stock. One discussion in 1993 centered on whether the company should buy back shares of employees' stock to compensate for the fact that net profits were projected to be down that year. Should the company invest some of its cash flow in the buy-back, thereby decreasing the number of shares outstanding, thus boosting the value of each share? What if profits exceeded projections? That would mean the buy-back would actually have reduced some employees' portfolio values.

Not all company matters are so financially oriented. Still, says Stack, "Those are interesting dialogues between hourly, salaried, and managerial people. Typically, employees are more likely trying to figure out why the parking lot isn't plowed, or why don't we have lockers— trivial things. Instead, we're trying to make some tough decisions about where the company should go. And the hourly employees have the fundamental data to be able to discuss these things."

Another believer in full disclosure is Gary Hirshberg, president of Stonyfield Farm, the privately held maker of yogurt based in Londonderry, New Hampshire, that also has a generous profit-sharing plan. He describes his company's mission objectives, in which the company agrees to "Promise what you deliver and deliver what you promise." Says Hirshberg: "One of the ways that we integrate our objectives into our day-to-day operations is that I make sure every employee knows how we're doing financially—quarterly for the whole staff, monthly for the supervisory staff. Hopefully, if they're doing their job, they're telling their charges how we're doing. The reason is that, in part, I want them motivated by the profit sharing. I want them to know where they are. I don't want them to have any mystery about it. I think it empowers them; even if they're not interested in the details of the cost of goods, they at least know that this is a different kind of place that shares that stuff.

"We fully expect at some point that we're certainly going to have to level off, if not downsize," Hirshberg continues. "And if we start to go south, I want them to know as or before it's happening so that their expectations are aligned properly. If you have to let people go, you have to let people go. It's a fact of business life and you can't pretend it's not out there."

Does all this information sharing and insight really improve the basic performance or the product employees are making every day? Jack Stack believes it makes a big difference: "When they're playing the game of business, when they're calculating their stock, when they're estimating where they stand as part of a unit, they see that they're making a difference as a result of how well they do their part." Paul Daley, owner of Daley Enterprises, a house and apartment

For hundreds of years they whipped people to build the Pyramids. It seems to me that it would have taken a lot less time if these people were enthralled with the idea of building Pyramids and excited and felt more like they were partners in the relationship. My guess is they would have come up with more ingenuity—how to build them faster, bigger, smaller, whatever they wanted to do. An employee that's beaten into submission, whether it's about profit or loss or building some edifice, is not going to be effective if they're under duress and working in conditions that only make demands without offering any fulfillment.

—PAUL FIREMAN,
CEO, Reebok International Ltd.

builder in Tulare, California, expressed a similar sentiment to *Inc.* magazine in 1994: "I've become convinced that the neurological connection between the ear and the brain runs through the pocketbook."

The benefits of gain sharing extend beyond fatter employee paychecks, says Stack. He sees his company squarely at the forefront of a much-needed sea change in business's role in creating jobs and building a healthy economy. "We always saw business as the Evil Empire," he says. "If you continually see it as the Evil Empire, we're going to have a self-fulfilling prophecy. Whereas we can show people that business can really make a difference. We talk about declining standards of living in the United States and the world, but we don't see too many people coming up with formulas to show how we can turn the standard of living around.

"The irony is that in order to increase the standard of living, you've got to create wealth. To increase the standard of living, you've got to distribute the wealth as equitably as you possibly can. I think that's a fundamental of capitalism. I don't think you're going to increase standards of living by arm-wrestling 4 percent wage increases at a bargaining table every year. The true wealth is in the equity and ownership of the corporation. That's where you're really going to see tremendous gains in standards of living. The only difference between the haves and the have-nots is the 5 percent of the people who've got the money know how to play the Great Game of Business."

Stack has a point. If companies genuinely want their employees to act like owners—to fully give of their bodies, minds, and spirits each day—they'll have to treat them like owners. That means giving them the power to understand the links between their actions and the bottom line, and providing them with incentives to do what's best for their company—and themselves.

Jack Stack is fond of saying "It's all mathematical" to describe his mode of empowerment. But he's only partly right. It's also respectful and responsible. As the folks at Springfield ReManufacturing have learned, when employees work with employers toward their mutual self-interest, it creates a synergy in which one plus one equals three.

THE WAY WE WORK

Frey, Stack, Hirshberg, and others have demonstrated that gain sharing, employee ownership, and empowerment are potent tools for transforming companies. They represent only some of the socially responsible strategies being used to build companies by building their employees in a fast-changing work environment. But you don't need a master's degree in business administration to see that the world of work has changed dramatically in recent years, creating a host of new issues and possibilities:

• Manufacturing has largely given way to the service and retail sectors. Jobs are becoming less permanent; it is now expected that we will move from one job opportunity to the next, maybe even change careers, every few years.

• The number of small businesses is growing as more people leave their jobs—voluntarily or otherwise—to strike out on their own. Many more women and minorities are among these entrepreneurs. Some of these enterprises grow into bigger companies, more fail, and still others prosper or struggle on as small companies. They provide a significant number of jobs and are the models for larger companies to become more innovative and competitive.

• Customers are demanding higher quality, more competitive prices, and faster turnaround—and, in some cases, adherence to a set of social or environmental philosophies and practices.

• The demand for technical skills is growing at the same time that educational skill levels are falling in much of our society. That's putting additional pressure on companies to invest in the training needed to create competent workers, where previously they had relied on school systems to do that.

• The makeup of the work force itself is changing: while white males still predominate in the upper ranks, growing numbers of women and minorities are vying for the same limited pool of management and executive positions. Workers' values, needs, and desires are changing, as more people face less job security and more financial pressures, opt for more leisure time, and shun traditional married-with-children family roles.

• Unions have been left with a diminished role in the American workplace, although many of the benefits for which they once pressed are now recognized by some companies as good for business. As unions have faded, their power to force or resist change has faded, too. But in some cases, the unions are leading the changes, helping craft new kinds of relationships that call for increased training and educational opportunities for their members.

• For companies, there is fierce global competition—often from countries with few if any socially responsible workplace practices—at the same time as companies at home struggle with a seemingly unending list of new regulations that affect daily work life, covering recycling, cigarette smoking, time off for parents of newborns, improved access to facilities for disabled workers, and many other factors.

All of this and more has made the 1990s workplace a dynamic, exciting, and challenging place for companies. And what's true for companies is doubly true for their employees, who are faced with greater demands, higher stress, and less security than any work force since the Depression. As the wear and tear on employees continues to grow, both they and their employers pay a price. The effects at some companies are tangible: higher absenteeism, lower productivity, higher medical claims, increased alcohol and drug abuse, for example. Other symptoms are less visible: lower motivation, commitment, and loyalty, and more personal distractions that keep them from "being there" even when they do show up.

A 1992 study of 600 full-time workers by Northwestern National

Life called "Employee Burnout: America's Newest Epidemic" painted a rather grim picture. It found, for example, that "one in three Americans seriously thought about quitting work in 1990 because of job stress, and one in three expects to 'burn out' on the job in the near future."

"I think there is a trend quietly going on in this country," says Robert Rosen. "Americans are going through an identity crisis, redefining what success is. You see it with thirty-five-year-old working parents who are struggling to balance work and family, searching for a way to do it and get a good night's sleep in the process. You see it with middle-aged white men who are kicked out of their large corporations and suddenly they're not so willing to run back into the same work environment."

Part of the problem, says Rosen, who is developing learning networks among U.S. companies, is that a few individuals and companies are beginning to redefine success. And what they are beginning to understand is that the way companies have pushed people—putting them in rigid jobs, with little flexibility to accommodate those who have families, ailing parents, or the desire to volunteer—is not healthy either for people or for companies over the long run. "Companies have said traditionally that success means that you grow 15 percent every year and you return that to your shareholder," says Rosen. "But the question around 15 percent growth is an interesting one. Can individuals grow 15 percent every year? At a time when organizations are so dependent on increasing the commitment, confidence, and capabilities of their people, can people learn fast enough? Can they manage change fast enough? Can they grow personally and technically and professionally fast enough to allow the company to grow 15 percent every year?"

Rosen's questions are good ones, and they point up some of the tough challenges facing business leaders. Some are turning these challenges into opportunities, harnessing the power of socially responsible practices to change attitudes and motivate and stimulate their employees. These companies are led by enlightened leaders who, like many of those described in this book, recognize that a large proportion of workers' abilities are being underutilized at work, a valuable untapped resource that can give companies a competitive edge.

There is considerable evidence demonstrating that companies that anticipate and respect employees' needs—as workers, parents, spouses, community members, and concerned citizens—are re-

You're welcome to talk to any employee in my company. I would bet you a case of Ben & Jerry's ice cream that you'll find a much higher degree of happiness here than elsewhere. I'm not saying life's a panacea here. But in general if you ask them what their favorite job was of anywhere, I'm willing to bet that most are going to tell you that it's here. Even though they're getting paid less. Most of them realize that there was a price that they paid for that high-tech-era employment. They never saw their wife or husband or children. Or they were discarded on the streets when things went sour.

—Gary Hirshberg,
president, Stonyfield Farm

warded in a number of ways, not the least of which is their employees' commitment, motivation, productivity, and general physical and psychological well-being. For example, Northwestern National Life's researchers concluded that employer policies could go a long way toward minimizing stress: "Companies with supportive work and family policies, health coverage for mental illness and chemical dependency treatment, effective communication, and flexible work hours have nearly half the burnout rate of employers who don't have such policies."

Social responsibility in the workplace moves beyond human resource programs to integrate a new breed of thinking throughout the company, from top managers down, based on the recognition that how employees are treated can have a powerful impact throughout the company and in the larger community. This is where corporate vision meets the front office and the factory floor.

The range of programs, philosophies, and practices is vast. They differ for large and small companies, manufacturers and service firms, startups and old-line operations. However disparate, they combine human resource issues—issues that contribute to the well-being and productivity of employees, such as work-family policies, wellness programs, diversity training, and the whole range of employee benefits—and organizational development issues—issues that affect the nature and structure of the organization, such as employee ownership and empowerment, increased job flexibility, and layoff reduction strategies.

BALANCING WORK AND FAMILY

There's probably no better example than Fel-Pro Inc. to demonstrate what can happen when socially responsible business leaders apply their philosophies to human resource practices. Based in the Chicago suburb of Skokie, Illinois, Fel-Pro is one of those privately held, family-owned companies that tries to stay out of the limelight and stick to its knitting, which in this case involves the mundane business of manufacturing gaskets for internal combustion engines that power cars, trucks, and other vehicles and equipment. Founded in 1918 as the Felt Products Manufacturing Company to make products for Henry Ford's Model Ts, Fel-Pro's products are sold only to manufacturers and advertised only to the automobile trade.

Despite its preference for a low profile, Fel-Pro, with sales of more than $300 million a year, has been getting a lot of attention lately, winning awards and praise for its innovative and generous family-oriented policies. The company has been written about everywhere from *Newsweek* to the *Harvard Business Review*. It has been listed among the best companies to work for in *Working Mother* and *The 100 Best Companies to Work For in America*, given an "America's Corporate Conscience Award" by the Council on Economic Priorities, cited by the Congressional Caucus for Women's Issues, and named "Employer of the Year" by several organizations.

The policies behind all this praise stem from the owners' long-standing tradition of treating employees like family. That's somewhat natural: the owners comprise three families, all blood relations, who are also related in temperament, according to Paul Lehman, grandson of the company founder and now Fel-Pro's president of administration. "My grandfather always operated in a very informal way, with his door open," he says. "There were few executive perks; there still are. He just treated people decently. He loaned employees money. He got involved in their personal problems. He tried to be helpful."

Today, there is a lengthy list of ways in which the company tries to be helpful to its 2,300 or so employees, both inside and outside the workplace.

Early on in its history, the company established policies that reflected the owners' own commitment to family and community. The company wears that commitment proudly. "We believe that if workers feel their company has consistently dealt with them openly and fairly, they will give full support to productivity and quality programs," reads one part of the company's position statement.

We implement this philosophy through a carefully conceived communications program with the following goals:

1. To promote a feeling that we are truly a Corporate Family.
2. To give employees an opportunity to air grievances openly and address these grievances promptly and effectively.
3. To monitor the pulse of the work force to adequately deal with minor grievances before they become major problems.
4. To make each employee feel important.

Beyond these heartfelt goals lies a foundation of employee programs and benefits that may qualify it as "the best employer in the land," in the words of Robert Levering and Milton Moskowitz, co-authors of *The 100 Best Companies to Work For in America*. Indeed, Fel-Pro employees and their families are covered literally from cradle to grave:

• Employees are given money or other gifts when they get married, become parents, have birthdays (when they get an extra day's pay), on the anniversary of their employment with the company, and when they suffer the death of a spouse, parent, child, in-law, or sibling.

• Their children benefit, too, beginning with a $1,000 Treasury certificate given by the company at birth, which matures on the child's twenty-first birthday, as well as a pair of bronzed baby shoes engraved with the baby's name and birth date. Employees who participate in the company's free Healthy Start Prenatal Program also receive a $100 gift certificate for disposable diapers or a diaper service. More than 300 employee children attend summer day camp at the company's 220-acre "Triple R" (for "rest, relaxation, and recreation") recreational facility about 40 miles from headquarters.

• Kids come to work with their parents, eat breakfast with them before the start of the work shift, then board yellow school buses to Triple R for the day. The bus returns to headquarters at shift's end. Families pay $25 a week per child for use of the camp, for up to three children per family (there is a $5 discount for early registration). Triple R also provides facilities for family recreation. Employees can invite their friends and families; the camp is a favorite facility for reunions. Employees who are interested in farming their own land are given a twenty-by-twenty-foot tract of land at Triple R, along with water and gardening tools, to plant a "mini-farm." All the mini-farms are plowed by Fel-Pro before the planting season begins.

• The company also offers a day care center, adjacent to the plant, only the second such facility opened in the state of Illinois. In 1988, Fel-Pro began offering emergency child care, where professional care-givers provide up to five days of care for a Fel-Pro employee's child, at a cost to employees of $16 per day.

• The benefits continue as employees' children grow. For example, there are college scholarships of up to $3,300 annually, and profes-sional counselors to help high school kids and their parents select a college and arrange visits. Children with functional or emotional disabilities receive one-on-one tutoring in their homes three days a week, paid for by the company. And the company encourages em-ployees' children to work for the company in the summer and during winter and spring breaks, where they earn above minimum wage.

There's more:

• an elder care consulting and referral service to help employees care for elderly relatives;

• a physical fitness center located in the Fel-Pro factory, offering equipment and classes along with a wellness education program;

• an artist-in-residence program, in which works are created out of scrap materials and using Fel-Pro manufacturing processes;

• a weekly visit by a lawyer, available to consult with employees on legal matters;

• a voucher for free income tax preparation by a professional firm; and

• full tuition reimbursement to encourage employees to further their education.

How can the company afford all these programs and benefits? If you ask Fel-Pro chairman emeritus Elliot Lehman, he'll likely respond with, "How can we afford *not* to? We feel that if an employee is preoccupied with personal, legal, or psychological problems, his job performance is affected. If our counselor program alleviates that preoccupation, our company benefits." Clearly, Lehman's philosophy has paid off. Its investment in its people has been a key to building the company's bottom line.

One proof of Fel-Pro's success can be seen in its low turnover rate, currently under 6 percent. The company has never had a layoff or experienced a work stoppage in its seventy-five years (although during hard times it has gone temporarily to a four-day work week), going so far as to reduce the company's liquidity in order to keep its workers employed.

How did Fel-Pro manage to put together its package of programs and benefits? "It wasn't an elaborate management philosophy," admits Paul Lehman. "It was a common-sense approach to dealing honestly and decently with people and paying them well and trying to understand that they had needs beyond nine to five. It was much more a sense of managing by gut and managing by human decency."

Paul's father, Elliot, agrees. "You deal with the fact that these are people, they are not merely an extension of a machine. And the minute you say that you then establish all of the human reactions to all situations, both tangible and intangible. You listen to what they need and how you can attempt as best you can to answer those needs, and what you can afford and what risks you are taking, and whether those risks are affordable. And you then proceed."

The bottom-line result of Fel-Pro's policies was underscored in a pioneering study conducted by researchers at the University of Chicago, who studied the links between the company's family-friendly policies and job performance. Susan Lambert, assistant professor at the University of Chicago School of Social Service Administration and the study's principal investigator, said of the 599 employees studied, those using the programs at Fel-Pro the most had the strongest sense of "corporate citizenship." She said these employees were more likely to volunteer for extra work and participate in team problem solving, and that they suggested twice as many product and process improvements as employees who did not use the benefits.

Lambert's study found that high-benefit users—employees using five to sixteen benefits per year—had the highest performance evaluations and the lowest intentions of leaving Fel-Pro. Few of these workers had received disciplinary actions. Employees using few benefits had lower performance ratings and greater intentions to leave Fel-Pro; a larger proportion had been subject to disciplinary actions.

The researchers tested the relationship between benefits use and job performance to make sure it couldn't be explained by other factors. They found that it held up no matter how long workers had been at the company, how much they earned, or other variables.

There are intangible benefits as well. As one five-year Fel-Pro office worker told the University of Chicago researchers: "Benefits are in some ways like money in the bank—you don't have to use them to make you feel good. Just knowing they're there gives you a secure feeling." She might have added that the benefits are like "money in the bank" for the company, too.

For Fel-Pro's management, the process of responding to employee needs never ends. "These are evolutionary concerns," says Elliot Lehman, "mainly because the nature of people's problems changes." For example, as the rise of two-worker families has increased, the company has begun to focus on the needs of employees' children to see if additional benefits or policy changes would ease the burden for Fel-Pro employees. "You just take a variety of influences that people are subjected to, and if you place yourself in the position where you encourage them to talk, and you encourage yourself to listen, you then start to move in directions that you feel are helpful that may not be possible for them to do on their own without great difficulty."

Like any company—large or small, public or private—Fel-Pro has felt the effects of economic and market shifts. In 1993, the company began moving toward self-managed work teams, which require fewer managers. That move potentially could involve laying off managers. But as we'll see later in this chapter, the company's owners have tried to do everything possible to avoid putting its employees on the street.

INVESTING IN PEOPLE

The idea of accommodating employees' needs outside work is relatively new for many companies. One reason is that the top people often haven't naturally related to their employees' needs. "Something like 70 percent of professional men still have wives at home," explains Fran Sussner Rogers, CEO of Work/Family Directions, a Boston consulting firm that helps companies such as American Express, Citicorp, General Electric, Hewlett-Packard, IBM, and NationsBank put together work-family programs. "So there isn't the experience of having to juggle both the home and business. The rules essentially are set for people who don't have responsibilities. It's not necessarily done with business rationale, just with tradition." In other words, the reason that some chief executives don't sympathize with work-family conflicts is simple: they don't have them.

Rogers believes part of the problem is that top management still doesn't listen carefully enough to those farther down the line. "You've got these companies talking empowerment, talking teamwork, talking cultural change, but they still aren't listening to people on these issues. It's as though those are really business issues and this is some other kind of social do-goodism, and never the twain shall meet. I think there is a disconnect that this is really a business issue. I think it's easier for people to write checks than to examine themselves and the way they manage people. Companies will sometimes start out fearing that if they get into this field they will have to set up day care centers, but by the time they understand it more deeply, they wish they could solve it by writing a check and building a day care center."

Rogers practices what she preaches. Her own 260-employee company—which itself has been named one of the "100 Best Companies for Working Mothers" by *Working Mother* magazine—has helped set up work-family programs at more than 100 companies serving some 2 million employees. In addition to creating programs for these companies, Work/Family Directions offers support services, such as a toll-free phone line staffed by experts in areas such as day care, schoolwork, and elder care. Employees can get individual answers to questions as well as a variety of brochures and workbooks full of tips, checklists, and suggestions on everything from planning a child's after-school activities to safety guidelines for leaving pets unattended.

Rogers cautions that simply offering day care or other work-family programs solves only some of the problems employees are encountering. "A company that does a day care center and makes people work ninety hours a week without any flexibility isn't going to have a happy population," she notes. Another way some companies undermine themselves, says Rogers, is by evaluating their employees on rigid time-based criteria. "People's families can't lead lives that are neat and tidy about what hour you get there, what hour you get back. They'll tell you, 'I can't get anywhere in my career because I'm written off because I can't stay late.' They'll tell you, if they work in a factory, that 'We have this absence policy that if I'm late three times, I'm out,' despite the fact that a parent can't not be late three times. The company cannot justify why these policies are in place for

I think there is a difference about the way that men and women approach problems. I think that the need for the feminine part of business is very real. When you look at the models of management styles that have been promulgated in the last fifteen years, if you had to break them down into male-female values, I think you would say that a lot of them are female values. It's working for the betterment of the whole. Sharing. Team playing. Open, honest communication. And I don't see a lot of men who really hold those values near and dear.

—DEBBIE AGUIRRE,
principal, Tierra Pacifica Corporation

these people. That's just the way it's always been. Things that may have been designed twenty years ago to catch malingerers end up catching families."

Rogers underscores the importance of a broader perspective on the value of employees, one that looks beyond individual policies toward a strategy that embraces individuals' need to flourish.

"Employees are entrepreneurial by nature," says Helen Mills of Soapbox Trading Company. "If you give them a chance to open up and blossom in their environment, they will produce ten times more than if they are stuck in the daily grind and left in their graven step in the corporate compensation scheme, and not given the opportunity to meet new challenges and be stimulated into learning, growing, thinking, and contributing." Mills has integrated this belief into her own company. In an industry—retail sales—known for high turnover and low retention, she has managed to achieve low turnover and high retention.

Johnson & Johnson, the giant pharmaceutical and personal care products company based in New Brunswick, New Jersey, has for years been developing programs that recognize the need for companies to invest in employees' overall well-being. In 1978, Johnson & Johnson introduced Live for Life, a wellness program providing employees with free, comprehensive health promotion programs. A decade later, the company implemented an even more ambitious and equally groundbreaking initiative, the Balancing Work and Family

Program. Like Live for Life, the work-family program offers a wide range of benefits and services: child care services; on-site child development centers; dependent care assistance plans; paid family leave to care for newborns, adoptions, and illnesses among family members; and flexible work schedules. There are also adoption benefits, a resource and referral service that assists parents in choosing public or private schools appropriate for their children, elder care resource and referral, and relocation planning for families.

Johnson & Johnson's programs have been scrutinized by academic researchers as well as executives at hundreds of other companies. One study, the first of its kind, attempted to weigh the claims made for Johnson & Johnson's work-family programs against the actual effects the programs had on the work environment and on the attitudes and behavior of employees. Employees were asked five questions to assess the extent to which their jobs made it difficult for them to have time and energy for themselves and their families and to get everything done at home each day. Researchers concluded that for the majority of employees, "Johnson & Johnson has become a better place to work." Specifically, they found that more than 53 percent of the employees surveyed felt their work environment had improved and that their jobs interfered less with their family lives. This decrease in what the researchers called "negative spillover" from work to family occurred despite the fact that the average employee worked longer hours, spent more nights away on company travel, and reported that his or her job had become more demanding in the preceding two years. Other studies, using the same measures of spillover, found that the more jobs interfere with family life, the higher the levels of marital tension and conflict, and the poorer the developmental prospects for children.

Moreover, the company's generous and flexible leave policies had not been abused by employees. The researchers found that absenteeism and tardiness had not increased following the introduction of the Balancing Work and Family Program. And, as at Fel-Pro, employees' loyalty and commitment to the company appeared to have increased with their use of the work-family benefits, while those who didn't use the services appreciated their existence: 71 percent of those who had used time-off and family-leave programs cited them as "very important" in their deciding to stay on at the company, for example, but the same sentiment was also expressed by 58 percent of those who did *not* use the programs.

In the end, the study concluded, Johnson & Johnson's programs didn't just ease stress and improve job satisfaction. They changed the way people worked, providing direct benefits to the company. "What is most remarkable about Johnson & Johnson's Balancing Work and Family Program," wrote the researchers, "is not that it announced new and progressive work-family policies and provided additional work-family benefits for employees, but rather that in just two years it has begun to transform the work environment in ways that promise to reap greater benefits for both employees and the company than could ever be achieved through policies and programs alone."

THE CASE FOR FAMILY LEAVE

Fel-Pro and Johnson & Johnson may be pioneers, but these days they are by no means alone. Hundreds of companies now offer some kind of program to increase employees' flexibility in meeting ever-changing family needs. Many are doing so because they are required to. In 1993, the Family and Medical Leave Act mandated all employers with fifty or more workers to provide up to twelve weeks of unpaid leave for family medical emergencies, childbirth, or adoption. While passage of that law—the first major legislation of the Clinton administration—provided what some saw as generous benefits, they are far less generous than those offered in Japan and parts of Western Europe (regions known for high-productivity workers), where companies are often required to offer longer leave with pay. In Japan, for example, women are entitled to six weeks' maternity leave both before and after childbirth, at 60 percent salary. In Germany, parents can receive six weeks' paid maternity leave before childbirth and eight weeks' paid leave afterward, with an optional partially paid four-month leave. Swedish parental-leave policy provides for twelve months' leave, with the state making up 90 percent of lost income. Mothers may take an additional six-month leave at 70 percent pay.

Early on, the U.S. law was bitterly fought by most business groups—until its imminent passage, that is, when a few companies and trade associations stepped up to support it. (In 1993, BSR—represented by Lotus Development Corporation—was the only business organization that testified in favor of the Family Leave Act before a congressional committee.) Most opponents cited the cost to companies, especially smaller ones.

Yet companies large and small with several years' experience with family-leave policies usually find them relatively easy and inexpensive to administer and—as Fel-Pro, Soapbox Trading Company, Johnson & Johnson, and others have found—ultimately beneficial to a company's bottom line. When Aetna Life & Casualty Co. introduced a generous leave policy in 1986, turnover dropped from 23 percent to 9 percent in four years. With nearly 90 percent of family-leavetaking employees returning to work, Aetna estimates it saves $2 million per year in not having to train new workers. Smaller companies have fared well, too. A 1994 survey by William M. Mercer, Inc., a benefits consultant, and the University of California at Berkeley found that despite initial fears that smaller companies might be hurt by the federal family-leave law, they actually have felt the law's impact less than larger companies. More than 90 percent of employers complying with California's family-leave law—essentially the same as the federal version, but enacted two years earlier—said they had experienced either insignificant or minor costs. The 4 percent who incurred major costs were all businesses with 10,000 or more employees.

There is good public policy rationale for family leave. Such policies ease the burden on working parents by reducing the conflict between job and family. That's especially helpful when dealing with problems: marital strife, children's problems at home and school, and family members with substance-abuse or other serious problems. If these matters can be handled within the family, it can often prevent higher social costs down the line—school dropouts, child abuse, and drug-related crimes, for example—that cost individuals, government agencies, and companies more money. Most of the companies supporting family-leave legislation said they did not view it as good social policy, however, but as a program directly beneficial to business.

INCREASING FLEXIBILITY

Even employees without dependents are finding that they can flourish at work when their personal and work lives aren't driven by the rigid constraints of a company's time clock. And in the same way that such programs and benefits as day care facilities, adoption assistance, and tuition scholarships help engender dedication and motivation, so, too, can a range of organizational policies and structures, from flextime to compressed work weeks, job sharing, and telecommuting. Each of these can provide employees with the ability to manage their personal lives more effectively, leaving them less distracted at work. Such policies have exploded in recent years among major corporations and smaller companies, who recognize that they bring a variety of benefits to the company. According to a survey by The Conference Board, recruiting employees, increasing productivity, and reducing turnover were three of the top seven reasons given for initiating flexible work plans.

Some companies are afraid to give up the control they have over employees' schedules. "They think they're going to open up Pandora's box and have worse results," says Fran Rogers. But, she says, "the evidence is that flexibility makes people commit more." Another barrier is that flexibility requires a different management style, says Suzanne Smith, co-director of New Ways to Work, a San Francisco—based group that works with companies to develop alternative work programs. She says managers and supervisors often have difficulty overseeing employees who aren't physically there all the time, such as telecommuters, who may work at home one or more days a week. "It means that it's incumbent upon every supervisor and manager to be flexible managing employees," says Smith. "And quite a few of them aren't. The critical point is that they need to be trained so that they do feel comfortable." But, says Smith, training programs that teach managers to deal with flexibility are still few and far between.

Another barrier to flexibility, says Rogers, is a major gap in understanding between companies and employees. "If you ask women with families, 'What is the thing you need most to do better at work?' the answer is, 'I need my flexibility.' If you ask their bosses, 'How do you view a person who asks for flexibility?', more than half say, 'Somebody who's not very serious about their career here.' So you have the very tool people need to be successful being viewed as a sign that they're not serious." That sets employees up for a dilemma: If they take advantage of a company's invitation to make their lives less stressful—and, by extension, their work lives more productive—they may be short-changing their chances for advancement and promotion. "You don't want to be punished simply because that's your lifestyle," says Rogers. "You want to be judged by results."

What's required is a cultural change, a need for companies to measure employees less by how much they work and more by the quality of their work and professional relationships. Changing that

Rapid growth has been really difficult. And one of the things that we never really checked was how you systematize values. How do we put it into a briefing when you come into the company? It has to be on every printed word: How you enter and exit; how you are interviewed. One of the things that eroded our culture very fast was the bringing in of such a huge amount of new people from blue-chip corporations.

We used to have a process where anyone who came in had a three-week induction course, where they went out on community programs. That dropped out of practice for a year. And to bring that back has taken an astonishing amount of energy. What we've done now is gone through a three-month process of talking to every member of our company in groups of twenty for two hours at a time, seeing how we can take those values and put them into every practice.

—ANITA RODDICK,
founder, The Body Shop

culture may require training managers to appreciate different expressions of motivation and commitment, and perhaps revamping the criteria used to evaluate performance. Says Rogers: "A company has to at least make an effort to take out of its culture things that penalize people for no good reason."

DAY CARE, FROM CRADLE TO GRAVE

Stride Rite's in-house day care center is now an intergenerational facility, a model for the business community, but when it was opened in 1971 it was viewed as revolutionary and was not universally well received. Some 6,000 companies—only a fraction of the 6 million employers in the United States—currently offer day care for employees' children as a regular benefit, according to the Families and Work Institute, though that represents a fourfold increase over the past ten years. The day care facilities and programs offered vary widely, as do the costs, if any, to employees. Some programs are in house, others take place off site. There are also consortiums of smaller companies pooling resources to make day care more affordable to all. But underlying all of the programs is the recognition that parents simply cannot work as effectively—or in some cases work at all—without quality care for their children. The continued growth of two-career couples has spurred growth in the number of "latchkey" children left at home after school without supervision. And then there's the financial stress: Working women in the United States routinely spend 25 percent of their take-home pay for child care. Even the grandmother next door—if she is willing to risk cutting her Social Security stipends by reporting baby-sitting income—can command up to $125 a week.

The lack of quality child care presents additional problems for working-class parents, who are caught in a double bind, according to a 1993 study by the Harvard University Graduate School of Education. On the one hand, they cannot afford to pay for private care; on the other, they earn too much money to get the subsidies that poor parents receive to pay for preschool programs like Head Start. As a result, many of these parents make do with low-quality care, which can have an adverse affect on their children's futures. The Harvard researchers contended, as many educators do, that some formal day care experience helps prepare children for elementary school.

Caring for elders—parents, grandparents, and even aunts and uncles—can take an even greater toll. Several surveys found that up to 45 percent of employees with adult dependents work less effectively because of concerns about their relatives. A survey conducted by the Older Women's League and the Families and Work Institute found that elder care duties led to nearly a fourth of workers changing jobs, quitting, or becoming self-employed; about a third arrived late to work, left early, or were absent; some reported turning down training, new opportunities, and relocations in order to devote time to caring for older relatives. Absenteeism and turnover among employees who are caring for elderly or disabled relatives cost companies about $2,500 a year per employee, according to Andrew Scharlach, a professor of aging at the University of California at Berkeley.

Companies can benefit by offering employees some kind of help in caring for aging parents, according to research by Work/Family Directions. A survey of its client companies' employees found that every call employees made to the organization's toll-free help line

Back in 1986, we had a whole day that we dedicated to AIDS awareness. It was really early; hardly anyone spoke of AIDS in those days. We had workshops, speakers, from doctors to hospice, and the final speaker was this very passionate, articulate man who was living with AIDS. It was so shakening. Everybody was crying and shaking afterwards. I felt such a sense of responsibility and pride and I got so much support from all the employees. They said "Thank you. It's so great to know that companies are doing this thing." It really empowered me. We realized that it was a very rewarding opportunity that we had to help our employees. We took a lot of pride and responsibility in being a company where people were getting more than just a salary. We were really helping people have more enlightened lives.

—Susie Tompkins,
founder, Esprit de Corp

(paid for by the employers) saved the worker about fifteen hours of time they would have spent trying to solve a problem. About 80 percent of that time would have been taken off of work, they said. A handful of other companies are helping employees in other ways. NationsBank in Atlanta has free lunch-hour seminars on what to expect as someone ages. IBM subsidizes a home care nursing service for its employees in New York. Other companies offer special payroll accounts with tax advantages, long-term elder care insurance, flexible work schedules, and therapy groups.

Again, proponents of child care and elder care focus on these programs' positive effect on morale and productivity, although a succession of studies have been inconclusive in this regard. The more widely held belief is that such programs enhance corporate reputation and enable companies to attract and retain employees. "There's a difference between what people think and what the objective measures say," says Ellen Galinsky, co-president of the Families and Work Institute. "People think helping with child care is going to improve morale, loyalty, and reduce absenteeism. In fact, the behavioral studies show it is much more crucial in recruitment and retention."

DOES DAY CARE PAY?

Stride Rite's Arnold Hiatt sees intergenerational care as a direct means of giving his company a competitive advantage. "Stride Rite is perceived as a company that cares. We didn't go out and say, 'We care.' We just made these investments in day care. When we made the investments, we thought it was in our interest to do so. By attracting and retaining better people and having less turnover, we're able to achieve what may be the key to this country's future in the global market—that is to be more productive, to circumvent the low-wage competition, because we're never going to be the lowest wage unless we want to become a developing country again. My impression is that the traditional businessman must expand his consciousness or his range of options in terms of what investments are going to have a payback."

Clearly, child care has had a payback for Stride Rite, says Hiatt. "The only natural resource we have, particularly in Massachusetts, is people. And unless we continue to have a highly trained and educated work force, we're going to have increasing difficulty in competing. Records show that we have lower turnover than other companies in this area. And in the mid- to late eighties, when there was a phenomenon known as the Massachusetts Miracle, it was hard to find really good people. Stride Rite never wanted for a large pool of skilled applicants. We always had people wanting to come to work at Stride Rite, whether it was the more difficult positions to fill, like programmers or analysts, when everyone was expanding their management information systems, or marketing people or human resources people. We could always attract them."

Stride Rite's social programs not only helped attract employees, says Hiatt, it helped keep them. "On average, it costs $21,000 a year to advertise for, attract, and train a new employee who is filling a position that is vacated. Furthermore, the loss of productivity until the new employee achieves the level of productivity of the old employee is expensive. We were spared much of that cost. That to me is a nonproductive investment. That's a good example of an expense—an investment in training costs that could have been avoided."

Hiatt's bottom-line thinking about child care, elder care, and other work-family strategies is what's needed if these programs are to spread as broadly as possible to both large and small companies. What's also needed is for companies to pool their resources locally, enabling all to offer their employees more than each of them can do alone. That's the idea behind the American Business Collaboration for Quality Dependent Care, a groundbreaking initiative begun in 1992. The project, coordinated by Work/Family Directions, brings together nearly 150 companies and other organizations to commit more than $25 million toward a broad range of child and elder care programs in 44 cities in 25 states and the District of Columbia. The goal of the collaboration is to invest in diverse types of care, including day care centers, family day care training, adult day care, senior volunteer programs, and programs for school-age children. The collaboration has funded more than 300 different projects serving more than 106,000 people. It's not just big companies, of course. Examples abound of small and mid-sized firms that support day care for employees, whether on site, off site, or through community collaborations.

For all the attention these programs give to working mothers, or even working parents, there are few that explicitly target working fathers. While many companies profess support for fathers' family roles, only a few put money and effort into this area. One that does is the Los Angeles Department of Water and Power, the nation's largest municipally owned utility, with 11,000 employees—80 percent of them male. Over the past few years, the department has established a set of innovative services that support men from impending fatherhood through their children's adolescent years. Fathers can take up to four months of unpaid leave for a birth or adoption, and use department-affiliated child care programs. There are lunchtime workshops for expectant fathers on such things as how to coach and support their wives during breastfeeding. There is also a "Tips for Dads" information hotline and a peer support group, as well as a "Dad's Department" within the company's Parent Resource Library.

Whether for dads or moms, the point of these efforts is the same:

Our people come first, then customers, then shareholders. We can't exceed the expectations of our customers unless we exceed them for our employees first.

—Howard Schultz,
chairman and CEO, Starbucks Corporation

Today's working parents need much more than a paycheck. They desperately need to balance their lives at work with their lives at home if they are to be happy and successful in either environment.

DIVERSITY: THE COMPANY OF MANY COLORS

In 1987, the Hudson Institute stunned corporate America with a study done for the U.S. Labor Department, "Workforce 2000," which concluded that fully 85 percent of new entrants into the work force between now and the end of the century will be comprised of members of minority groups, women, and immigrants; that is, only 15 percent will be white, native-born males. With already working white males retiring in record numbers, the U.S. Bureau of Labor Statistics predicts that by the year 2000, the American work force will be 47 percent female and 26 percent minority.

Integrating all this diversity into one seamless work force is a formidable task, and a vital one. Indeed, there are those who see diversity as a powerful force that, harnessed effectively, can enhance productivity and propel a company to success well into the twenty-first century. Mismanaged, it can become a drain on a company's time and resources.

One good example of the power of diversity is Reebok International Ltd., the athletic footwear and apparel company. At Reebok, the need for diversity came about as part of an evolution that took place as the company grew from a small $12-million-a-year shoe company to a $3 billion footwear powerhouse in less than a decade. "When we were growing very, very fast, all we did was bring another friend into work the next day," recalls Sharon Cohen, Reebok's vice president of public affairs and executive director of the Reebok Foundation, as well as a longtime company employee. "Everybody hired nine of their friends. Well, it happened that nine white people hired nine of their friends, so guess what? They were white, all about the same age. And then we looked up and said, 'Wait a minute. We don't like the way it looks here.' That's the kind of thing that can happen when you are growing very fast and thoughtlessly."

The financial breakthrough for Reebok came in the early 1980s, when a group of women in the company bemoaned the fact that there was no good shoe available to use for aerobics, which had caught on as a major fitness activity. So, Reebok began marketing aerobic shoes, which within two years became a phenomenally profitable business and pushed Reebok to the forefront of the athletic shoe competition. The company didn't necessarily recognize at the time that their success was due in part to a diversity of perspectives—in this case, of women. But while they didn't refer to the new perspective as diversity, they reaped its benefits just the same.

These days, Reebok executives talk about diversity a lot. "When I speak of diversity, I speak from experience," says Paul Fireman, chairman of Reebok, who has become an outspoken advocate on the subject of workplace diversity. "The corporation that wants to be a congenial old boys' network or cling to its nostalgic memories is making a choice. And the choice it is making is to hang on to yesterday rather than to grab hold of tomorrow."

Workplace diversity has become the hot human resource issue for the 1990s, extending well beyond racial and cultural differences to focus on a broadly defined group generally known as "the disenfranchised": women, minorities, the aged, the disabled, gays, and lesbians. And whereas the affirmative action movement of past decades was seen largely as a fairness issue, the diversity challenge is viewed by a growing number of executives as a strategic business issue. According to a 1993 survey of 131 U.S. companies by The Conference Board, 42 percent of companies viewed diversity as a competitive opportunity, while 24 percent called it "part of good management." Only 4 percent said it would have no serious impact on their operations.

Another study, done in 1992, gives executives good reason to care about diversity. This study, funded by the Center for Innovative Management Studies, examined the work environment of 2,000 scientists and engineers in the research and development divisions of 18 major U.S. corporations. The study, using surveys and questionnaires, found that managers consistently rated women lower than men in the area of innovation and rated foreign-born contributors lower than U.S.-born on scales of promotability. The researchers noted that "If a large and growing population of the labor force in R&D believe they are not getting rewarded for the contributions they believe they are making, they are likely to become frustrated. Frustration, in turn, often leads to poorer performance, a less-productive work environment, and higher turnover." Although this study covered only one small slice of the professional spectrum, most experts agree that one would find similar results throughout American business.

Despite the growing acknowledgment of its importance, engen-

Diversity as a Survival Tactic

If we do not learn to celebrate diversity, all the dreams and aspirations we hold for ourselves and for our children will be moot. As both society and the work force become more diverse in terms of race, culture, ethnicity, lifestyle, age, and gender, we must replace fear and stereotypes with knowledge and respect for other cultures, histories, and traditions. In this way, we can foster a climate in which each group can move forward and flourish, and we can build on each other's strengths and work together to advance agendas that will ultimately benefit us all. Because our moral and economic health—indeed our growth and survival as a nation—depend on it.

—FROM A TIME WARNER BROCHURE

dering diversity does not come naturally to many managers or employees, who often have had little meaningful exposure to those outside of their own racial, cultural, generational, or socioeconomic circles. Nor is the issue limited to increasing the number of minorities and women being hired. True workplace diversity demands a system for ensuring that these employees are fully integrated into the company, with equal opportunity for advancement. Exactly how to do that—by setting rules or guidelines, linking managers' pay to their success in fostering true diversity, or whatever—is up to each individual company.

Turning this vision into reality has created a challenge for companies to foster in top leaders and middle managers an appreciation for what genuine diversity can bring to the workplace. Indeed, a cottage industry of professionals—from anthropologists to MBAs—has grown up around helping companies manage a multicultural work force. And more and more companies, recognizing that diversity means good business—not to mention fewer discrimination suits, union clashes, and equal employment regulatory actions—are setting aside time and resources to cultivate what they hope will be a more tolerant, cooperative, and productive work force.

The need for diversity extends beyond the general work force to boards of directors, which are overwhelmingly white and male. The rate of change at that level is even slower than that lower down in the company. The greatest progress has been at the so-called Service 500 companies, in fields such as retailing, finance, and publishing, which have placed slightly more women on their boards than have the industrial and manufacturing firms of the *Fortune* 500. According to a 1992 census by Catalyst, a nonprofit group in New York that tracks women in the workplace, women comprised 6 percent (375 of 6,268) of the directorships on Service 500 companies, compared with 5.3 percent (289 of 5,421) at *Fortune* 500 companies. Those 664 directorships were held by just 495 women; nearly 90 are members of more than one board.

Paul Fireman will be the first to admit that seeking diversity isn't easy, and that the subject alone can make many business leaders uncomfortable. With good reason: dealing with diversity means wading into unfamiliar territory. Consciously or subconsciously, people naturally prefer to hire those who resemble themselves culturally, racially, and socioeconomically. Breaking those habits means entering a world of unknown sensitivities and cultures, an uncomfortable world for many. Beyond that, some executives feel that confronting diversity issues means a never-ending stream of demands on their companies.

"Part of the discomfort is entirely understandable," Fireman told the Business for Social Responsibility annual conference in 1993. "For all its fashionability, diversity is still a new word and an unsettling idea. My industry, the sporting goods industry, ten years ago was an industry overwhelmingly dominated by blond men with long legs. Ten years ago, if you saw a black man at Reebok, you knew there was an athlete visiting for the day. And while we've started down the road to change, we still have a long way to go." Fireman says that most business people are inclined to think of diversity grudgingly, as something forced upon them by government regulation—which is not the case.

But Fireman has come to view workplace diversity as "an idea whose time has come—one we ought to actively welcome." He believes the power of diversity lies in the different perspectives that new employees bring to company decision making. "You can hire all the consultants you want, set up a dozen or a hundred focus groups," he says. "In the end, no outsider can take the place of a working team within your corporation that has the vision to give birth to an idea and the grasp and understanding to make the idea work. And that kind of working team cannot be a team of clones. If you put five centers on the basketball court, you're going to lose the game. You need, we all need, people of different strengths and talents—and that means, among other things, people of different backgrounds."

Fireman is also quick to point out what diversity is not. "Diversity is not about hiring an African-American or a woman with a fancy title and no real responsibility." Moreover, statistics showing how many blacks, women, Asian-Americans, and Hispanics work in your company aren't a particularly valid gauge of diversity. "In the final analysis, human diversity is about qualities that don't bunch up into convenient categories. It's about the fact that we come from different places and bring with us different stories. It's about our differences in taste and temperament. We may need laws and regulations to get us from here to there, from yesterday to tomorrow, but in the end it is not habits of compliance we seek to change, it's habits of the heart.

"If you want to get from here to diversity," stresses Fireman, "you have to seek out, at every level of employment, the people who have new and different stories to tell. And then you have to make real room for them, you have to learn to listen, to listen closely, to their stories. It accomplishes next to nothing to employ those who are different from us if the condition of their employment is that they become the same as us. For it is their differences that enrich us, expand us, provide us the competitive edge."

How Diversity Made Inroads at Inland

One of the more celebrated diversity programs at American companies is at Inland Steel Industries, a 100-year-old Chicago-based producer of cold-rolled steel, used for cars, appliances, electric motors, and other products.

In 1987, four young African-American employees—Tyrone Banks, Vivian Cosey, Robert Hudson, Jr., and Scharlene Hurston—were frustrated with what they perceived as a lack of opportunity for advancement for minorities at Inland. Lacking minority mentors among top management, they approached a white manager, Steven Bowsher, to express their feelings about this. They told him that they liked the company, and most of the people with whom they worked, and preferred not to seek jobs elsewhere.

Bowsher, who for over fifteen years had worked his way up to become a divisional sales manager at the company, had a reputation for being a fair and sincere leader. His discussions with the four

Working Together

At Herman Miller, problem definition and problem solving result in products, systems, and services that improve productivity and the quality of life in working and healing environments. In a special way, we are committed to design excellence and leadership. Through research we seek to discover new solutions to our customers' needs. We recognize that this commitment requires us to adapt to significant change, and we are prepared to do so....

At Herman Miller, we are committed to the participative process of working together and understand our obligation to perform in a manner consistent with our values. We achieve our goals by having the right and responsibility to contribute in our individual areas of competence, to own problems, and to be held accountable for results. We believe that people are our most important resource and we are committed to enabling their development and to providing equal opportunity for each person.

We believe that all career employees should be able to own stock in the corporation. We believe that participative ownership, practiced with fidelity, can make this an exceptional company....

We seek to be socially responsible. We share a concern and responsibility for the quality of the environment in which we and our neighbors live and work. We recognize that we are more than participating owners in our company: We are also members of families and communities. We are committed to the nurture, support, and security of the family....

At Herman Miller, growth and job security must be a consequence of our problem solutions, of the potential in our programs, and of the performance of our people

—From the Herman Miller Mandate

disgruntled employees led him to attend a two-day workshop on race relations being held in Atlanta. That turned out to be what he later described as "the single most important training I've been through." So moved was he by the experience that, on his return to company headquarters, he persuaded the company to send more than one hundred other managers and executives to similar workshops, and helped form an Affirmative Action Focus Group. A year later, then president and now CEO Robert J. Darnall attended an Atlanta workshop with two African-American employees.

The result of Bowsher's conversion, and ultimately Darnall's, was an aggressive affirmative action program within Bowsher's own department, in which selected minority employees were promoted several steps up the ladder, commensurate with their years of experience. He also instituted a five-year career-planning program for all employees to shift their expectations from who they were to who they could become.

Things have changed dramatically at Inland. What had been described by one minority employee as a "veil of discomfort" has been lifted, as more minorities and women have been given the opportunity to advance into key positions. And while barriers remain, the momentum—and the resolve—exist to remove them. The efforts of Banks, Cosey, Hudson, Hurston, and Bowsher to promote diversity were recognized in 1992 with an award by the Business Enterprise Trust.

Darnall, for his part, now sees diversity as a key to competitiveness. "I think years ago it was strictly a moral issue, and perhaps a legal issue as you got into EEOC, but today I think it's increasingly becoming an important business issue. Given the changes that are going to occur in the work force in the years ahead, a company that is diverse and manages that diversity well is going to have an upper hand in terms of the way they conduct business. We need to stimulate, lead, and get the best efforts out of our entire work force in order for this company, in a very tough business, to be competitive in the years ahead."

Tabra Inc.'s "Little United Nations"

Another glimpse into the potential power of diversity in the workplace can be found at a small California company called Tabra Inc.

The moment you step onto the shop floor at Tabra, you realize that you have entered the workplace of the future. Not because of any robots, computers, or other high-tech wizardry. And not because of the facility itself, which is located in a nondescript, cinderblock warehouse in a suburban industrial park in Petaluma, California, about 35 miles north of San Francisco. Rather, it's because of the people.

Tabra's modest work force—ranging seasonally between 60 and 120 people—is a congregation of Third World immigrants, from Cambodia, China, El Salvador, Ethiopia, India, Laos, Mexico, Thailand, Tibet, Vietnam, and other countries. Hanging from the ceiling of the main production facility are flags representing the countries of origin of Tabra's employees; there are typically ten to twelve different flags aloft.

Tabra makes jewelry and accessories—mostly high-end necklaces, earrings, bracelets, and belts—sold by a network of sales reps to boutiques around the country and overseas, as well as to Tiffany's. The items sell for prices ranging from $35 for a simple pair of earrings to as much as $2,000 for an ornate belt encrusted with stones, jewels, and other ornaments collected from around the world, usually by the company's founder and owner, Tabra Tunoa, in person.

Tunoa herself is not an immigrant. Born in the Midwest, she moved to Samoa and then spent several years traveling around the world before setting up a small jewelry-making business. In the mid-1980s, needing a bookkeeper, Tunoa hired a Vietnamese woman, then a woman from Laos, both of whom still work for her. Things got better, business doubled, and she began seeking out other immigrants to hire. Over time, Tabra Inc. became known as a port of entry for immigrants.

But Tabra Inc. is no sweatshop. Tunoa pays her employees above-average wages, gives them health coverage, and offers other benefits. She pays for classes to teach English to employees. When business is good, there is profit sharing for employees with two years or more of employment. Her light, spacious, and airy factory exceeds federal and state worker health and safety standards.

Tabra Inc. may seem far removed from the corporate corridors of big business, but it has proven that there is strength in diversity. Bringing a variety of nationalities and cultures together and helping them understand one another is not only possible, it can be a powerful force in building a company as well as fostering commitment and productivity among the disparate individuals who walk through the front door each workday morning. "I would like for this to be a little United Nations, everybody getting along and learning to appreciate each other's culture, instead of just tolerating it," she says. "I want them to appreciate it and celebrate it."

How Teamwork Transformed Timberland

If Fireman, Tunoa, and others make it seem easy to bring diversity to a company with a few simple programs, don't be fooled. "You can't just become diverse," says Richard Morgan, vice president for human resources at Timberland, the New Hampshire–based $700-million-a-year manufacturer of shoes, boots, and other outdoors apparel. "It's not like just hiring people of color or hiring women and putting them into a senior position. That's way too easy and also the kiss of death, because generally what happens is they don't succeed and the whole thing falls flat on its face.

"Timberland is competing on a worldwide basis," Morgan goes on. "Our competition, our brand, competes in global markets. A most definite competitive edge that a company like ours needs is an appreciation for diversity: diversity in culture, in language, background, and perspective. So many American companies that are trying to do business globally think very locally. They think about how to sell in Europe as if they're in the United States. Although we believe in our brand and there is a lot of brand continuity on a worldwide basis, our employees need to be empowered with the skill to engage with people from different walks of life."

Jeffrey Swartz is one firm believer in the power of diversity to boost the bottom line. Swartz, chief operating officer at Timberland, sees diversity as far more than the ability of people of different races and cultures to work together harmoniously. He considers it nothing less than the key to building the productive and dynamic teams he sees as critical to the future success of his 900-employee company.

Timberland's diversity program is somewhat unusual, to say the least. Swartz bypassed outside consultants and internal training programs, opting instead for a synergistic relationship with an innovative Boston-based nonprofit group called City Year. The brainchild of Harvard Law School graduates Michael Brown and Alan Khazei, City Year enrolls more than 200 young people between ages 17 and 22 from a variety of racial, cultural, and socioeconomic groups in a program that has been called a combination of boot camp and the Peace Corps. They serve the community for a year and are paid a $100-a-week stipend; when their year is up, they get a $5,000 scholarship. The public-private partnership, begun in 1987, became a model for Bill Clinton's vision of voluntary national service, one of the cornerstones of his 1992 presidential campaign. City Year aims not just to transform communities through volunteer projects—

cleaning and restoring vacant lots, creating after-school programs, mentoring physically and mentally challenged senior citizens, rehabilitating rundown neighborhood business districts—but to transform the volunteers themselves.

In 1989, Timberland became a major sponsor of the program, contributing $1 million to sponsor Team Timberland, one of City Year's eight twelve-member teams. That $1 million was no small investment at a time when Timberland's net income was only about $8 million. In addition, the company has outfitted the entire corps with Timberland boots and apparel. Team Timberland's mission is to focus on urban environmental issues—the environment is a key concern for Swartz—cleaning up empty lots, reviving urban parks, landscaping, planting, and so on.

City Year is no passive investment for Timberland. The company has leveraged its funds by actively involving its own employees with Team Timberland, to the benefit of both. Bringing diverse employees together to work side by side with a diverse group of youth helps build better teams and foster teamwork, as well as an appreciation for diversity. "Working with City Year is a very different mode of problem solving than the traditional business manager is used to," says Swartz. "A cross-function team—where we are stuck together, and we may be of different ranks, but it doesn't matter, we have a common goal—it's a very uncomfortable position for some traditional people to be in. City Year is fundamentally about cross-functionalism: ten to twelve young people of diverse backgrounds and life experiences working together to solve common problems. You have college graduates and high school dropouts. You have inner-city kids and suburban kids. You have men and women, black and white, yellow and green, and they're forced to work together against this common mission, and problem-solve in a way that's dynamic. That model is extraordinarily educational to the Timberland people."

Richard Morgan sees City Year as a boon to his efforts as Timberland's human resources head. "I have been in the human resources business for twelve years and I have been involved in the affirmative action movement, had specific training around equal employment opportunity, and I understand how that applies to the workplace. Yet there are very few real good examples of what's good about diversity in the work force. If you could spend a day with a team of people at City Year, that is one of the best empirical pieces of evidence of diversity in its pure form and how it is working, how it gives you an advantage. If you want a really good example of how they're a better team as a result of diversity, go down and spend a few days with City Year. I have, personally, and it all started to click for me. I began to understand that once you get through the barriers and once you get the essential trainings learned, that team of people is a very strong team. I'd like to re-create that same environment here at Timberland."

Swartz underscores the fact that the value of this hands-on, real-life approach surpasses traditional human resources programs. "I say to some of my business colleagues, 'How much did you spend on Outward Bound courses last year? How much did you spend on leadership-development seminars? How much did you spend on these externalities?' " says Swartz. "And the answer is always something like, 'Oh, you mean our training budget? We spent $750,000.'

"I ask, 'Well, how'd you do?'

"They respond, 'Well, it was interesting but I'm not really sure it made a difference.' "

In contrast, says Swartz, "City Year creates value for us. We don't do any executive training except City Year. We do all our team building with City Year; we consume services from City Year in that regard. We do team building four times a year with City Year. I know what that would cost to do on the outside with seven hundred employees—a hell of a lot more than we're currently investing in City Year. So you could say we're saving money."

Timberland is also *making* a lot of money. Its 1993 profits rose more than 60 percent to $21 million on sales of $410, a 41 percent increase. During the third quarter of 1993, Timberland's stock doubled in value. And Swartz predicts that heady growth will only get better: $700 million for 1994, heading toward $1 billion. "Not only are we getting bigger, we are constantly reinventing ourselves," he says. "We have to reinvent ourselves because our competition is smarter, our consumer is more informed."

Diversity is one road to a smarter organization. It can be a difficult road to travel—with potholes, roadblocks, and detours galore—but the journey is usually well worth the effort. Transforming a business into a competitive, high-performance organization demands everyone's creativity, cooperation, and can-do spirit. Tapping into those resources will require that business leaders not only bring out the best in everyone but also foster a new appreciation of the power of differences, and the idea that fresh thinking, though at times unsettling, brings opportunities as well as challenges.

Our Most Important Asset

We are responsible to our employees, the men and women who work with us throughout the world. Everyone must be considered as an individual. We must respect their dignity and recognize their merit. They must have a sense of security in their jobs. Compensation must be fair and adequate, and working conditions clean, orderly, and safe. We must be mindful of ways to help our employees fulfill their family responsibilities. Employees must feel free to make suggestions and complaints. There must be equal opportunity for employment, development, and advancement for those qualified. We must provide competent management, and their actions must be just and ethical.

—FROM THE JOHNSON & JOHNSON CREDO

SURVIVING TOUGH TIMES

One of the toughest workplace issues facing nearly every industry is how to close a plant or reduce a company's work force with the least adverse impact on the people affected. Certainly, this is one of the toughest issues facing socially responsible companies.

Getting companies "lean" is one of the key thrusts of creating the high-performance workplace. The quest for "high performance" means creating new ways of doing old jobs better, often using fewer people to accomplish the same tasks. The irony is that at the same time some companies are paying more attention to the need to support their employees, their employees' families, and their communities, many are implementing management strategies that cause hardship to employees, families, and communities. Some companies have come to learn that there's a downside to downsizing that can cost companies more than it can save. There may be negative impacts on reputation, for example, and on morale and productivity among survivors.

Another irony is that massive retrenchments may prove to be shortsighted, rendering companies even less competitive in the long run. Studies show that making substantial work-force cuts doesn't necessarily improve a company's bottom-line standing; indeed, it can harm it over the mid to long term. A 1993 study of more than 500 companies by the Wyatt Company found that although three quarters had cut their payrolls, most reported that the cuts had failed to achieve their expected results. Of those surveyed, over half of the companies that cut personnel had refilled some of the positions within a year. So wholesale job reductions may not be the answer, nor cutting benefits, but rather creating a new model inside companies—one that elevates employee-employer relations to a new level of communication, respect, and trust.

As we will see, companies in both the industrial and service sectors have found that this new model can bring benefits not attainable by "cutting the fat," "getting lean and mean," or performing other "butcherlike" acts, as U.S. Secretary of Labor Robert B. Reich likes to call them. In his metaphor, "butchers" trim the fat to get things lean and mean—that is, by cutting away whatever seems unnecessary—while "bakers" capitalize on the unique qualities of each ingredient they bring to the task. "The baker strategy is to invest in the skills of employees by providing them with training, both on and off the job," Reich said in a 1993 speech to BSR members. "It provides front-line workers with substantial authority, so they can make decisions about how to improve the production process and increase sales. And it gives employees a degree of security by tying their wages to profits or to productivity gains. That way, when hard times come, they are shared by everyone rather than only by those who are axed. When profits return, everyone will share in them as well."

No one ever said that creating a high-performance workplace automatically means laying people off. "High performance" is a way of doing business, creating an environment that gets the job done as quickly, effectively, and efficiently as possible. There are a variety of creative solutions that can put a company on that track without causing undue upheaval.

So, what should companies do when they have more people than they need? Are there socially responsible and economically viable ways to reduce personnel? Are there ways to avoid layoffs altogether without hindering a company's ability to become more competitive?

Solutions to these tough questions must be found on a case-by-case basis, with each company examining the options among their employees and within their communities. The good news is that there is a growing pool of success stories to which to refer.

Lotus's Soul Committee

The following is excerpted from a 1994 memo sent to all employees worldwide by Jim Manzi, CEO of Lotus Development Corporation:

It's time to take a more focused look at our "soul," by which I mean the sometimes tangible and sometimes intangible efforts and energy that define the quality of life and spirit here at Lotus. . . . At Lotus, we've always paid attention to our soul, striving to balance *what* we do with *how* we do it in a way that makes our organization supportive as well as profitable. Our operating principles are one outgrowth of this effort.

   Another outgrowth is a newly created Soul Committee, comprising primarily middle and senior managers from various functions through the company. I realize that establishing a committee to explore something as subjective as "soul" may seem oxymoronic. But this committee's intent is not to legislate what our soul should be but rather to take a focused approach to continuing the process of evaluating the aspects of our organization—be they policies, attitudes, perceptions—that influence our life at Lotus.

Consider, for example, the landmark 1994 agreement between NYNEX and the Communications Workers of America (CWA), the union representing 35,500 of the telecommunications company's 66,000 employees. In early 1994, NYNEX reported a net loss of $1.24 billion for the fourth quarter of 1993, and announced that as a result of "re-engineering," the company would eliminate 16,800 by the end of 1996. The layoffs were only the latest in a series of cutbacks for NYNEX, which in 1984 had nearly 95,000 employees.

NYNEX isn't the only phone company striving to cut back. The seven "Baby Bell" phone companies together announced about 60,000 job layoffs between 1989 and 1993, with plans to cut thousands more as they prepare for an era of relaxed regulation and increased competition. Cable television companies were planning to offer residential service, smaller companies were using fiber-optic lines to pursue NYNEX's prime business clientele for local and long-distance phone service, and forthcoming wireless technologies threatened cellular phone markets. Moreover, NYNEX claimed it was less efficient than other Baby Bells. According to one estimate, for example, NYNEX had 43.3 employees per 10,000 phone-access lines as of the third quarter of 1993, compared with 34.3 for Bell Atlantic Corp.

Prior to the announcements, CWA officials had been talking with NYNEX officials to find ways to avoid involuntary layoffs. After the announcement, CWA made a formal request to enter collective-bargaining negotiations to discuss "some humane, compassionate ways to deal with the downsize," says Jan Pierce, vice president of CWA's District 1, which includes the seven northeastern states in which NYNEX operates. After what Pierce calls "a lot of fits and starts," CWA and NYNEX announced in 1994 a plan to deal with what CWA calls "rightsizing" NYNEX without involuntary layoffs, forced transfers, or downgrades.

The plan had two basic parts, one affecting the people laid off, the other affecting the people who stayed:

• At the centerpiece of the plan is what Pierce calls a "pension enhancement," a means of sweetening an employee's pension plan as an incentive for him or her to seek early retirement. The plan, referred to as the "6, 6, and 30" incentives, adds six years to participating employees' age and years of service, accelerating their pension eligibility, and increases their pension by the greater of 30 percent or $500 a month. A craft person with thirty years' service could retire from NYNEX with 57 percent of his or her last year's base wage; for a telephone operator with the same amount of service, the percentage would be 61 percent, and 63 percent for a clerical employee. Without the sweetener, all of these employees would have been eligible for only about 35 percent of their last year's wage. Like all of NYNEX's unionized employees, they would also get full health care coverage during their retirement. If the pension sweetener doesn't attract enough voluntary retirees, a half-dozen additional provisions kick in. For example, there's an Income Protection Plan that would permit employees who are not pension-eligible to receive lump-sum payments ranging from $2,900 to $7,000, in addition to monthly payments of around $400 for forty-eight months.

• For employees who stay on, there is an innovative retraining program that enables qualified workers to take leaves of absence of up to two years with no loss of seniority and benefits, and receive up to $10,000 a year in company-paid tuition to learn new skills; participating employees have guaranteed reinstatement upon completion. Another program enables employees to attend school one day a week at company expense, and at the end of the training qualify for an additional $50 a week. The idea of both programs is to help NYNEX employees become better suited to the growing technological changes affecting the phone company.

The era of cooperation between NYNEX and CWA represented a major change from the confrontational atmosphere that in recent years had led to a seventeen-week strike in 1989, after which the union continued attacking the company before state regulatory agencies. But CWA recognized that confrontation was no longer an adequate strategy in the current landscape. "When the union learned of the company's decision to downsize by significant numbers, the union accepted that as a challenge," says Pierce. "We said to the company, 'If you have the compassion, we have the creativity to deal with rightsizing this company.'"

"We think we have in place here a concept, a vision, and direction where everybody comes out well," says James Dowdall, NYNEX vice president for labor relations and the company's chief negotiator. "The union takes care of its membership. And we come away with a work force that is in position for the twenty-first century."

Alternatives to Layoffs

With or without union influence, a growing list of companies is addressing plant closings and downsizings with greater concern for the fate of employees—those who go as well as those who survive. For example, when H. B. Fuller, the $1-billion-a-year maker of adhesives, sealants, coatings, and paints, decided to close a plant in Texas during the 1980s, laying off twenty-seven employees, it offered each employee a job at another Fuller plant. The company also offered a $10,000 bonus to employees if they could find a new job within six weeks and if they worked right up to the shutdown. "We feel responsible to do everything we can to help our people when there is a layoff," says Anthony Andersen, the company's chair and CEO.

Andersen is among those who have come to recognize the short- and long-term costs associated with layoffs. First there are the direct costs—more than $7,000 worth of such items as severance, processing of dismissals, and other paperwork, according to estimates by the Saratoga Institute, a California consulting firm. The costs are based on the typical tab for dismissing 100 employees with five years' service and an average salary of $30,000. In addition, there are the indirect costs, including a temporary decline in quality as survivors learn the jobs of the departed and a possible loss of sales because of short staffing. And then there are the costs of eventual restaffing, should that be necessary. The Saratoga Institute put those costs at about $5,000 per employee.

Some consider such estimates to be conservative. Dow Chemical, which has bent over backward to avoid layoffs, estimates that laying off a technical or managerial employee costs the company between $30,000 and $100,000. Hiring replacements typically costs about $50,000 per employee if relocation expenses are part of the deal. "Layoffs are horribly expensive and destructive of shareholder value," says Dow's CEO, Frank Popoff. When you lay people off, he says, "you lose all the loyalty you've busted your butt to build." Moreover, he testifies to the fact that when companies express their loyalty by avoiding cutbacks, employees express theirs by working harder. "The quality of work you get from motivated people is literally light-years ahead of what you get from people who aren't well motivated."

Popoff's observations are underscored by studies that show some of the backlash of downsizing. For example, a 1993 study by The Conference Board of 353 companies that had cut workers in the late 1980s found that nearly half reported increased health care costs after the downsizing. Two out of five companies reported a greater need for employee retraining, three in ten said overtime increased, and two out of three found that morale plummeted among surviving employees. Another 1993 study, this one by the American Management Association, found that despite the massive layoffs of the 1990–91 recession, most companies were not realizing increased profits or productivity.

Beyond that, there is the impact of layoffs on the larger community. Each company's cuts produce "externalities," bad effects borne by the rest of society, according to the economist Frank Lichtenberg, of the Columbia University business school. There is a multiplier effect, as the loss of business and jobs contributes to the breakdown of families and an erosion of tax dollars to pay for schools, roads, and other services. This is especially true in scores of towns throughout the United States that rely heavily on the employees of one company or industry. So there is much to be gained, internally and externally, from companies that strive to keep employees working.

Socially responsible companies aim for a level of growth that can be sustained over time, without the retrenchments required when markets turn—and the personnel cutbacks that inevitably follow. "For the last fifty years or so, our goal has been to build a company, not maximize income in any given point in time," is how Tony Andersen puts it. "If you really believe that, and if you really practice it, there will be a ripple effect amongst all kinds of things that have a profound effect on the company. Since the earliest days, our sales objective has been to double the size of the company every five years. Not just to grow, but to provide opportunities for people. If you've got a career growing, and you're sharp and you work hard and you get good results, but the company doesn't grow, it is highly unlikely that you as a person in your career will grow. Therefore, a great motivator for all people in the company is to know not only that they can build a career in the company, but it's going to be an increasing challenge if the person wants it to be."

Fel-Pro is another company that tries hard to keep its employees employed. "As we're going to teams throughout the organization, we're finding that we don't need as many managers as we used to need," says company president Paul Lehman. "We're also finding that as we go to self-managed teams, we don't need as much direct labor as we did to get the same kind of work out. So, we're trying to manage that in every other way than to lay off people." But, he adds,

The Body Shop's AIDS Policy

We recognize that HIV and AIDS constitute a new and still misunderstood threat to health.

We will provide a program of education and training for all employees which will help them to safeguard their own health and that of their families and friends.

Through this program, we aim to create an atmosphere of understanding in which anyone who is HIV positive or has an AIDS-related illness will feel free to come forward, in the knowledge that they will meet with care and sympathy and that appropriate support will be offered.

There is no obligation on any member of staff to disclose their HIV status, but if disclosure is made, that information will be treated in strict confidence unless the individual wishes otherwise.

No member of staff will be dismissed or re-deployed because they are HIV positive and/or have an AIDS-related illness, unless they request it or medical advice suggests it is in their best interest.

Disclosure of confidential information relating to HIV status or continued discrimination of any kind against an employee who is HIV positive or who has an AIDS-related illness will lead to dismissal.

The Body Shop is determined to lead by our example. We will campaign internationally to dispel the myths which are contributing to the continuing escalation of the AIDS epidemic and to improve conditions for those who are part of the epidemic.

"I do imagine in the next couple of years, as we become more efficient, as we implement self-managed work teams more fully in the company, there will be people that will lose their jobs."

On those rare occasions when Fel-Pro has had to consider cutbacks, the company has gone to extraordinary lengths to help its employees. For starters, the company offers a full year's notice. During that period, it seeks out opportunities for other positions within the company, taking account of employees' skills and interests. If, as the end of the year approaches, it is clear that there aren't suitable opportunities for them, the company offers career counseling for jobs outside the company. On top of that, the company offers liberal severance pay.

Why bother with all this? "It's consistent with the company culture," says Lehman. "There's so much more to lose by not treating people decently than by treating them decently. If, in the end, a couple percent of our people lose their jobs as a result of our becoming more efficient and more effective, whatever savings the company might enjoy could be far offset by reduction in morale and productivity. So, one of the reasons we do it is to be decent to the people who are going through this process. But the other reason we do it is to send a message to the rest of the organization that even though Fel-Pro has to change every day and has to improve, there's something that we're going to hold sacrosanct around here, and that's our basic respect for people and treating them decently. So it's really helpful for the people who are staying, which is really almost everybody. It's good for morale. It's as important to address the needs of the survivors, the people who make it, as it is the people who are leaving the organization."

Other companies, too, have layoff and plant-closing policies that place a high value on employees' needs:

• Pratt & Whitney's East Hartford, Connecticut, plant, whose workers are represented by the International Association of Machinists, avoided plant closures through a partnership between the company, state government, and labor. The three parties worked to reduce costs and provide incentives for the plant to remain open. By switching to a new team-based production style, lead and set-up times at the plant were drastically reduced. Production teams were reduced from seven to four members. The displaced workers were transferred to other facilities.

• Federal Express Corp., a nonunion company, has a no-layoff policy. Employees whose jobs are eliminated have the first opportunity to apply for internal job openings. Employees who cannot find equivalent jobs can take lower-level jobs and maintain their salaries for up to eighteen months, until they find an equivalent or higher-paying job.

• Nucor Steel, a nonunion company, also has never resorted to layoffs in its more than thirty-year history. In slow times, the steel producer's employees work fewer hours, but continue to receive pay bonuses based on productivity. In return, they are expected to work up to seven-day weeks when the company has a high number of orders to fill.

• Rhino Foods, a 55-person specialty dessert manufacturer in Burlington, Vermont, avoided layoffs in the face of efficiency improvements and a drop in orders. The company initiated an innovative employee-exchange program with nearby companies in need of workers.

• Sky Chefs, a $450 million in-flight services company based in Arlington, Texas, worked with the AFL-CIO to ease layoffs due to restructuring. The restructuring announcement was made at an all-employee meeting where people were encouraged to ask questions and voice concerns. Employee-driven teams decided where to make most of the cuts and helped design a voluntary severance package. As a result, most of the departing employees left voluntarily, and all were offered retraining and transition services.

• At Hewlett-Packard, jobs made obsolete by the discontinuation of a product line, relocation of manufacturing facilities, or declining sales are designated as "excess." Employees who find their jobs labeled "excess" have ninety days to find another job within the company, during which time they are given no other assignments except to find work. If they are unable to locate another job in that period, they are placed on "direct placement," meaning their manager has responsibility for finding the employee a job at a company site anywhere in the United States. If the employee is offered a job within a 30-mile commute and turns it down, he or she is eligible for a severance package of two weeks' pay for every year of service, with a minimum of four months. Since 1989, more than 85 percent of those labeled "excess" are still with the company.

In the end, you can tell a lot about a company's character and culture by the way it does business during tough times. When business is good, it's easy to be generous, to contribute to profit sharing, to give raises and bonuses and endless perks. It's the hard times that bring the biggest challenges—not just from financial upheaval, but from crises of conscience that test the values of companies and their leaders.

The solution to coping with bad times isn't a lot different from the

How to Be Happy at Hanna

1. Be kind and intelligent with others, especially our customers, without whom we are nothing. Fairness and respect make good things happen. Apply them in all you do.

2. Bring energy to your work . . . if you feel you don't, talk with someone in management. It's important for both you and the company.

3. Changes within the company are not a sign of weakness. Where there is growth, there must be change. And where there is change, patience is in order. Sometimes the long-term good is difficult to see at first.

4. Stay away from office politics. They take energy away from important work and divide rather than unite. Talk is just talk. But work will put you ahead.

5. Get behind your task no matter how big or small. If it needs doing, it needs doing well. Think of each task in terms of how it strengthens the whole effort. "None of us is as good as all of us."

6. Keep a balance between work and play. Our work load varies seasonally. When the demands of your job are light, we encourage time off to recharge, and when the season is busiest, performance is a must.

7. The Hanna habitat is clean, healthy, and comfortable for everyone. Your part in maintaining this is vital. Keep your work organized and tidy. It's your job to pick up after you.

8. Rest assured that success will reward us all. Working at Hanna can be demanding but rewarding. We have wages and benefits that match or exceed industry standards. We encourage personal growth. Give us your best and we'll share that great feeling that comes from being the best. When success means profit, we'll share that as well.

How to Be Happy at Hanna (Continued)

9. Never stop growing. Because all of your ideas and comments are welcome, the policies in this book will change as we continue to grow. You can help us to affect that change. You're encouraged to learn as much as you can about your job, the company, and the mail-order business so that you may grow with us.

10. Apply love and respect in all you do. Love for your work, respect for others. It works wonders.

—From the Hanna Andersson employee handbook

solutions to operating during good times: Put your faith in people, create a working environment where both employees and companies can prosper, give employees the power and the tools to let them do their best, respect their needs and ideas, build their trust and respect—and they will turn you and your company into winners.

Chapter Eight

Thinking Corporately, Acting Locally

"I really believe that business has to play a larger role in chang-ing our society. Business people know how to get things done. We tend to think outside the box. We need to bring that cre-ativity to our community."

—ELLIOT HOFFMAN,
CEO, Just Desserts

It is difficult to spend much time talking to business people in the Twin Cities of Minneapolis and St. Paul without coming away with a strong sense of community. In this hearty midwestern metropolis, there is a shared commitment to helping the local citizenry—a com-mitment that seems stronger, and has endured far longer, than in most other large American cities. Some people attribute it to the city's Scandinavian culture, which brings with it a tradition of caring for one's neighbors. Others attribute it to the region's high-quality education system or to the traditional American values still evident in the nation's heartland.

Whatever the reasons, there is an undeniable can-do spirit among companies here, from *Fortune* 500 corporations—seventeen are headquartered in the Twin Cities—to countless small and mid-sized firms, many of which contribute generous amounts of money and manpower toward making their part of the world a better place. And, as many of their executives will tell you, that involvement in the community makes the company a better place, too.

Just ask the folks at Fingerhut Companies, Inc., a highly successful catalogue-marketing company that sells general merchandise and services, primarily through the mail, to middle-income households. The company, based in the Minneapolis suburb of Minnetonka, has so effectively targeted its 13 million active customer base that Fingerhut is either virtually unknown (if you are not part of its demographically targeted market) or a household name (if you are). In 1993, the company's revenues exceeded $1.6 billion, its fifteenth consecutive year of record sales.

While Fingerhut's loyal customers stretch from coast to coast, the company has kept a close watch on its local community, actively involving itself in the Twin Cities' environmental and social issues. For example, Fingerhut pioneered in Minneapolis what has become the nation's largest recycling program for mixed mail—magazines, catalogues, and the small mountain of direct-mail solicitations each of us gets each year—which is generally not collected or accepted in most communities' recycling programs. Fingerhut used its clout as a major paper buyer to prod paper mills in nearby Wisconsin to accept the collected paper for recycling into such items as toilet paper and paper towels. The company has also taken a lead in efforts to locate several lost or abducted area residents—both children and elderly—including donating or helping to raise more than $100,000 to allow the Minnesota State Patrol to procure a helicopter-mounted thermal-imaging device used in night searches of wooded areas. In addition, Fingerhut has sponsored an ongoing tree-planting project in a state forest about three and a half miles from company headquarters, which has resulted in the planting of more than 65,000 seedlings. The 95-acre site has been named the Fingerhut-Blandin Forest in honor of Fingerhut's employees and customers. Still another company-sponsored program is Take-A-Taxi, in which Fingerhut picks up the taxi fare for anyone in the Twin Cities area who feels he or she isn't able to drive home safely due to alcohol consumption; Fingerhut employees voluntarily staff the Take-A-Taxi phone lines. The program started in 1976 after a Fingerhut employee was killed in an automobile crash while driving under the influence. It is not surprising, given such involvement, that the company and its chairman and CEO, Ted Deikel, have been the recipients of a host of state and local awards and have received generous kudos from the local press.

Why does Fingerhut do all this? The combination of giving and doing comes from no grander notion than that community matters. "If you take seriously that you are part of the community, that your employees live there, that they are part of it, and that therefore you are an important institution in that community, you can elect to make a difference or not," says Elizabeth A. Bothereau, Fingerhut's vice president for consumer and environmental affairs. "We believe that this is a community that we want to reinforce, and a community work force that we value, and a customer base that we care about. So we try to do something about it."

THE BENEFITS OF BENEVOLENCE

The idea that companies give something back to the communities where they do business is nearly as old as business itself. As the impact of business in society has become stronger—and such problems as violence and homelessness, deteriorating schools and social services have increased—the need for companies to step in has grown increasingly urgent. Unfortunately, companies are facing their own challenges, and when they make cuts, they often target the personnel charged with the mission of working with the local community. Sometimes, community responsibility is shifted to those in the human resources or public affairs department (who themselves may be working harder due to downsizings or cutbacks), who must find a way to add these worries to their existing workload.

Fortunately, some companies are managing to balance a high-performance workplace with active community involvement, even recognizing the internal benefits that ensue. These companies are embracing a wider role than the traditional one of philanthropic donor. Their efforts range from encouraging employees to volunteer in community programs to company-sponsored initiatives that directly invest money, talent, goods, and creativity in schools, neighborhoods, community centers, and other areas of need.

Most companies view these efforts as enlightened self-interest. By providing leadership and restoring local economies, these leaders recognize that the same issues challenging society also challenge their companies. For businesses to isolate themselves from the prob-

Would we cut back on some of the givings in the community if we didn't have the funds to do it? Probably so. We'd shrink the proportionate amount of gifts we were giving. It's possible we might have less staff, have to pull a little harder on the rope. But it would be no different than we would do for any of the other parts of our business. The focus on human rights and social responsibility shouldn't be measured by surplus dollars or a good year. They should be measured as part of the standards of your business every year. It doesn't take a wealthy person to give money or time. Poor people give charity and their time also. Businesses shouldn't consider doing that coming out of good times and excess; it should be standard every day.

—PAUL FIREMAN,
CEO, Reebok International Ltd.

lems around them represents a shortsightedness that could be detrimental to their prosperity.

So, supporting local communities makes as much sense for your company as it does for your neighbors: If your business helps improve your community's quality of life, you create goodwill among local citizens—including, perhaps, local politicians and regulators who may be influential in overseeing your company or shaping public policy. Of course, many of your company's neighbors are also customers or employees, or at least potential customers or employees.

For years, most business community involvement focused on philanthropy. But corporate giving is no longer the growth industry it was during the decade from 1978 to 1987, when donations grew by an annual average rate of nearly 15 percent, according to the Council for Aid to Education, which tracks donations to all causes. In 1992, the latest year for which data are available, company donations dropped for the first time since 1970. Contributions in 1992 totaled about $6 billion, representing 1.6 percent of company pre-tax income, nearly a third below that of 1986, when American businesses donated 2.35 percent of pre-tax income. (The figures are somewhat skewed by changes in tax rates that caused many companies to accelerate donations during 1986 in order to exploit tax advantages that were set to diminish the following year.) In real dollars (unadjusted for inflation), the level of corporate giving during 1992 was even more anemic, roughly comparable to what companies had donated eight years earlier. About a fourth of the total—roughly $1.5 billion—went to community and civic causes, and to culture and the arts. (Most of the rest went to education and health and human services organizations.)

Needless to say, this reversal of fortune has many service and cultural organizations concerned, and has intensified the competition for an already limited pool of financial resources. The sudden prospect of a decline in contributions from the corporate sector—compounded by the diminishing contributions of the federal and state governments, and the overall financial anxiety among the general public as the result of a weakened economy—has put a further squeeze on the ability of these groups to meet local needs.

While philanthropy is important, no amount your company gives at the end of the year can have the impact on the community that changes in the way you run your business can have. That usually requires a deeper level of commitment. Such involvement by small and large companies in local community affairs cuts to the heart of social responsibility.

"Ultimately, the success of business is linked to the prosperity and stability of the society that hosts it," says Bob Dunn of Levi Strauss. "As individuals and as businesses, there's a way in which we're inextricably linked to the fortunes of society. I think most businesses understand that when there's a crisis or calamity—the Los Angeles earthquake, the Newark riots, Hurricane Andrew—it has a profoundly adverse impact on business. What people understand with greater difficulty is that over time, if you neglect educating people, you don't have a competitive work force. That over time, if you don't provide for the poor and they sleep in the doorways of retail stores, they damage the prospects for commerce in the marketplace. So, if you take any issue—whether it's health care, education, crime, homelessness, all the ills of our society—there's a way in which in the long run it has very dramatic consequences for business.

"So then, one choice for business is to say, 'Well, I pay taxes, and I'm satisfied that the most efficient use of resources to address social problems is what can be done with government. And therefore, I'm going to favor government that has a maximum role to play in all these issues.' It seems to me that's not a view that's very compatible with what most people in the business community favor. Most of them favor a limited role for government and a reliance on the private sector to meet needs directly for profit; or for individuals, families, communities, and nonprofit organizations to work on the local level when possible to point the way—to put up venture capital, to explore options, or to craft solutions."

Another option is for companies to absolve themselves of any responsibility beyond what is required by law. But, says Dunn, "if that attitude is translated into the operating principles of our society, our society is the worse for it. It would be like citizens saying, 'The only responsibility I have as a citizen is not to violate the law. I'm not required by law to vote, so I'm not going to do that. I'm not required by law to make the schools better in my community, so I won't bother.' We have to think about what kind of a society we want to have and ultimately what the consequences are of having one kind of society versus another." When such outcomes are considered, says Dunn, the path is clear: If business protects its ability to function as an institution by making communities strong, it increases its opportunities to prosper in the marketplace, both locally and globally.

The benefits of involving company resources in community affairs are also more direct. Such efforts engender publicity and goodwill, for example, foster skills development and teamwork, and may even result in increased sales and customer loyalty. Even when activities are done without much public fanfare (as is the case in many companies), the satisfaction of contributing to the local welfare can contribute to increased pride and loyalty among employees—who, after all, are part of the community themselves.

Indeed, a pair of studies conducted for IBM by David Lewin, a professor at the University of California at Los Angeles business school, found a direct link between a company's level of community involvement, its employee morale, and financial performance, expressed in return on investment. The studies, conducted in 1989 and 1992, concluded that employee morale was higher in companies that were actively involved in the community. Moreover, concluded Lewin, "the study shows that the companies that increased their community involvement were more likely to show an improved financial picture over a two-year period (measured by ROI) than those that did not increase their community involvement."

Lewin's study has been criticized by some as lacking methodological rigor, and it did not track whether the increased performance continued beyond the two years studied. But even viewed strictly as anecdotal, it lends credence to what many CEOs know from gut instinct: the relationship between companies and communities is symbiotic. Companies that fail to recognize this interdependence— merely taking from the community and giving little or nothing back— may find themselves less able to attract and retain qualified employees, and in general may be viewed less favorably by customers, regulators, the media, and other local stakeholders.

The notion that turning employees into involved citizens creates better workers makes sense. Volunteerism and community service make people feel good. If companies assist in their efforts, that can only boost employees' attitudes about their employers. Bosses who fear the loss of productivity that may result from employees leaving occasionally during the work day to participate in community activities may be shortsighted. "My experience is that people tend to get their jobs accomplished whether they take an hour off for a doctor's appointment or two hours off to work at a homeless shelter," says Dunn, whose company has long had a formal program for encouraging volunteerism and community involvement. "They're still going to get their work done, but there is a way in which having permission to do some things on company time makes a big difference."

"Until a management trainee serves soup to a homeless child, those homeless children are only like fictional characters they see on TV," says Helen Mills of the Soapbox Trading Company. "And the experience of learning triggers an inbred ethos that we have as humans—a

I don't know one woman business owner that's not giving back. But I don't see men doing the same thing. I think they think they're taking their wealth with them. And they're going to be surprised. I don't know one woman business owner who is not doing something to help. And some of them cannot afford to do it. Their businesses are right on the edge and yet they are always giving back. If it's not money, then it's their time. Maybe it's that women really do understand that it's all about the next generation. We're the ones that have the children. So it's a different dynamic.

—ELLA WILLIAMS,
president and CEO, Aegir Systems

morality and a sensitivity that we have allowed to grow dormant in ourselves as neighbors and citizens. Volunteerism is one of the ways companies are trying to glue back the erosion of continuity and camaraderie and commitment in their companies. And it's working. Employees feel a greater allegiance to their company if they're working together to do something other than push paper. We see it in our retail stores. We have managers who have been there four or five years, which is unheard of in retail. I attribute that to the enriched job environment. They're not just pounding around all day, selling soap on hard marble floors. They're feeding homebound AIDS patients, teaching English as a second language, playing Bingo with the elderly, or serving sandwiches to the homeless; these are active programs we have with our employees right now. They feel an empowerment they did not have at their other jobs. It enriches their lives."

But community involvement produces more than satisfied workers. "We're in the process of transforming our factories to team manufacturing," says Dunn, "and we're finding that a lot of the skills that people need are skills that some people have cultivated as a result of the work they've done in community volunteering. Experience that our employees have had in their volunteer capacities as individuals and as board members has really developed them and made them more valuable employees in ways that far exceed anything we could cook up in a training program. We have lots of illustrations of people who have moved up into supervisory ranks, and people who were supervisors who are now plant managers. I think that if you were to talk to these people, they would tell you that a lot of the self-confidence, interpersonal skills, group process skills, analytic skills, and their broadening of perspective occurred as a result of their volunteer experience. We see this happening with people at the management level as well. Encouraging people to get out into the community and be a volunteer or serve on a board has real benefits in terms of what people are like as managers. So there are enormous benefits to the individual, there are real benefits to the company, there are benefits to the community, too."

Sometimes, the benefits are as simple as the increased camaraderie that comes from working together. At the Jefferson Group, a seventy-employee government relations and public affairs firm in Washington, D.C., a program called TJG Cares brings all its employees together on a regular basis to tackle community projects. During those efforts—at a local Ronald McDonald House, for example, or a shelter for homeless women—management and lower-level workers shed their business clothes and don "teamwork T-shirts." Carolyn McLaughlin, the firm's chief administrative officer, believes the program has had a measurable effect on productivity. "It's given people an ability to be more comfortable with one another on the professional side after you've had an opportunity in a more giving social situation to get to know someone," she says. "It breaks down those barriers when you don't have those corporate uniforms on."

Anita Roddick, managing director of The Body Shop, the 1,100-store, $650 million British-based chain of personal care product retailers, believes that such interaction is essential for employees' growth and well-being. "One of the things that needs to be discussed is the workplace as the new community," says Roddick, "because communities are being devastated in a hundred and one ways, whether it's because of the shopping malls, television, or whatever." She views the workplace as a sort of family substitute for many employees, because they may spend more time in close contact with co-workers than with actual relatives.

At The Body Shop's corporate offices in West Sussex, England, Roddick combines the two notions, encouraging the hiring not just of employees' friends but also their families. "We have kids, we have their moms and dads and their grandmas and their grandpas, all working together." Relatives or not, there's a sense of family at The Body Shop that engenders a spirit of community and volunteerism— not just at its international headquarters, but at each of its small, locally owned or managed stores in more than forty countries. "I think these activities make for an education for life," says Roddick. "Companies have an absolute responsibility to keep the education process going. I don't mean training them to put another widget in that makes you work faster or more efficiently. There's a dimension beyond the training to do a job more efficiently that should go on in the workplace." For Roddick, that means fostering employees' education about "real life," with all its joys, passions, and challenges.

Roddick's implicit point is that going to work each day is "real life," too. And companies that give employees permission to bridge the two spheres often find that their workers are better off. The ideal employee may once have been perceived as someone who thinks of nothing but work for eight hours or more a day; but Roddick, Dunn, and other enlightened executives increasingly recognize that such single-mindedness doesn't always serve a company well over the long run. They have seen that encouraging employees to embrace the fullness of their communities can result in more well-rounded, stimulated individuals, who bring the same enthusiasm to work that they bring to "real life."

HONEYWELL'S HELPING HAND

Sometimes, companies arrive at their community-minded consciousness by necessity. That's the case at Honeywell, another company based in the Twin Cities area, which has become deeply involved in a range of issues, including helping to renovate houses in the neighborhood around its headquarters, one of the poorest areas in Minneapolis. Over the past two decades, more than one hundred abandoned dwellings have been rehabilitated and sold to local residents at costs well under market value. As a result, local neighborhood groups, which used to be extremely critical of the company, are now among its biggest supporters.

The history of community involvement at Honeywell is interesting. The company, which sells about $6 billion a year in high-tech control systems for commercial buildings, factories, residences, airplanes, and other environments, has had a rocky relationship with its host city. During the 1960s, Honeywell—which manufactured electronic devices used on weapons during the Vietnam War—was the target of persistent antiwar protesters, who established a nearly permanent encampment adjacent to the company's headquarters, picketing the building and pummeling it with rocks and bricks. Employees were harassed on their way to work. The protests continued through the 1970s and into the 1980s, when the company finally got out of the weapons business.

In 1968, largely to counter its negative image, Honeywell set up a community affairs department. Ron Speed, who headed the effort, set out to create a dialogue with the protesters in hopes of easing tensions. The dialogue continued for the better part of two decades, gradually changing the relationship between the two sides from one of hostility to grudging acceptance and even mutual support. "I can remember in the early eighties coming to work and there would be maybe a thousand protesters outside," recalls M. Patricia Hoven, today Honeywell's vice president of community and local government affairs. "They got so that the protesters would call the police, say, 'Here is when we're coming.' Everyone would work together and it was real congenial, it got almost routinized." Honeywell would put up a fence whenever demonstrations were expected. The company allowed protesters to enter the building to use the bathrooms until doorways became so blocked and employees so irritated that Honeywell reversed its policy, promising to arrest those who trespassed. "The buses would be lined up to take [violators] to the courthouse and the police chief would be here serving coffee; his wife was one of the protesters," says Hoven. "It was almost kind of silly." By the mid-1980s, Honeywell began co-sponsoring a program in Washington, D.C., called Prospects for Peacemaking, a four-part series of nationally broadcast discussions on war and peace.

As tensions eased, Ron Speed's community affairs department shifted its efforts to other issues, especially improving local schools, a *cause célèbre* for a succession of Honeywell CEOs. With Minnesota's white, Scandinavian stereotype, many people are surprised to find that the Minneapolis public school system is more than 50 percent nonwhite, including many urban poor from Southeast Asia and a sizable population of Native Americans. "We've got the same inner-city school issues that other parts of the country have," says Hoven, citing a host of social service problems facing educators. "The teachers can't teach because they're dealing with all these other issues." Honeywell lobbied the U.S. Department of Health and Human Services for a grant for the school system to study how better to deliver social services within the schools without disrupting the educational process.

But Honeywell's most prized educational effort is located right in its own headquarters. It's called New Vistas High School, and it offers pregnant teenagers and teenage mothers a chance to stay in school and get a high school diploma. The school, which opened in 1990, is a collaborative effort involving Honeywell, the Minneapolis public schools, and several community and social service organizations. The first year's class had eleven students; New Vistas now accommodates sixty students and up to seventy infants, toddlers, and preschoolers in child care. There are four teachers and two counselors. In addition to a standard high school education, students receive a wide range of health and social services, including medical care and parenting classes. Children's Hospital maintains an examining room on site, ensuring that the children get proper medical attention. Every two weeks each student is required to work a day in the child care facility to gain experience.

The program's success has been phenomenal. In 1993, there were twenty-two graduates, nearly all of whom went on to college. Very few of the participants have subsequently gotten pregnant again. Says

Hoven: "Most of these students had been on Aid to Families with Dependent Children. If we can help get them off the welfare rolls, that benefits us. We don't have to pay as many taxes."

Employable citizens is not all Honeywell stands to gain. In recent years, the company has entered the educational market with its climate-control systems. "As you can imagine, old school buildings are wonderful markets for us," admits Hoven. "They are not energy-efficient at all. I have observed school superintendents and board members being more receptive to what Honeywell is trying to sell because they realize we really are concerned about education, we're not just talking that education is important. We have been involved. So I think that the schools think we are a good corporate citizen."

But there's a larger agenda at work, too. "I think we do a lot of the things we're doing because we believe that communities have to be viable or companies can't function," adds Hoven. "And so we work to keep the community functioning as well as it can. We do these things to help the community, but also the company benefits. If we don't have an educated citizenry, they're not going to buy our products, nor are they going to be good employees. And I think one of the reasons that companies have gotten so involved in the public education system over the last ten years is that to stay competitive worldwide, we've got to have better public schools."

DOING WHAT COMES NEIGHBORLY

And then there's Ceridian Corporation, a scion of Control Data Corporation (CDC), the Minneapolis company founded by William C. Norris, whose operating principles included its policy of "addressing unmet societal needs as profitable business opportunities." In 1992, a floundering Control Data split into two entities: Control Data Systems and Ceridian; the latter provides such services as employer payroll processing, media and market research (through its Arbitron subsidiary), and point-of-purchase check authorizations.

The reorganization came after years of hard times at CDC. Among other things, the company reacted badly to Japanese competition and the advent of mini- and microcomputers, which radically changed the computer industry in the early 1980s. CDC, which had been a leader in mainframe computers used for scientific research, reacted far more slowly than other big computer firms. The company's focus on time sharing—in which dozens of companies shared

Rhino Records' Volunteerism Policy

As Rhino, Inc., is dedicated to contributing to the community, we encourage and support our employees' involvement in community activity. Rhino now offers its employees the opportunity to earn time off—6 days per year maximum—in exchange for community service. Community service is done on company time or on a weekend in exchange for time off during the week (and will be above and beyond any community service already performed by employees for the Christmas season).

The employee may pick his own organization, or may refer to organizations managed by the [company committee]. Organizations must meet the "3-NP Rule": Non-profit, Non-political, Non-partisan. Employees must show proof of community service activity by providing an official letter from the organization confirming hours worked. All time off during regular work hours must be approved in advance by your department head.

—FROM A RHINO RECORDS EMPLOYEE HANDBOOK

a remote mainframe—was quickly outmoded by the advent of smaller, faster computers. As a result, CDC teetered on the cusp of bankruptcy. In 1986, Norris stepped down; after a series of retrenchments and reorganizations, the company was back on sound financial footing by 1991, having narrowed its focus to a few principal products and services.

Meanwhile, CDC's profitable offspring, Ceridian, has carried on part of the Norris tradition. "I don't even know if it's a visceral reaction, if it's something unusual about this place, but people seem to want to in some way contribute back to the communities in which they work," says Shirley Hughes-English, Ceridian's vice president for human resources and administrative services. Linda Falch, Ceridian's manager of corporate communications, agrees: "I think that people want to be seen as individuals and not replaceable cogs. And that if they work for a company that worries about whether people out in Dakota County have enough to eat, that same company is going to care about me and you and everybody here as a valued person. That's still a very strong motivator here."

If, as Falch and others suggest, employee bonding motivates a company's work force to excellence, businesses would do well to institutionalize employees' community involvement. And many companies have made this part and parcel of their operating principles and practices. A few examples follow.

• Reebok is one of several companies that sponsor annual volunteer fairs, showcasing opportunities for employees to get involved. Organizations that need volunteers are invited to the companies to display their activities and talk with employees about their needs. "As [CEO] Paul Fireman said at the kickoff of the first fair we had in 1991, 'Volunteering is a very personal decision,'" recalls Doug Cahn, director of human rights programs for Reebok International Ltd. "It's not necessarily right for everybody all the time, but if it is right for people, we want to be in a position to offer those opportunities to people and to use the workplace environment in order to make those opportunities available." Says Sharon Cohen, Reebok's vice president of public affairs and executive director of the Reebok Foundation, "We provide a fitness center so that working out is convenient for our employees. So let's make volunteering just as easy."

• The Body Shop encourages its franchisees to set up employee volunteer programs in the local community. "In each of our shops, all the employees get together and decide what it is that they want to invest their time and energies in," explains Helen Mills, who operates five Body Shop franchises. "What do they really care about? Where do they think that they can make a difference? And they select the project. They are compensated somewhere between a half day a week to a half day a month, depending on the person, the project, what the demands are, and what staff availability we have. And then they go out and punch out their daily punch card and punch the clock just as though they were on the job. They go off and work in community service and come back, punch the clock in, and finish the day on the floor or go home." As a result, says Mills, "people know about us because of our work in the community. They're working side by side in different community projects. We're sitting there tutoring people who are learning English as a second language. We're working with the elderly and the homeless. We are working side by side with other groups and individuals helping to change our society and make it be a visible, meaningful contribution—community by community, person by person."

• Rhino Records, a $20 million record company based in Santa Monica, California, rewards employees who engage in charitable activities. For example, employees who contribute sixteen hours of personal time to community service programs can take Christmas week off with pay. Nearly all of the company's 100 employees participate.

• Honeywell has a program called HELP—for Honeywell Employee Launched Projects—which offers grants of between $100 and $500 to support community volunteer projects in which Honeywell employees, retirees, and their families are directly involved. To qualify for funding, a minimum of four Honeywell employees or retirees must be involved in the project. The company gives out an annual community service award, which is accorded the same recognition as its engineering and sales awards. Another program is the Honeywell Retiree Volunteer Project, which since 1979 has channeled retired employees into youth and adult educational programs, technical and health services, and other civic projects. Says Pat Hoven: "It costs us practically nothing. It's a win for the retirees. Some of the people that started it fifteen years ago are now over eighty and they still are here almost every day. And it's a win for the community. Last year we figured that if you consider even minimum wage, over $3 million was contributed in time."

• Loews Hotels has had a Good Neighbor program since 1991 that lends support to communities where Loews owns and manages its hotels, in areas ranging from environmental protection to aiding the homeless. Among other things, the hotels donate excess food to local food banks and support local literacy programs by providing space for classes to be held and volunteer instructors from hotel staff. The Loews Anatole Hotel in Dallas donates more than 16 tons of food a year to the North Texas Food Bank. "Between the employees themselves and the resources available at our hotels, we are in a position to have a very positive impact on the communities in which we operate," says Loews Hotels president and CEO Jonathan Tisch. "When you assist your community, you're not only helping your employees, you're helping yourself. I don't think any of us want to be operating businesses in morally bankrupt communities."

• Levi Strauss recognizes and encourages employee volunteerism and awards grants to community projects identified and actively supported by employees and retiree teams. In addition, the program offers grants on behalf of sewing machine operators who either volunteer in the community or join a community nonprofit board of directors; the money goes to the nonprofit group in the employee's name. "In small communities where we're located, someone who can leverage a cash contribution of $600 for an organization is a major donor," says Bob Dunn.

Community involvement and volunteerism is one area where smaller companies can have as much impact as larger companies. If the local school has twelve children who need mentors, whether those mentors come from a twelve-person organization or a thousand-person organization makes little difference. And so hundreds of smaller companies are making big contributions. For example:

• The Longfellow Clubs, a $4.5-million health and recreation company in Wayland, Massachusetts, donates the use of facilities to kids with special needs. Laury Hammel, general manager and principal owner, points with pride to his company's involvement with the Handi-Racket Tennis Program, in which about twenty-five handi-

> We are all for giving money to causes we believe in, but in the type of competitive environment that I am in, if I don't ensure that my philanthropic and social investments absolutely contribute to improving my profitability, then I am failing to truly serve my employees, my stockholders, my customers, and in fact even the nonprofit causes themselves. For only by ensuring that the fountain continues to get higher and higher, with a larger and larger financial spread and spray, can I be certain that my company will be a sustainable part of the solution. A one-time grant here or there that doesn't generate goodwill toward my company fails to serve our higher goal.
>
> —GARY HIRSHBERG,
> *president, Stonyfield Farm*

capped children learn to play tennis weekly. Along with two other programs involving swimming and basketball, Longfellow reaches about 80 percent of the community's children with disabilities.

• Just Desserts, the San Francisco–based bakery, persuaded thirty-five other companies to join with it to adopt an elementary school in a low-income area. In one event, the group organized about 700 volunteers to paint and refurbish classrooms, the library, and other school facilities.

• Gardeners' Supply, a $20 million mail-order company based in Burlington, Vermont, collects and composts at no charge grass clippings and leaves for residents of the Burlington area. The program has become so successful that the county now runs it, collecting up to 4,000 tons a year, then making the compost available to gardeners. Among other things, the compost is used to grow produce for a local medical center cafeteria.

• Hanna Andersson, a children's clothing mail-order catalogue based in Portland, Oregon, asks customers to recycle its products by donating them back to the company. The company then donates the goods—called "Hannadowns"—to local shelters and other children's organizations. Customers receive a credit worth 20 percent of the returned item's original price, which is applied to a subsequent purchase. Since 1984, the company has donated more than 100,000 garments to needy children.

As these and other companies have learned, encouraging employees to get involved in their communities doesn't take much arm-twisting: employees generally *want* to be involved. Putting a company's resources behind those efforts not only motivates employees, it can energize an entire work force. And as communities prosper, so do the companies that help them.

But things aren't always that simple. Even the most enthusiastic employees can be stymied by managers who may view community activities or volunteerism as disruptive to the daily work flow. Managers have had a traditional mandate to increase sales and profits; volunteerism may appear to conflict with that mission. In their minds, there hasn't been a change of vision in the means to that end. So anything that appears to take time away from the profits goal may seem to them a distraction. That points up the need for a formal company policy, spelling out employees' rights and responsibilities, as well as those of their supervisors, in the context of the company's total mission. Such a policy also underscores the value to and commitment of the company to provide corporate time and resources.

TEAM TIMBERLAND'S CITY YEAR

No one knows more about the benefits to companies of community involvement than the 1,000 or so employees at Timberland, Inc. The company has elevated community involvement to an art, integrating an amalgam of corporate philanthropy and employee activism into its company values and visions. "Working at Timberland is not just a job," reads a company brochure, "but an avenue of opportunity which makes it possible to find fulfillment in not only a career but in personal values that really matter."

At some companies, such language might amount to a well-intentioned but relatively meaningless slogan. But at Timberland, it's a way of life. Chief operating officer Jeff Swartz has infused his company with a sense that taking responsibility for the well-being of one's community is a key element of a successful human being—and a successful Timberland employee. Timberland's close association with City Year, described in chapter 7, has been one of Swartz's principal means of accomplishing both goals.

One of the company's early projects with City Year was a joint effort with Timberland employees to refurbish Odyssey House, a residential center for troubled teenagers located about a mile from Timberland's Hampton, New Hampshire, corporate headquarters. Odyssey House, badly in need of a paint job, became an exercise in which Team Timberland taught Timberland employees how to conduct an effective community service project. Over 100 Timberland employees showed up for the work-day afternoon project, more than enough available hands to do in a day what otherwise might be a week's worth of painting.

But the exercise proved to be far more refreshing than a mere coat of paint. "What I found most intriguing was the next day," recalls Richard Morgan, Timberland's director of human resources, who oversaw the project. "After everyone came back, there was a definite buzz within the work force, a real vitality. People were real excited about the friendships they had made, the insights they had gained working elbow-to-elbow with different folks.

"Our employees' lives were impacted," Morgan continues. "I can tell you that without sounding too poetic. It was really just a change—certainly my own perspective changed. I had some serious flashbacks to my earlier days as a teacher and in social services. That good feeling that I had back then I had again and I was really kind of excited about—Wouldn't it be nice if I could combine my job with some of this type of work, to strike a balance—which is truly what I think people were responding to the next day. For those that weren't able to participate, they probably heard more than they cared to hear that day, because everyone was involved, was extremely into it, and definitely had a heightened level of energy around coming to work and feeling good about the fact that they work for a company that cares about the community and cares enough about me to offer me that opportunity."

As a result of the experience, Timberland initiated a policy allowing all employees sixteen paid hours a year—the equivalent of two work days—to volunteer in the community. About a third of Timberland's employees took advantage of the policy the first year, with participation growing after that. To further entice employees, Morgan created a program featuring quarterly service projects that the company sponsors and encourages employees to sign up for.

Timberland's wholehearted involvement with community action provides a number of benefits to the company, says Morgan. "I think it shows up in the caliber of people we're able to attract here. I think we have a competitive edge as a company because we are seen as an enlightened company which, in fact, we are. We're seen as a company that does more than just talk the talk. We're a company that gets out there and does it, which, personally, as a recruiting tool, there's definitely added value there for me. I can talk about Timberland with a great deal of pride, and eyeball to eyeball say this is a good place to work. That enables me to hire and retain more talented people."

Among the benefits community involvement brings is a sense of ownership and empowerment among employees who create their own solutions to problems. The lack of such initiative among employees is a common complaint of executives, says Swartz. "I think if you asked any CEO or any COO running any company in America, 'What's the biggest limit to your success?' I think they'd tell you what I'd say: 'The inability of our team to unlock itself.' There's so much crap that goes on right outside my office door. So much waste, so much stupidity. The people who are participating in it know it's waste and stupidity. They just don't feel the need to solve that problem. They don't have the notion of individual ownership as deeply and as profoundly as I wish they did."

What's desperately needed, Swartz adds, is the ability to foster within the work force not just a can-do sense of empowerment, but also a *must-do* sense that for the company to prosper, employees must take charge of their own actions and pitch in on behalf of others, too. "If the City Year message got internalized—*Speak out. You are responsible, damn it!*—then 90 percent of the things we don't do right at Timberland would get corrected in a week," says Swartz. "Half the problems that we have as a company—late deliveries or bad quality or invoices that didn't get mailed—are not acts of omission. They're acts of commission—people walking past problems, just like people walk past the homeless on the street: it's somebody else's issue. If we can get this value as deeply internalized here as we need to get it internalized, we would earn twice what we earn as a company. The waste would disappear. Good ideas would flow like water.

"What we really need to do is shut the company down for a year and send everyone to do a City Year experience. And then we'd come back here and we'd put Nike and Reebok out of business."

Swartz's refrain—that a company's involvement with its community can generate direct returns for the company—is heard repeatedly among socially responsible business leaders. And not all are from big, booming businesses like Timberland. In Vermont, for example, a host of smaller companies have taken a keen interest in local affairs, both social and political, working both alone and together to support and protect their region. "People grant immediate credibility to being active in your community," says Pat Heffernan, a former president of Vermont Business for Social Responsibility as well as co-president of Marketing Partners, a public relations firm. "It is counterintuitive in many people's minds for a business person to do that. My experience has been that anything that is somewhat counterintuitive makes people take notice more, which automatically provides greater impact. Smaller ripples become larger ripples that way. That's the real arena, rather than being on the sidelines in the business sector. That's where you can have the greatest impact."

HARVESTING HOPE AT THE GARDEN PROJECT

A single small business can make a significant and lasting impact on the local landscape. If you have any doubts, venture into the Hunter's Point neighborhood of San Francisco and visit God's little half-acre—which only a few years ago was a garbage-strewn back lot—behind

Building Better Communities

For over thirty years, the Cummins Engine Foundation has offered to pay the architectural fees for most new public buildings in its home town of Columbus, Indiana—schools, firehouses, the city hall, the post office, even the new jail—if the entity erecting the building agrees to hire a world-class architect from among three recommended by the foundation. The result has been an architectural renaissance in Columbus unmatched by any other American city. Today, more than fifty buildings by I. M. Pei, Paul Kennon, Harry Weese, Eliel and Eero Saarinen, Kevin Roche and John Dinkeloo, Richer Meier, Cesar Pelli, Robert Venturi, Gunnar Bikerts, Edward Larrabee Barnes, Norman Fletcher, and others grace Columbus and its environs. The foundation's commitment to good architecture has been emulated by local churches and by business and other private organizations as they have built their own buildings.

All of this represents the lengthened shadow of J. Irwin Miller, who served as CEO of Cummins from 1934 to 1977. His intense belief in the uplifting and spiritual power of architecture has helped Cummins attract graduates of the top schools in the country to work for the company and to make Columbus their home.

the Just Desserts bakery. There, society's former outcasts are nurturing and harvesting their futures.

This plot of land is home to the Garden Project, an innovative program that helps former prisoners ease the difficult transition back to society after their release from the San Francisco County Jail. The project aims to empower its "students" to heal their environment, their communities, and ultimately themselves.

The project was the last wish of a profoundly ill woman. In 1984, Cathy Sneed, a counselor with the San Francisco Sheriff's Department, was in the hospital with a life-threatening kidney disease. While there, a friend gave her a copy of *The Grapes of Wrath*, John Steinbeck's novel about itinerant California farm workers. Inspired by the tale, Sneed persuaded her boss, Sheriff Michael Hennessey, that inmates might find meaning and redemption by working the soil. Her idea was to revive a working farm that had been part of the original San Bruno Jail when it was built in the 1930s, but which had subsequently been abandoned. Hennessey, Sneed's mentor and friend, agreed to try the experiment if Sneed was released from the hospital, a doubtful prospect at the time. When she was finally released—still with little hope for recovery—Hennessey granted her four inmates and $300. Together, they began clearing the field. Miraculously, Sneed recovered.

Today, Sneed is in good health, and the 10-acre San Bruno Jail garden is alive and well, too. It grows more than 50,000 pounds of produce a year, much of which is purchased by local restaurants, notably Chez Panisse, the Berkeley-based temple of California cuisine. Most of the rest goes to local soup kitchens.

But once released from jail, the former inmates had nowhere to continue plying their newfound trade. In 1991, Elliot Hoffman, president of Just Desserts, met Sneed and offered her the small plot of land behind his company's headquarters. Now it boasts row after row of flowers and produce—lettuce, leeks, beans, potatoes, garlic, spinach, mustard greens, lilacs, calendula, algerinium, over thirty types of herbs, and more—planted, cultivated, and harvested by former inmates using organic gardening methods. The gardeners share in the bounty and are paid a small stipend for their twenty-hour work week.

But it isn't for the money that the former inmates stick around. Paul Rogers, a thirty-two-year-old former drug addict, the youngest in a family of twelve children, began gardening in 1992 while spending a year in the county jail for receiving stolen property. After years on the street (his addiction began at age nine) he was steered toward the garden as "a way to relieve my stress and a way to find myself," as he now puts it. "I didn't necessarily have to deal with people, and I needed to get to myself." As Rogers began to garden, he also received guidance counseling. "I started out weeding and [my counselor] talked to me in a language that weeding is like taking plants out of your life. When you weed from the garden, you help the plant to grow, and you also do that with your life, which will help you grow. So I started looking at it like that and things started opening up for me. That's what made me very acceptable to what was happening to me, which was change."

After his release, he joined the project going on behind Elliot Hoffman's bakery. "I wanted to continue what I was doing for myself," explains Rogers. "I was making change for myself, feeling different. And I knew that I could better myself because it was in me.

"My favorite thing to do in the garden is weeding," Rogers goes on, "because that gives me time to think about what's in my life that I need to weed out, what do I keep needing to cultivate in myself. I take what I do in the garden and apply it to my life in the same manner. I know that each day for me to grow I need to water myself. What I call 'water' is knowledge, and the more knowledge I put on myself, the more I will grow. That's just like a fertilizer. The more fertilizer you keep within your garden, and you keep weeding, the better and stronger it will grow every day."

Rogers explains that the garden is a means for people like him to break the streets-to-prison-to-streets cycle they grew up with. "So many times we go back and forth to jail and we feel like we're never going to get a chance or nobody is ever going to believe in us," he says. "When you get programs such as this, then we know there is hope. Hopefully other people that are in prison will see that we're doing good, that people do want to help us if we help ourselves, and it will turn them around, too." In the garden, he says, people "know that they're worth something, that their life is not meaningless. Once they know that change is possible, then change brings around growth, and that's productiveness. That's what the program is based on. We have our problems up and down with certain individuals, but we all sit together as a team because it won't work without us working together. It's just like the water and the dirt help the plant to grow. We're like the water and the job is the dirt. To keep everything growing, you have to keep it together. When something bad happens, we have to weed it out."

Rogers, who has a fourteen-year-old daughter and three stepchildren, ages six, four, and one, knows he could make more money at other jobs. "The money for me is not the issue because I take what I have and utilize it in every area. My kids are not very money-hungry, they're just thankful for what they get because they know that I'm doing what I can. For them that's enough. And the fact that I'm there, because so many times I wasn't. This is the first job I've held in six years. So this is something that I'm very proud of. I love being out here. Like I said, the money issue isn't what's happening for me right now. What I'm more interested in is that I stay productive for myself and keep growing in myself. I know that as long as I do that, the opportunities will always be there for me."

For Elliot Hoffman, the garden is just one more component of a thriving business operation, albeit one that brings him a great deal of personal joy and satisfaction. He gives frequent tours of the garden to other business executives and encourages groups to hold meetings at the garden's long picnic tables; among those that do so is the Sheriff's Department. Nearly everyone who stops by is moved by what they see taking place there. Hoffman says his business thrives as a result of efforts like the Garden Project. "My employees are more motivated, our customers are a little more loyal. They are going to buy from us because I really believe they take that into account in their decision making." In addition, Just Desserts has hired several graduates of the Garden Project to work in its bakery.

Hoffman believes that the Garden Project is the kind of effort needed to help cities survive and thrive. "I am not going to spend 100 percent of my time doing this," he says. "I am not going to give all my money away to charity or the Garden Project. But I am going to spend some of my time, money, and energies on change. I want my kids to live in a crime-free society. I don't believe that you're going to deal with crime, drugs, and homelessness unless we create jobs. Jobs will come from one place, and that's business. The only other alternative is to build more jails and more walls, if that's how we want to spend our money. I want us to be one of those model businesses that says, 'You can make a great product or provide a great service and be a great place for people to spend their work lives. You can contribute positively to a community, and you can make money doing it.' I think we need more of those models."

It is more than that. Hoffman sees the Garden Project as a symbol of what business—indeed, society—needs to do to improve its very infrastructure. "I really believe that business has to play a larger role in changing our society," he says. "Business people know how to get things done. We tend to think outside the box. We need to bring that creativity to our community. We need to look to creating jobs rather than ending jobs. We need to put money and resources into job training and new jobs if we are ever going to address the tough issues."

Hoffman's point is critical: Creating sustainable, well-paying jobs *is* key to many cities' success in ending the spiral of poverty, crime, and hopelessness. And socially responsible companies like Just Desserts see a direct role for themselves in a variety of community-building activities, including creating jobs and serving as catalysts for new opportunities. The fact that Hoffman and others are doing this quietly, without major publicity, is a fitting antidote to the public's poor perception of business, born of the seemingly endless stream of headlines trumpeting the massive job-slashing initiatives of bigger companies. Collectively, these smaller companies' job-creating efforts haven't yet countered the bigger firms' cuts, but they offer hope in communities where hope is an endangered species.

WHERE CREDIT IS DUE

Creating economic opportunities in communities that lack them has become a leading cause for some companies. Some deliberately site new factories in poor communities, for example, much as Control Data chief Bill Norris did in Minneapolis during the late 1960s. Indeed, a handful of entrepreneurs have founded companies based on the idea that there is money to be made creating job and housing opportunities for others.

That was the principal idea behind South Shore Bank in Chicago, founded in 1973 to help reverse the process of urban decay in one part of one city, and to prove that it was possible to make a profit while doing so. The founders—two Caucasians and two African-Americans—are idealists whose beliefs and skills were honed in the civil rights movement and the community development efforts of the 1960s. They had become discouraged with the impact of the Great Society programs created by President Lyndon Johnson as part of his War on Poverty, viewing such initiatives as piecemeal efforts with no perspective on the integrity of urban neighborhoods. "We had to find some way to create permanent institutions that could work in these neighborhoods and could work in the whole range of needs that exist within urban neighborhoods," recalls Ronald Grzywinski, one of the founders, who is now chairman of South Shore Bank's parent company, Shorebank Corporation.

Grzywinski and his three partners had been working together at another bank, Hyde Park Bank & Trust, where they started the first minority loan program in Illinois, lending mostly to small businesses. But they recognized that "the needs were not limited to only the small business lending we were doing at Hyde Park. There were things like housing, jobs, remedial education, and child care" that were not being funded.

Over the years, the South Shore neighborhood, once predominantly white and one of Chicago's most fashionable shopping areas, suffered from white flight, poverty, and crime. (In the 1960 U.S. Census, the neighborhood was 100 percent white; by the 1970 Census, it was 70 percent black. Today, it is 98 percent black.) By the early 1970s, the neighborhood was rife with abandoned buildings and empty lots. Economically, it teetered on the edge of oblivion.

When Grzywinski and his partners took over South Shore Bank, it was a thirty-four-year-old institution that had fallen on hard times. They immediately set out to transform the company to address community needs, searching out opportunities to lend money to businesses and projects that would help revive the neighborhood. "What we recognized from the beginning," says Grzywinski, "was that as important as the money was going to be in rebuilding the South Shore community, that equally important was going to be the issue of turning around the psychology of the community." Nearly everyone—from the folks at City Hall to the police commissioner to local school principals—assumed the neighborhood was going to fail, as so many other impoverished neighborhoods around the country had failed already. Grzywinski and company set out to rebuild the community's faith in itself, and to build a bank in the process. They attended scores of community meetings—"every PTA, every block club meeting, every church basement we could find," says Grzywinski. "We told people who we were and what we intended to do, and we invited them to tell us what they considered to be the community's greatest needs. For months we talked and listened, and if nothing else, we learned a great deal."

Little by little, they persuaded local residents to pull their savings from downtown banks and put them into South Shore Bank, and they encouraged entrepreneurs and developers to take another look at doing business in the community. Their goal was to implant in the neighborhood an assortment of locally owned businesses and residential buildings, and to spur the rehabilitation of existing homes that had been abandoned or were badly decayed. As the community became more viable, so too would South Shore Bank. To ensure this metamorphosis, the bank's new owners instructed loan officers that before they could turn down a loan application from someone living in South Shore, or who wanted to buy a home or start a business in that neighborhood, they had to bring the application to one of the four owners to approve the rejection.

Slowly, the idea worked. And as it did, South Shore Bank's owners fine-tuned their efforts, setting up other organizations to assist in the process: a for-profit real estate development company, for example, and a nonprofit organization, The Neighborhood Institute, which rehabilitates abandoned housing units while also offering remedial education and job training for the unemployed and those on welfare. The institute also founded a small-business incubator to give inexpensive space and management assistance to small businesses and to provide training for entrepreneurs—including welfare mothers—who want to run their own businesses. And they established The Neighborhood Fund, which specializes in financing small businesses, and Shorebank Advisory Services, a consulting firm that offers technical assistance on development banking and other community economic development strategies.

Today, Shorebank is a thriving corporation that is credited with turning the South Shore neighborhood around, though the area is still troubled by many urban ills. Since 1973, the company has rehabilitated more than 7,000 nearby housing units, plus thousands more in other areas. Its loans and development efforts have spread to other Chicago neighborhoods it has targeted, and in recent years the company has helped set up similar institutions in Michigan, Arkansas, and Kansas. In Arkansas, for example, Shorebank helped set up Southern Development Bancorporation in 1986 to accelerate the pace of economic activity in a thirty-six-county area in the southwestern part of the state. More recently, the company has been helping set up small businesses in Poland.

For twenty years now, South Shore Bank's good work has met with continual success, fueled by deposits from socially minded individuals across the country. In 1993, the bank's balance sheet showed record assets and the company enjoyed record earnings. Its rate of loan charge-offs is well below the industry average. Back in the South Shore neighborhood, the bank has helped to turn a number of residents into millionaires, from their investments in rehabilitating and reselling property once considered too risky to handle. "It is truly old-fashioned banking," says Grzywinski. "It is what banks used to do when they really focused in on their community, their neighborhood, their borrowers, and understood them intimately."

Since South Shore Bank's founding—and partly as a result of its success—hundreds of community lending institutions have sprouted up across America, helping transform abandoned inner-city neighborhoods that other lending institutions would not touch into viable communities. (Government has played a significant role in this through the Community Reinvestment Act of 1977, which mandates banks to invest in poor communities.) All of these new local lenders acknowledge one of the hard realities of life in the 1990s: Access to the credit needed to create new, locally owned, profit-making enter-

> Our business objective is to become the market leader in urban banking in New England. We have never for a moment seen this as philanthropy or do-goodism, but rather have taken the same approach to the urban market as to every other market that we consider valued and valuable: to tailor a relationship-banking approach to that market that would meet its needs and allow us, therefore, to succeed.
>
> —GAIL SNOWDEN,
> *president, First Community Bank at Bank of Boston*

prises is as important to a community's economic viability as are safe streets and good schools. Some would say that the two go hand in hand. Without such credit, the underprivileged become vulnerable to a variety of economic inequities that can border on the scandalous: pawnshops and rent-to-own furniture stores that charge interest rates often exceeding 20 or 30 percent; supermarkets (if they're even in the neighborhood) that charge premium prices for groceries, which their owners justify as the cost of security for doing business in crime-ridden neighborhoods; and check-cashing operations that charge hefty fees for the privilege of cashing welfare checks or paychecks, or paying rent or utility bills. More often than not, these businesses are owned by individuals or entities residing outside the neighborhood, further compounding the exodus of capital. Those residents who do maintain savings accounts also may be inclined to place them in banks located outside the neighborhood, often viewed as more stable than local institutions. When he took over South Shore Bank, Ron Grzywinski was astonished to find that some $90 million of local savings was being held in downtown Chicago banks.

To be sure, there are profits to be had from lending money in poor neighborhoods, even at nonusurious interest rates. A handful of mainstream lenders are beginning to recognize this and are taking the first few timid steps where their banking brethren have feared to tread. In California, for example, American Savings Bank, once the target of protesters complaining of redlining—unwritten (and illegal) policies by some banks to restrict lending in low-income and minority neighborhoods, regardless of an applicant's creditworthiness—is now being hailed by community activists. The reason: Mario J. Antoci, the bank's CEO, decided to boost low-income lending. By 1993, loans to low-income neighborhoods had increased nearly tenfold over 1990 and accounted for a fifth of the bank's mortgage originations—about $10 million worth. Moreover, these loans are among the best-performing loans the company makes. (Ironically, the profits from these loans are helping to offset losses on loans made by American Savings in wealthier communities in southern California, where property values have plummeted.) In Los Angeles, delinquencies on loans in low-income neighborhoods are about a third of those on loans in more affluent neighborhoods.

Antoci, who came to American Savings after working at a savings and loan with a strong low-income lending record, knew the profit potential of such lending. To woo borrowers, he created a community outreach program that sponsored such activities as neighborhood "paint-a-thons" and a fashion show at a child care center. He opened branches in Watts, as well as in East and South Central Los Angeles. (Previously, the South Central neighborhood had been covered by a branch seven miles away, in Hollywood.) Elsewhere in the state, Antoci has set up branches in such underserved areas as San Francisco's Chinatown, where the bank offers home-buying seminars in Chinese. The bank has hired loan agents from local neighborhoods and given them the flexibility to bend the rules a bit when making loans. Lending officers can accept utility bill receipts in lieu of credit card payment records as proof of a good credit history. "A typical credit person might have a problem with that," Antoci told *Business Week* in 1993. "But we are proving it doesn't have to be that way."

Antoci is proving that there is a lode of profitable banking to be found by mining the niches of society once written off as not worth the effort. In the process, American Savings Bank, Shorebank, and other enlightened lenders may be the saving grace of South-Central Los Angeles, Chicago's South Shore, and other poverty-plagued neighborhoods. By reversing the downward spiral of poverty, despair, and crime, these leaders are writing the future growth of the American city—on loan applications and deeds of trust.

FREDDIE MAC'S FAMILY WAYS

One question facing nearly every company seeking to help out on the local level is where to put one's resources so as to have maximum impact. Is it better to contribute time (in the form of volunteers or loaned employees, for example), or money, or other resources? Which will yield the greatest bang for the buck—for the community as well as for the company and its employees? And then there's the matter of focus: Is it better for a company to spread its philanthropic and volunteer resources over a wide range of issues, perhaps reflecting the diversity of concerns among its leaders and employees, or zero in on one or a handful of issues, perhaps garnering greater results in the process? There are no right or socially responsible answers to these questions. Each company must reach its own conclusions, based on its unique culture and resources.

In the case of Freddie Mac, the answers came from Leland C. Brendsel, chairman and CEO of the company that underwrites one of every eight home mortgages in the United States. Freddie Mac (formally chartered by Congress in 1970 as the Federal Home Loan Mortgage Corporation; the Freddie Mac moniker, coined by Wall Street traders, has become the official name) is a stockholder-owned company that buys investment-quality mortgages from lenders, packages them as securities, and sells the securities to institutional investors, such as insurance companies and pension funds. By doing so, Freddie Mac (and its principal competitor, the Federal National Mortgage Association, or Fannie Mae) helps facilitate the flow of affordable mortgage funds. It is a handsomely profitable business. In fiscal 1993, Freddie Mac enjoyed its twenty-third consecutive profitable year, with net income at a record $786 million, up 24 percent from the previous year. In fiscal 1994, it was on track to net $1 billion.

Brendsel's passion is children—specifically, disadvantaged youth, from newborns through age six. "When it comes right down to it, if children don't have healthy and nurturing young lives, they won't develop into happy, productive adults," he says. "An investment in young children is by far the investment with the highest returns as a nation." As a result, Brendsel's company has focused its philanthropic arm, the Freddie Mac Foundation, and most of its community involvement programs, on what J. David Robinson refers to as "children, youth, and families at risk"—specifically those on its home turf: the Washington, D.C., area, where the company was founded in 1970 before moving to suburban Virginia in 1987. Some 2,700 of Freddie Mac's 3,000 employees live and work in the region.

"At the risk of sounding altruistic, we really want to make a big difference," says Robinson, Freddie Mac's vice president, Corporate Giving, who oversees the foundation. "And we decided that we can't make a big difference in the lives of every child or youth at risk in this country, and if we spread our resources too thin, we can't make a big

How Lotus Combats Racism

Lotus Development Corporation has taken a strong stand against racism both at home and abroad, and has invested considerable sums of money in helping community groups. In fact, "anti-racism/classism" is one of two main areas of focus for the company's philanthropy program; the other helps provide access to information technology.

Lotus programs are highly action-oriented, supporting community organizing, advocacy, and economic development. For example, the company funded a confidential campaign to test housing authorities in the Boston area on whether they were discriminating on the basis of race. "They found that if you were a single mother of African-American descent, you got a different sense of assistance from local housing authorities than a white person," according to Lotus philanthropy director Michael Durney. The company also has funded advocacy groups working against redlining by mortgage lenders in minority neighborhoods, which resulted in legal actions against several Boston-area banks.

Despite his company's longstanding involvement with such efforts, Durney is frustrated by the lack of other companies joining in on these issues. "It's a hot button for a lot of people," he says. "Community organizing and advocacy, which in my mind is the most effective approach to issues of race and class, is something that companies by and large are uncomfortable with."

One reason, he says, is that it is difficult to measure these programs' success. "You can't do it on the basis of jobs created or houses built; they're only components of a larger issue. What you need to be measuring is how leadership is being brought into organizations, how much people are interacting across neighborhoods and across racial barriers. Those are the things that will lead to a more inclusive and productive society in general." But, he adds, these things take years to develop, which frustrates philanthropy managers who want more immediate and tangible results.

difference in the lives of very many children. So if we concentrate our resources, we can make a big difference in the lives of a few—though it turns out to be more than a few." The effort, which began modestly in 1988, resulted in more than $2 million in grants to Washington-area organizations, plus countless hours of employees' time devoted to helping children, youth, and families in and around the nation's capital.

Most of Freddie Mac's money went to local organizations targeting Washington's inner city; a few grants went to national organizations, such as the Children's Defense Fund and the National Committee for the Prevention of Child Abuse. The local donations zero in on a handful of D.C.'s most troubled neighborhoods, such as Anacostia, Shaw, and Columbia Heights. Recipients ranged from Bright Beginnings, which provides free, high-quality child care to children of homeless and transitional families, to Food & Friends, an organization aimed at improving the nutrition and health of HIV/AIDS-infected families. In addition to the financial grants, Freddie Mac has a wide range of employee volunteer programs, such as its Reach Out to a Child campaign, which raises national awareness about the problem of child abuse and neglect. The company sponsors five-kilometer races at mortgage industry conventions, at which it has raised more than $1 million since 1990 for children's charities. The company's employees donate hundreds of hours of volunteer time to the races.

In addition, Freddie Mac donates its employees' time to local government agencies, schools, and social service organizations. Two Freddie Mac–paid employees have toiled for the past two years in the labyrinthine offices of the District of Columbia government, helping to improve the computerized technology of its foster care tracking system.

What does all this have to do with Freddie Mac's stated mission of "making the American dream of decent, accessible housing a reality"? Robinson says, "We could make loans all day long in low-income neighborhoods, but if the support services required to make those neighborhoods really vibrant communities that will last for a long time aren't in place, then our loans won't be any good and people won't be able to keep their houses. The neighborhoods will deteriorate and it will have a direct negative impact on our business in the long run." While Robinson can't point to any hard evidence that proves his company's grants and other programs are having a positive impact on Freddie Mac's loan portfolio, he cites other findings that suggest there is an impact. "For example, we know that default rates increase as neighborhoods decline. We know that it is tougher to find people who qualify for loans in declining neighborhoods. It is more difficult to maintain property values in declining neighborhoods. All of that is backed up by empirical evidence. It's one of those things that we accept as a de facto situation: If we help a neighborhood stabilize and improve, over the long run there will be more opportunities for residents to own homes or live in decent multifamily apartment buildings."

And then there is the positive impact Freddie Mac's commitment to children and families has on its employees. "It makes employees feel good about themselves and it makes them feel good about the company," says Robinson. "We get lots of positive feedback from employees about the things that Freddie Mac does in the community. It makes them feel pleased that they're working at Freddie Mac. We believe that translates into greater loyalty to the company, more productivity, and greater longevity in the work force."

"All people want to be associated with organizations that are responsible, that contribute, that have integrity," says Brendsel. "In a certain sense, our philanthropic activities reinforce the values that the people share in working at Freddie Mac—values of service, of integrity, of helping customers and communities. The image we are creating or reinforcing is that we are good stewards of the resources to which we are entrusted."

CREATING ECONOMIC OPPORTUNITY

As Freddie Mac has come to understand, transforming communities takes more than just sound buildings. And much of what must be done is beyond the scope of even the most ambitious corporate agenda. Business alone can't save communities. Communities have to develop and grow from the inside out in order to truly tap their potential. Where companies are most effective is as a catalyst and support system, not as the sole provider.

What's ultimately needed are jobs. Creating jobs is something that business can do very well—or at least did until relatively recently, until companies "re-engineered" a significant number of their employees onto unemployment lines. That has left tens of thousands of families—and countless communities—hurting.

But some companies, both large and small, are growing, creating jobs along the way. Companies like The Body Shop, whose founder,

We should absolutely not expect our corporations to be social service providers because it confuses their agenda tremendously. We should expect the corporations to act in a
way that is sustainable and restorative in terms of how it
impacts the environment, there is no question about that.

At the same time we have to understand that there are so
many systemic obstacles for them to do that we cannot expect it without also as a policy examining the context within
which they operate. For example, as consumers we want our
companies to produce the lowest-priced products at comparable quality. As citizens, environmentalists, and people who
care, we want them to do the opposite, internalize costs to a
great degree, to a point it would make them uncompetitive.
And so we send business a mixed message, and it's very confusing and not surprising that they do confusing things, given
that information.

This confusion of roles is manifesting itself in people turning toward business and saying, "Well, government is broke
and now we need you to step in here and fill in." And actually,
although I admire companies that do have programs that do
that, in a sense, that's not what business is designed to do. I
don't think it does it well.

I admire that. In fact, if I were in business, that's what I
would want to do because that's extremely interesting to me.
I would want to go to either a country or a place in this
country where people are tremendously disadvantaged,
where there's poverty, lack of education, and opportunity. I
find that real exciting. It's interesting, dynamic. But that's a
personal choice. That's different than saying every business in
the country should somehow take care of a deteriorating
social infrastructure.

—PAUL HAWKEN,
co-founder, Smith & Hawken

Anita Roddick, has made it her mission to create economic development projects around the world. Roddick is best known for forging partnerships with indigenous people in Third World countries, creating trading links to such countries as Bangladesh, Brazil, India, Mexico, Nepal, Nicaragua, and Zambia. (More about those in chapter 9.)

"I have a good eye for setting up small-scale economic practices," Roddick says. In Baltimore, Maryland, for example, local Body Shop franchises set up a business called Tico Enterprises, which hires graduates of a state-sponsored program that teaches carpentry to at-risk youth. After graduating, there weren't many opportunities for these young people to ply their trade. Tico Enterprises now hires them to produce a product called Soap Savers, a kitchen and bathroom gadget made out of recycled wooden warehouse pallets, which is sold in Body Shop stores nationwide. Tico's half-dozen or so employees now own the enterprise, which also sells Soap Savers and several other handmade goods to some of The Body Shop's competitors.

Stonyfield Farm has taken a different tack. For company president Gary Hirshberg, the focus has been on the survival of the family farm, an endangered species in a nation that has turned agricultural economics in favor of larger producers. Stonyfield has worked hard to support family farmers in New Hampshire, who provide milk, the raw material for the company's principal product. It works with farmers to support their efforts to use less polluting, less energy-intensive farming methods, rewarding them with higher prices and other forms of recognition. The company also waged a campaign to educate its customers and the public about the importance of family farmers, which Hirshberg views as more resource-efficient and less likely to use additives that end up in the environment or the foods they produce. One Stonyfield program is "Adopt-A-Cow," which provides participating customers with a certificate and a photo of an actual dairy cow (with an actual name), and regular updates about the cow's life on the farm. The idea is to help bring family farmers and consumers in more direct contact. Still another effort is the company's "Moosletter," providing customers with regular updates on the yogurt company and the farmers from which it buys its milk.

Hirshberg has a personal stake in these and other efforts. "I grew up in New Hampshire and my father ran shoe businesses all over the state. He literally was the employer that kept three towns alive. And in the seventies, when you suddenly could produce shoes in Brazil for eighteen-cents-an-hour wages, that industry disappeared. I watched the devastating effect it left on the towns. These communities have never recovered." His efforts at Stonyfield are done with the hopes that they can help New England's family farmers avoid a similar fate.

Other companies are also setting up shops in impoverished neighborhoods. Ben & Jerry's, for example, has set up "scoop shops"—what used to be known as ice cream parlors—in places like New York's historic Harlem, long a symbol of urban decay. The Harlem shop, opened in 1992, hires homeless people to work behind the counters, providing a way off the streets and into a productive life. Seventy-five percent of the store's profits are plowed back into a Harlem shelter and drug-crisis center. Ben & Jerry's gave its imprimatur to a new flavor created by the store's manager—Harlem Blues Berries (raspberry ice cream, blueberry swirl, and chunks of strawberry)—which is available only at this store.

Setting up and running the Harlem shop, and others of its kind, isn't easy, and Ben & Jerry's has taken its licks in keeping these operations running smoothly. "The stores have been tremendous successes from a social standpoint," says Will Patton, the company field operations manager. "But they've been tougher to run because they haven't had as clear a direction financially. They don't run as smoothly. This is not a nice, clean, write-a-check-to-charity kind of thing. This is a real dirty, roll-up-your-sleeves, I'm-going-to-work-alongside-of-you operation." Still, he says, "We've already made some big impressions on the business community in Harlem. We've changed some individuals' lives."

Chapter Nine

A Global Vision

"We are not a government, not an all-knowing, all-powerful force in the world. But I strongly believe that corporations have a responsibility to the consumers who purchase their products to assure that those products are manufactured in ways that are consistent with the values of those consumers."

—Doug Cahn,
  director of human rights programs, Reebok International Ltd.

In 1987, Chiat/Day, the advertising agency, suggested to executives at Reebok International Ltd. that it sponsor what seemed an unusual event for an athletic footwear and apparel company: an effort by Amnesty International, the human rights organization, to increase awareness of human rights around the globe in commemoration of the fortieth anniversary of the United Nations Declaration of Human Rights.

Amnesty had decided to target young people through a "Human Rights Now!" concert tour, featuring some of the top performing artists of the day: Peter Gabriel, Sting, Tracy Chapman, and Bruce Springsteen, among others. The universal language of music would help Amnesty reach youth throughout the world—places where literacy rates weren't as high and people were less aware of human rights abuses.

"It was going to be an expensive proposition," recalls Reebok's Sharon Cohen, who heads the Reebok Foundation, the company's philanthropic arm. "I don't believe Amnesty International had ever approached a corporation before for a major underwriting endorsement of this kind." It certainly was a huge chunk of cash for Reebok: close to $10 million, a significant piece of the company's annual advertising budget. "Clearly, the business interests of Reebok would have been better served if we had just taken the money and used it to increase our ad buy," says Cohen. But the Chiat/Day proposal had come after several very profitable years in which Reebok had grown from "almost insignificance, literally barely living, to a pretty powerful billion-dollar company with significant profits," in the words of Paul Fireman, Reebok's chairman and CEO.

What was compelling about Reebok's potential relationship with Amnesty, says Cohen, was "the idea of giving back to the community in a way that touched people, and that created awareness of human rights." So Reebok agreed to sponsor the tour—not just as a sponsor, but *the* sponsor.

Reebok's involvement developed into far more than writing a check. As things progressed, company employees were caught up in planning nearly every aspect of the international concert tour, from stage design to event promotion to backstage hospitality. "Once we got in the program and enough of our people [got] involved, it really became infectious and pretty soon we all got bit with the bug," says Fireman. Recalls Cohen: "When we became involved in human rights, it struck a very warm heart here, which became more compelling as that summer went on."

The Amnesty tour turned out to be one of the musical highlights of 1988. It played in twenty-one cities, from Philadelphia and Los Angeles to London, Paris, Athens, Tokyo, and Bombay.

And when it was all over—after the final chords of the last ebullient jam session had finished reverberating through the summer night in Buenos Aires—Fireman, Cohen, and colleagues began to ponder the future. "The tour was a very positive thing," says Cohen. "Everyone at Reebok was very proud to be associated with it. The question was what could we do to continue our involvement in this issue." Their answer: to make human rights a year-round part of Reebok's culture and concerns.

And so was born the Reebok Human Rights Awards, presented annually "to honor young people who, early in their lives and against great odds, have significantly raised awareness of human rights and exercised freedom of expression," according to Cohen. The award was the first human rights prize offered by a corporation. It was also the first targeted at people under age thirty; most other such awards, such as the Robert F. Kennedy Awards, typically honor individuals toward the end of a lifetime of activism.

The first Reebok Human Rights Awards were given in December 1988, in a ceremony held across from the United Nations in New York, although all subsequent ceremonies have been held near company headquarters in Boston. Among the eleven recipients honored that year were Janet Cherry, a twenty-seven-year-old South African human services worker who had become a visible champion and symbol for the multiracial struggle to end apartheid; Arn-Chorn Pond, age twenty, a survivor of the Cambodian killing fields that claimed the lives of his family, and founder of an organization called Children of War, aimed at educating others about the horrors of armed conflict; and Winona LaDuke, a twenty-nine-year-old Native American who founded organizations that promote economic development on reservations. Each winner received $25,000, to be used directly by the organizations with which they work.

The company-sponsored annual awards ceremony has become something of a community event. Entire classrooms attend, as do several hundred Reebok employees. The event helps everyone keep things in perspective, says human rights programs director Doug Cahn. "We go through our travails every day. It is always humbling and perspective-building to learn about the remarkable accomplishments of young people who have in the face of considerable odds changed the lives of their communities in significant ways. They improve the human rights conditions where they live." And the impact is felt beyond the event itself. "One of the most frustrating and yet positive things that comes out of the ceremony, as people go back to work, is that they say to themselves and to others, 'What can we do in our own communities and our lives to make the world a little bit better place?' " In 1992, for example, a group of employees returned from the ceremony and decided to set up a community food drive.

Not surprisingly, Reebok's efforts on human rights have made the company a magnet for other groups seeking to improve the human condition throughout the world. Among the other innovative projects Reebok has funded is a program called "Witness," conceived by the musician Peter Gabriel and implemented by the Lawyers Committee for Human Rights. Created in 1992, "Witness" is designed to arm human rights activists worldwide with what its organizers call "weapons of mass communication"—specifically, hand-held video cameras and fax machines. The idea is to vividly record human rights abuses on video and in photographs, Rodney King style, and broadly disseminate the evidence. "Witness recognizes that if more people knew about human rights abuses around the world, more people would object to them and let their governments know that they object to them," says Cahn.

"Witness" not only provides the equipment but also maintains relationships with international human rights groups and the international news media. It's no easy task. Getting the equipment into some countries involves paying stiff duties. There's also the matter of training: most of the recipients are not very sophisticated about the world of state-of-the-art electronic technology. And then there's the issue of electric power: How do you obtain or recharge batteries in remote outposts of the world? Finally, there's the issue of political power: how to defend or protect individuals who are captured or otherwise punished by officials for using such equipment to embarrass their government. "It is an involved project," says Cahn, "but we believe it is a very important one. The human rights community can better do its job when it's using the same kinds of technologies that the abusers are using." Reebok employees have personally donated more than a score of video cameras to the "Witness" program.

Cahn believes Reebok's commitment to human rights rubs off on employees in other ways: "Lots of things go on as a result of our efforts that we don't know about." He's seen volunteerism among Reebok employees rise since the company began its programs, and wherever possible, the company has tried to encourage and support such efforts. For example, after Hurricane Andrew devastated parts of Florida in 1992, a group of employees asked for leave time to go to Florida to help clean things up. Reebok not only gave over two dozen employees a full week's time off, it picked up the tab for their flights.

Why would a company that's a household word for athletic shoes become committed to human rights? Indeed, why would any company become involved in international issues? Is it socially responsible for businesses to insinuate themselves into other countries' workplaces or environmental affairs? What rights do shareholders, executives, and employees have to try to alter the relationships between a company and its local contractors, let alone trying to press foreign leaders to adopt new social or corporate cultures?

And finally: How far should a company go in enforcing its beliefs when doing business in foreign countries—as far as pulling out of the country altogether?

Beyond these tough questions are larger issues: What kind of social role should companies take in the expanding global economy? How much should companies trading across borders actively participate in the social issues confronting the citizens of their trading partners: inadequate education and health care, environmental degradation, and human rights abuses? Should a company be as committed to community welfare abroad as it is at home?

These are among the questions a growing number of companies are asking of themselves and their colleagues. There is far from unanimity in the answers, even among socially responsible companies. One thing, however, is certain: Whether they wish to or not, all companies that do business globally inevitably find their operations linked to local standards, traditions, and politics, from the way their environmental effluents are (or aren't) monitored and controlled to the treatment and rights of workers. And when the realities of local issues fly in the face of a company's moral, ethical, or philosophical policies, companies like Reebok find that they have little choice but to take action.

These are extremely sensitive issues for most companies, both politically and philosophically. When they impose their cultures and values on the leaders and populations of countries half a world away, it can have serious and widespread repercussions on trade and foreign relations, local economic conditions, and the fortunes of thousands of workers, many of them living in extremely impoverished conditions. Far more than the bottom line can hang in the balance of such decisions. And yet some companies aren't shying away from making them.

In some cases, socially responsible policies have had a negative financial impact through increased labor costs, or in forgone sales opportunities. But these companies' leaders believe that the price is worth paying. Sometimes the decision is a result of personal experience, as when executives witness firsthand squalid working conditions or environmental havoc created by a foreign supplier and recognize that their clout as local employers and purchasers of goods and services can be a potent agent for change. "As a business we have a responsibility to act in a way that's consistent with our values," says Bob Dunn of Levi Strauss. "That includes making some positive contributions in the countries where we do business." Others see consumers increasingly concerned about the working conditions of those who make the products they buy. Some consumers already avoid brands they associate with exploitative or abusive practices in favor of those with socially responsible reputations.

The point here is not that American companies should expect to turn their foreign trading partners into Americans, but to bring a socially responsible way of doing business to suppliers and contractors that allow them to retain—and perhaps export—their corporate values. The idea is not to transform Third World workplaces into the automated factories found in industrialized nations, but to encourage such values as fair wages and healthy workplaces among foreign suppliers.

This is the new world of business, an era of international trade in which how you do business abroad is becoming as important as how you do business at home. It is a business philosophy that recognizes a values-driven bottom line.

MAKING DEMANDS ON SUPPLIERS

The price of ignoring such considerations may be steep. That was the message received by Wal-Mart, the largest retailer in the United States, when it was the subject of a December 1992 "Dateline: NBC" television program detailing abusive child-labor practices of companies in Bangladesh manufacturing clothing under the Wal-Mart label. Although the company denied the story—"I can guarantee you that we have an absolute policy against [child labor]," David D. Glass, Wal-Mart's CEO, assured a St. Louis business audience a few weeks later—the program's airing brought considerable embarrassment to a company that had invested heavily in a "Made in the U.S.A." advertising campaign. In the few days prior to the broadcast, as rumors circulated about the story's content, Wal-Mart's stock dropped two and a half points, though it would later resume its healthy upward climb.

In April 1993, Wal-Mart toughened its policy against child-labor practices, threatening to discontinue doing business with contractors who failed to comply. That didn't stop a union demonstration at seventy Wal-Mart stores by the United Food and Commercial Workers Union, which made Wal-Mart the focus of its annual Mother's Day protest against child labor. Several mutual funds with social screens divested their holdings in Wal-Mart stock, attributing their decision to child-labor abuses. To this day, Wal-Mart is working hard to counter its image as an exploiter of child labor.

Wal-Mart wasn't alone. During the months following the "Dateline: NBC" episode, the news media generated a succession of stories about how American companies exploit child labor in Third World countries. In one typical story, *The Washington Post* described conditions in several Asian nations. Reporter Lynn Kamm told of Praiwan Krasang, a thirteen-year-old living in Bangkok, who makes leather handbags from eight in the morning until eleven at night, with an hour off for lunch and again for dinner—for a wage of $24 a month. "After work," wrote Kamm, "Praiwan washes his clothes, waits in a long line for a shower and doesn't usually get to bed in his small, dirty room much before one a.m. On his days off—the second and fourth Sunday of every month—he heads for the Social Service Center in Bangkok. It's the only place where he can read and educate himself toward his goal of becoming a scientist." The article was headlined: "How Our Greed Keeps Kids Trapped in Foreign Sweatshops."

It turned out that Thailand and Bangladesh were only two of many hotspots. According to the International Labor Organization, an agency of the United Nations, child laborers number in the hundreds of millions worldwide. Moreover, the agency says, the trend is worsening because of a "global rural-to-urban migration" and a "breakdown of production into more decentralized units." These factors send children into the urban "informal sector" as street hawkers and workers in small, often illegal, manufacturing plants.

Pharis Harvey, executive director of the nonprofit International Labor Rights Education and Research Fund, attributes the rise in child labor to the globalization of production. "With computerization, you can produce fairly sophisticated goods, with the most labor-intensive parts singled out and shipped out to be done wherever it's the cheapest," he says. Developing nations typically lure multinational corporations by creating "export-processing zones" with tax incentives and abundant cheap labor. In many cases, companies who manufacture there are exempted from local and national environmental and labor laws. Among other things, that sets the stage for the use of child labor. Not only are children inexpensive to employ, they are easily intimidated, don't know their rights, and have little apprehension of the dangers of operating machinery, say international labor experts. Moreover, children in some developing nations are the sole or major means of support for their families. In a country like Indonesia, where the minimum wage averages only 40 to 60 percent of the amount necessary for a typical family to survive, parents are often forced to send their children to work. In some cases, the children's wages can be a family's only source of income.

Business Partner Terms of Engagement

Our concerns include the practices of individual business partners as well as the political and social issues in those countries where we might consider sourcing.

This defines Terms of Engagements which addresses issues that are substantially controllable by our individual business partners. . . .

1. **Environmental Requirements:** We will only do business with partners who share our commitment to the environment. (Note: We intend this standard to be consistent with the approved language of Levi Strauss & Co.'s Environmental Action Group.)

2. **Ethical Standards:** We will seek to identify and utilize business partners who aspire as individuals and in the conduct of their business to a set of ethical standards not incompatible with our own.

3. **Health and Safety:** We will only utilize business partners who provide workers with a safe and healthy work environment. Business partners who provide residential facilities for their workers must provide safe and healthy facilities.

4. **Legal Requirements:** We expect our business partners to be law abiding as individuals and to comply with legal requirements relevant to the conduct of their business.

5. **Employment Practices:** We will only do business with partners whose workers are in all cases present voluntarily, not put at risk of physical harm, fairly compensated, allowed the right of free association and not exploited in any way. In addition, the following specific guidelines will be followed.

   • **Wages and Benefits:** We will only do business with partners who provide wages and benefits that comply with any applicable law or match the prevailing local manufacturing or finishing industry practices. We will also favor business partners who share our commitment to contribute to the betterment of community conditions.

Business Partner Terms of Engagement (continued)

- **Working Hours:** While permitting flexibility in scheduling, we will identify prevailing local work hours and seek business partners who do not exceed them except for appropriately compensated overtime. While we favor partners who utilize less than sixty-hour work weeks, we will not use contractors who, on a regularly scheduled basis, require in excess of a sixty-hour week. Employees should be allowed one day off in seven days.
- **Child Labor:** Use of child labor is not permissible. "Child" is defined as less than 14 years of age or younger than the compulsory age to be in school. We will not utilize partners who use child labor in any of their facilities. We support the development of legitimate workplace apprenticeship programs for the educational benefit of younger people.
- **Prison Labor/Forced Labor:** We will not knowingly utilize prison or forced labor in contracting or subcontracting relationships in the manufacture of our products. We will not knowingly utilize or purchase materials from a business partner utilizing prison or forced labor.
- **Discrimination:** While we recognize and respect cultural differences, we believe that workers should be employed on the basis of their ability to do the job, rather than on the basis of personal characteristics or beliefs. We will favor business partners who share this value.
- **Disciplinary Practices:** We will not utilize business partners who use corporal punishment or other forms of mental or physical coercion.

—LEVI STRAUSS & CO., WORLDWIDE POLICY

Such reports and the increased media coverage helped put some companies on the defensive. Not at Levi Strauss, however. "We got a phone call from one of our largest retail customers saying their board had been meeting the day after the NBC broadcast and that they would not accept any products from us or anyone else that were made in Bangladesh because they thought it would be unacceptable to their consumers," recalls Bob Dunn. Fortunately, Dunn was able to describe to this customer his company's well-established code of conduct for its suppliers, which specifically addresses child-labor conditions, and to explain how the company already had taken measures to eliminate abuses encountered in its Bangladesh contractors' factories.

Actually, the company's solution here was instructive about the complexity and challenges business faces in such situations. When Levi Strauss inspectors found children working in two factories in

---

Guidelines for Country Selection

The following country selection criteria address issues which we believe are beyond the ability of the individual business partner to control:

1. Brand Image. We will not initiate or renew contractual relationships in countries where sourcing would have an adverse effect on our global brand image.
2. Health and Safety. We will not initiate or renew contractual relationships in countries where there is evidence that company employees or representatives would be exposed to unreasonable risk.
3. Human Rights. We should not initiate or renew contractual relationships in countries where there are pervasive violations of basic human rights.
4. Legal Requirements. We will not initiate or renew contractual relationships in countries where the legal environment creates unreasonable risk to our trademarks or to other important commercial interests or seriously impedes our ability to implement these guidelines.
5. Political or Social Stability. We will not initiate or renew contractual relationships in countries where political or social turmoil unreasonably threatens our commercial interest.

—LEVI STRAUSS & CO., WORLDWIDE POLICY

Bangladesh, they sat down with the contractors and ordered the kids out or the plant shut down. As Dunn tells it, "The contractors said, 'Fine, we'll kick the kids out tomorrow. You should know that the kids are the sole source of support for their families. If that's what you want, fine.'

"So we said, 'We'll cut a deal with you. Let's have them go to school [instead of working] until they're of legitimate working age. You pay the kids their wages and we'll pay for the books, uniforms, and tuition. And let's agree that you're not going to hire any more kids who are under age.' The contractors agreed. So we took fifty kids out of two factories and sent them to school in cooperation with the contractors." Because Levi Strauss had such initiatives in place, their products were allowed to go on the concerned retailer's shelves. "It was one of our large accounts in the Midwest," Dunn goes on. "The average per capita income in Bangladesh is about $200, so these kids were earning less than $20 a month. It wasn't a huge sum of money. But it was something we were willing to do."

Levi Strauss wasn't the only company to receive calls after the NBC broadcast, though not everyone was as well prepared as Dunn to respond. Still, the Wal-Mart episode got companies moving. The day after the NBC broadcast, Home Depot, a nationwide chain of do-it-yourself stores, developed a questionnaire seeking information on labor practices, which it subsequently required all overseas vendors to fill out.

It's doubtful that questionnaires alone will be sufficient to change centuries-old labor practices. More significant, perhaps, was that a single television show brought to the public's consciousness the largely hands-off foreign-labor policies of many multinational businesses. And companies were forced to reveal their practices to reporters, customers, investors, and the world at large. Those that had already confronted these tough issues were prepared for such disclosure and were less vulnerable to public embarrassment and lost sales. Those that hadn't could do little but try to control the damage.

THE CAUX ROUND TABLE PRINCIPLES

One of the problems confronting companies doing business in foreign countries has been the lack of an agreed-upon set of standards about what constitutes socially responsible behavior. The Caux Round Table Principles may help change that.

The Caux Round Table Principles, subtitled "Business Behavior for a Better World," and covering company operations on foreign soil, were modeled on the Minnesota Principles, created in 1992 by the Minnesota Center for Corporate Responsibility, based at St. Thomas University and focusing on socially responsible business issues. The Minnesota Principles, a "statement of aspirations" whose purpose "express a standard against which our often inadequate performance can be held accountable," describe socially responsible behavior between companies and their customers, employees, owners/investors, suppliers, communities, and competitors.

In 1993, a new set of principles focusing on international business was adopted by the Caux Round Table. The group, an international association of executives based in Caux, Switzerland, believes that "business organizations can be a powerful force for positive change in the quality of life for many in this world," according to Dr. Walter Hoadley, chairman of the Round Table steering committee. The Caux Round Table Principles consist of seven general principles (see box) and a series of stakeholder principles. "Business behavior can affect relationships among nations and the prosperity of well-being of us all," reads the introduction. "Business is often the first contact between nations and, by the way in which it causes social and economic changes, has a significant impact on the level of fear or of confidence felt by people .worldwide."

The principles are rooted partly in the Japanese concept of *kyosei,* roughly interpreted to mean "living and working together for the common good." Its appearance is due largely to the influence of Ryuzaburo Kaku, president of Canon Inc., the Japanese electronics company. For years, Kaku has taken an active interest in the behavior of companies operating overseas. In a publication entitled *Canon Around the World,* he writes:

> In accordance with the spirit of kyosei, we are determined to fulfill our growing social responsibilities and make a genuine contribution to the communities that provide the basis of our wide-ranging global operations. Canon is convinced that no global corporation can ever hope to prosper without contributing to the welfare of people and society at large.

It is too early to tell exactly how widely the Caux Round Table Principles will be adopted—and, of course, how much they will be put into practice. But the principles represent a clear statement of what is increasingly being expected of companies operating globally.

The Caux Round Table Principles

Preamble

The mobility of employment, capital, products, and technology is making business increasingly global in its transactions and its effects.

Laws and market forces are necessary but insufficient guides for conduct.

Responsibility for a business's policies and actions and respect for the dignity and interests of its stakeholders are fundamental.

Shared values, including a commitment to shared prosperity, are as important for a global community as for communities of smaller scale.

For these reasons, and because business can be a powerful agent of positive social change, we offer the following principles as a foundation for dialogue and action by business leaders in search of business responsibility. In so doing, we affirm the necessity for moral values in business decision making. Without them, stable business relationships and a sustainable world community are impossible.

General Principles

1. The Responsibilities of Businesses: Beyond Shareholders toward Stakeholders.

The value of a business to society is the wealth and employment it creates and the marketable products and services it provides to consumers at a reasonable price commensurate with quality. To create such a value, a business must maintain its own economic health and viability, but survival is not a sufficient goal.

Business has a role to play in improving the lives of all of its customers, employees, and shareholders by sharing with them the wealth it has created. Suppliers and competitors as well should expect businesses to honor their obligations in a spirit of honesty and fairness. And as responsible citizens of the local, national, regional, and global communities in which they operate, businesses share a part in shaping the future of those communities.

The Caux Round Table Principles
(continued)

2. The Economic and Social Impact of Business: Beyond Shareholders toward Justice and World Community.

Businesses established in foreign countries to develop, produce, or sell should also contribute to the social advancement of those countries by creating productive employment and helping to raise purchasing power of their citizens. Businesses also should contribute to human rights, education, welfare, and vitalization of communities in which they operate.

In order to contribute to the economic and social development in not only the communities in which they operate, but also in the world community at large, businesses should use resources effectively and prudently, compete freely and fairly, and innovate aggressively with new technology, production methods, marketing, and communications.

3. Business Behavior: Beyond the Letter of Law toward a Spirit of Trust.

While accepting the legitimacy of trade secrets, a business should recognize that sincerity, candor, truthfulness, the keeping of promises, and transparency contribute not only to their own credit and stability but also to the smoothness and efficiency of business transactions, particularly on the international level.

4. Respect for Rules.

To avoid trade frictions and to promote freer trade, equal business opportunity, and fair and equitable treatment for all participants, businesses should respect international and domestic rules. In addition, they should recognize that some behavior, although legal, may still have adverse consequences.

5. Support for Multilateral Trade.

Businesses should support the multilateral trade systems of GATT/World Trade Organization and similar international agreements. They should cooperate in efforts to promote the judicious liberalization of trade and to relax those domestic measures that unreasonably hinder global commerce.

The Caux Round Table Principles
(continued)

6. Respect for the Environment.

A business should protect, and where possible, improve the environment, promote sustainable development, and prevent the wasteful use of natural resources.

7. Avoidance of Illicit Operations.

A business should not participate in or condone bribery, money laundering, and other corrupt practices: indeed, it should seek cooperation with others to eliminate them. It should not trade in arms or other materials used for terrorist activities, drug traffic or other organized crime.

At the very least, they should provide a basis for socially responsible companies to create their own set of rules for business behavior wherever they may operate.

THE CHINA CONUNDRUM

There's probably no issue that better illustrates the complexity of making ethical decisions than the question of doing business in China. Following the Chinese government's 1989 crackdown on the student-led pro-democracy movement—an event that has become known to the world simply as "Tiananmen Square"—several companies began to rethink their growing business links with China. Then as now, China had been relinquishing its tight control on economic activity, luring hundreds of major corporations with a 1.5 billion populace as a new cheap source of manufacturing and a gigantic market for selling products. *The Economist* magazine, for one, has flatly predicted that China will have the world's largest economy within the next quarter century.

But the government's controls on its citizens have not faded as quickly. The government does not tolerate free speech or dissident political activists and tightly regulates citizens' lives and work habits, including whether and when they can have children. Violators can lose their jobs or even their lives. The situation has befuddled experts around the world and became the focus of a fractious debate within the Clinton administration and throughout the country in 1994, over whether to extend Most Favored Nation trading status to the Chinese government. As that debate revealed, determining the "right" course is far from easy. It has been no less easy for some company executives.

The Tiananmen Square uprising shook the world—including the business world. Large corporations, such as AT&T, Coca-Cola, and Ford Motor Company, already had invested tens of millions of dollars in China-based enterprises, with commitments of many millions more, all of which suddenly seemed in jeopardy. Meanwhile, executives at some companies that had begun or were considering manufacturing goods in Chinese factories asked themselves whether they should be doing business at all in a nation whose government killed countless unarmed students, among other atrocities.

Three companies known for their socially responsible policies—Levi Strauss, Timberland, and Reebok—took different approaches and reached different conclusions. Timberland executives had a visceral reaction to China's policies, citing human rights conditions, and decided immediately to pull their operations out of the country. Levi Strauss stepped back and studied the situation, ultimately deciding to curtail or forgo its Chinese operations. Reebok, like most other companies, reaffirmed its commitment to doing business in China. The company decided to try and work within the country to effect changes in China's human rights policies, and developed a framework for instituting workplace and human rights standards for people in its factories there. It began manufacturing shoes soon afterward.

"We were concerned about the reports we had heard about the use of forced labor in workplace settings," says Reebok's Doug Cahn. "We certainly didn't want to be a part of any factory that was engaged in human rights abuses. So we adopted a policy that no Reebok shoes would be manufactured in factories that used prison labor. We required our business partners to sign a statement attesting to that, and it became part of the arrangement between Reebok and the factories we contracted with."

In 1992, Reebok broadened its workplace standards to include such factors as child labor and the length of the work week. A Reebok task force devised a system for auditing all of its overseas business partners. Working with an inspection team, Cahn now visits all the

Reebok Human Rights Production Standards

Nondiscrimination. Reebok will seek business partners that do not discriminate in hiring and employment practices on grounds of race, color, national origin, gender, religion, or political or other opinion.

Working hours/overtime. Reebok will seek business partners who do not require more than 60-hour work weeks on a regularly scheduled basis, except for appropriately compensated overtime in compliance with local laws, and we will favor business partners who use 48-hour work weeks as their maximum normal requirement.

Forced or compulsory labor. Reebok will not work with business partners that use forced or other compulsory labor, including labor that is required as a means for political coercion or as punishment for holding or for peacefully expressing political views, in the manufacture of its products. Reebok will not purchase materials that were produced by forced prison or other compulsory labor and will terminate business relationships with any sources found to utilize such labor.

Fair wages. Reebok will seek business partners who share our commitment to the betterment of wage and benefit levels that address the basic needs of workers and their families so far as possible and appropriate in light of national practices and conditions. Reebok will not select business partners that pay less than the minimum wage required by local law or that pay less than prevailing local industry practices (whichever is higher).

Child labor. Reebok will not work with business partners that use child labor. The term "child" generally refers to a person who is less than 14 years of age, or younger than the age for completing compulsory education if that age is higher than 14. In countries where the law defines "child" to include individuals who are older than 14, Reebok will apply that definition.

Reebok Human Rights Production
Standards (continued)

Freedom of association. Reebok will seek business partners that share its commitment to the right of employees to
establish and join organizations of their own choosing. Reebok will seek to assure that no employee is penalized because
of his or her non-violent exercise of this right. Reebok recognizes and respects the right of all employees to organize
and bargain collectively.

Safe and healthy work environment. Reebok will seek
business partners that strive to assure employees a safe and
healthy workplace and that do not expose workers to hazardous conditions.

factories, making recommendations and following up on them. "It's
an ongoing effort," he says. "It's not a one-shot deal, something you
do on Tuesday and if there are any problems they're cleaned up by
Friday and that's the last of it. It's a corporate commitment on an
ongoing basis to produce the highest-quality shoes using factories
that engage in the highest-quality workplace environments."

The two are inextricably linked, he says. "You can't produce a
high-quality athletic shoe in an environment that isn't clean and safe.
You won't be able to retain the highest-quality workers and you
won't have shoes clean enough to put in the box at the end of the
line. So there is a direct correlation between the human rights standards, the workplace environment, and the quality of the product
that comes out."

Cahn admits there are limits to his company's impact on government policies. "We are not a government, not an all-knowing, all-
powerful force in the world. But I strongly believe that corporations
have a responsibility to the consumers who purchase their products
to assure that those products are manufactured in ways that are
consistent with the values of those consumers."

The folks at Levi Strauss would agree, though they came to view
the China situation somewhat differently. The company has a long-
held reputation for adhering to its social values in determining where

to set up shop. In the 1950s, for example, it pressured officials in some American southern states to allow the company to operate integrated facilities as a condition of doing business. Where it met resistance—in Alabama and Mississippi, for example—the company refused to open factories, despite the appeal of cheap labor and access to transportation and raw materials. Years later, Levi Strauss was at the forefront of companies refusing to do business in racially divided South Africa.

So when the question of China came along, the company already had a track record of putting its morals where its markets were. Along the way, Levi Strauss had established a set of ethical guidelines for suppliers—what it calls its "Terms of Engagement," covering the "practices of individual business partners as well as the political and social issues" in countries that serve as sources for the company's products. Among other things, they spell out the conditions on employment practices for potential business partners, from wages and benefits to working conditions and child labor.

As company executives discussed the China question, a few suggested that "we had to go beyond the individual contractor and recognize that there were times when we had to look at a country and think about whether there were reasons we wouldn't want to be there," says Bob Dunn. He and others formed a task force to examine the question. "We wondered whether there was a way to craft a standard that would apply," Dunn continues. "We came up with language stating that if there was a pervasive violation of basic human rights, that would suggest we shouldn't be there."

The group developed four criteria for determining whether violations were "pervasive": they had to affect nearly everyone; they had to be serious in nature; they had to be essentially supported by the policy of the government; and there had to be no indication that favorable change was under way. "If we felt that all four of these were true, then we probably didn't belong," says Dunn. "We weren't trying to be overly simplistic or pure and say we're only going to do business in Switzerland. But we wanted to acknowledge that at any given time there are a handful of countries that are really pariahs, outlaws in the community of nations. And given what we stand for, we have a set of core values that include respect for diversity and the dignity of individuals. How can we be in a place like that and claim these values have any meaning?"

To rate China's human rights policies, the task force created a system similar to the one used by *Consumer Reports* to rate automobiles and other products: a series of circles—empty, filled in one-quarter, half, three-quarters, or all black—reflected the severity of human rights abuses; the blacker the circle, the greater the abuses. Using a list of rights drawn from a U.N. declaration, Dunn and Elissa Sheridan, his assistant, rated China's policies. "When we presented it to the task force, what we had was virtually a page of all black circles. The group was very unhappy with that and said, 'Let's go back and go through these one at a time and compare China to a number of other countries that we think may have serious problems but that are okay.' So we did that. We went back and looked at China versus other countries and it was clear that China was worse."

To double-check its findings, the task force brought in consultants—human rights advocates, leaders of China's pro-democracy movement, business consultants, officials at other companies. "We brought as much information into the room as we could," says Dunn. "When we finished, the group voted unanimously that China satisfied our definition—that there was, in fact, a pervasive violation of human rights there. And then we had a real dilemma because most of the group really wanted us to be in China."

A debate ensued. Some in the group thought the company should change its guidelines so Levi Strauss could stay in China and try to make a difference. Others thought that the existing guidelines should be honored and that Levi Strauss should stay out of China.

The discussions continued for weeks. Would it be more compassionate for the company to create jobs and enhance the quality of life for people living under an oppressive system, or to withhold capital and employment in the hopes of ultimately promoting greater freedom? The group debated the nitty-gritty questions: Could Levi Strauss managers enforce the Chinese government's one-child-per-family policy, a policy in which not only could an employee be fired for having a second child, but the employee's *manager* might be fired, too? At the end of the estimated 2,000 or so person-hours, the task force was deadlocked.

In the end, the decision was made to stay out of China. Says Dunn: "Our chairman felt, consistent with what we had done in the past, that if we had gone into China, that we would not have honored one of our values, which says that we'll go to great lengths to keep our promises, even at some cost to us. This would have been a decision dictated purely by financial consequences and not by ethical consequences.

"You have to understand that one of our rules is that ethics trumps other considerations," Dunn goes on. "So if we are making a decision and there are ethical arguments to make one decision and nonethical arguments in favor of a contrary view, the ethical argument prevails. Ethics is one of our six core values. Ethics is a ground rule. It applies to all decisions and overcomes other arguments. So we considered briefly and abandoned the idea that we should go in because we could improve human rights in China. Some people wanted to make that argument at the beginning. We tested it and it seemed pretty presumptuous for us to think that this little company employing a couple thousand people was going to have a real impact on human rights in China."

Levi Strauss's struggle to determine whether or not to do business in the world's most populous nation is instructive to a point. While it provides a rare peek into the internal machinations of one business reviewing its responsibility as a global corporate citizen, even Dunn concedes his company's decision on China may not be applicable to others. "We never said that other companies should do what we did," he points out. "Given our values and what we stand for, we were trying to make a decision that was proper for us. We think that others with the same values could make a different decision that was proper for them." As it's turned out, not many companies have reached the same conclusion as Levi Strauss did about staying out of China.

In the end, the issue isn't only China, or even human rights. The debate could just as likely have taken place over any of a number of countries involving a variety of workplace, social, and political issues. As business operations continue to expand in scope abroad, it is likely that more such debates over corporate values and local conditions will take place.

LOTUS AND SOUTH AFRICA

Lotus Development Corporation, reconciling its ethical and financial goals, made a decision to open operations in South Africa in 1992. This decision was a reversal for the Cambridge, Massachusetts–based computer software company, known for its best-selling spreadsheet program *1-2-3*. Early on, Lotus had supported sanctions that barred trade with the white-controlled South African regime. In 1985, a year before the federal government enacted the Anti-Apartheid Act banning U.S. investment in South Africa, the company initiated a policy that it would not do business in that country as long as apartheid existed because of Lotus's stated commitment "to stand against discrimination in all aspects of our business."

So, Lotus's turnaround turned heads in the business community. Though the U.S. government's official ban against South African investment had been repealed in 1991, anti-apartheid groups were holding firm in calling for an international boycott against South Africa until a democratically elected government was in place. Moreover, Lotus had become recognized as a company that generally supports its work forces around the world. Just a month before the South Africa announcement, for example, it had become the first publicly traded U.S. corporation to offer health and other benefits to the live-in partners of gay and lesbian employees. Lotus also has had one of the most progressive diversity-training programs in American industry.

So why did Lotus renege on its South Africa commitment? In part because the company's executives believed they could do so in a responsible way and become a positive force for change in the beleaguered nation. Rather than merely set up offices in what was then the white-dominated business sector, as other companies had done, Lotus made a commitment to the development of the black business community, including training black South Africans to assume managerial positions. As Mackie McLeod puts it: "We thought we might be able to set new agendas and trends for other firms."

McLeod, an African-American computer hacker and anti-apartheid activist, was hired to run Lotus's South African social investment trust, a roughly $350,000 annual fund to assist black community self-help projects in South Africa. The trust was part of an international program Lotus had run for years to fund social responsibility programs in countries where it operates. McLeod's specific mandate was to work directly with black-run information technology projects. Among his early efforts was to send a group of South Africa's top black computer instructors to Lotus's Massachusetts headquarters for advanced training. He also created an internship program for black programming trainees in Johannesburg.

Lotus's initiative was a sea change from most previous corporate efforts in South Africa, which had been run by whites and favored placing its philanthropic gifts in the hands of large, well-established, white-run groups. In contrast, Lotus attempted to "use our business to do what we can in terms of nontraditional business development," according to Michael Durney, director of U.S. philanthropy and community affairs programs for the software company.

Durney explains the company's strategy: "We felt that apartheid was an abhorrent system and flew in the face of everything we were attempting to do, let alone that it was a basic human rights issue that should be addressed. So for us to reverse that in a way that could be viewed as opportunistic was of concern to us. We also wanted to be sure that we were doing the right thing. We were lucky enough that we did and still have friends in a wide variety of organizations and political organizations in South Africa and were able to poll those people and get some kind of consensus about how we might go in there in a way that conceivably could set a standard for other U.S. companies following us."

Lotus's involvement in South Africa has taken a couple of different thrusts. One has to do with using its business as an agent for change. The company formed a partnership with the only nonwhite software distributorship in the country, which has since become one of the largest distributorships in South Africa. Lotus invested time and resources providing the technical assistance to bring the distributorship up to the requisite professional level. The company also has sought out opportunities to develop other business entities among the black population, a challenge in a country where the overwhelming majority of educated professionals are white, and has worked with indigenous community-based organizations to enhance technological literacy and skills. Part of that effort involved bringing directors of community-training programs to Cambridge to show them firsthand the training program Lotus operates for nonprofit organizations. Lotus also made grants of cash and software, and created an internship program in which participants learn to operate computer networks.

Initially, the company was criticized by some in the business community for breaking the sanctions against doing business in South Africa. That criticism eventually mellowed into begrudging respect for the manner in which Lotus entered the marketplace. But creating a trained and technically proficient work force has proved challenging and costly, as demand has skyrocketed for the small number of professional black South Africans. Still, Durney and his colleagues feel good about what Lotus has achieved in South Africa. So, it seems, do other companies: Mackie McLeod spends a considerable amount of his time showing a parade of interested companies what Lotus has done.

Michael Durney expresses satisfaction with Lotus's small role in helping to move a new generation of black South Africans into leadership positions for the country's emerging integrated business community. During the months leading up to South Africa's historic 1994 elections—creating the country's first democratically elected government in more than 200 years—Lotus's philanthropy played a role. In 1993, the company donated both money and its *cc:Mail* electronic-mail software to the Matla Trust, one of South Africa's principal voter education and election-monitoring groups. It also provided training on computer networks to sixteen systems monitors in eight election districts. That system was vital in helping South Africa's independent electoral commission conduct a reliable parallel vote count, which was analyzed by the United Nations and other election monitors.

Durney says that from a business perspective, Lotus's investments in South Africa have met with mixed success. One reason may have had to do with the two-part nature of the company's activities there. Half of the company's focus was on philanthropic activities—donations, training, and so forth—while the other half aimed at tapping South Africa as a new market for sales of Lotus products. Although the philanthropic activities were generally deemed successful, the sales efforts have taken longer to bear fruit. For example, the white business community—the principal market for Lotus products up until the 1994 elections—seemed to be holding back on investments in new technologies, given the uncertainty of the post-election business climate. And Lotus hadn't viewed South Africa's black business community in anything other than philanthropic terms.

But all that was destined to change. "There's a major growth opportunity in the black community that we're just beginning to think about and figure out what our business approach is going to be," says Durney. "We need to treat it as a major market opportunity, not just a community affairs kind of thing." He is confident that over time, Lotus's philanthropic and business interests will merge in a vote of confidence for the socially responsible manner in which the company has conducted business in what used to be one of the world's most politically sensitive markets.

WHEN DOING THE "RIGHT THING" FAILS

The tales of environmental, ethical, and social violations by companies working abroad are well told. But sometimes what seems to socially responsible leaders to be the right decision proves wrong.

This points up the amount of care that needs to be taken in conducting business operations on foreign soil.

Consider the tortured tale of Tony Andersen, chairman and CEO of H. B. Fuller Co., the Minnesota-based maker of adhesives, sealants, coatings, and paints. The tale has to do with one of the company's more than 10,000 products, a line of solvent-based glues sold under the brand name Resistol, manufactured by a wholly owned South American subsidiary. Resistol products are used in a variety of industrial and commercial settings, including small shoe-manufacturing factories. Resistol is not sold in the United States or Europe, where manufacturers use different technologies and adhesives.

The problem with Resistol is that a key ingredient, toluene, has become a highly addictive inhalant favored by young street urchins— mostly orphaned and abandoned adolescents. For them, toluene provides a cheap thrill, a diversion from the poverty and hopelessness that engulfs their lives. When high on toluene fumes, users experience wild mood swings and often turn violent, fighting among themselves or attacking anyone unfortunate enough to happen along their path. Violence, though, may be the least of the problems. Toluene is a known carcinogen, and is associated with irreversible kidney failure and brain damage. (Resistol products are far from the only toluene-based goods sold in Latin America; in Mexico, for example, the chemical is found in more than 300 other products. Fuller also sells other toluene-based products in the United States.) So bad is the problem, say social workers in Central America, that virtually all of the 5,000 or so children living on the streets of Guatemala City are glue sniffers. They have become so common in Guatemala, Honduras, and other Central American countries that in some parts of the region they are known as *resistoleros*.

Andersen and other H. B. Fuller executives had been aware of the Resistol abuse problem since the early 1980s, though the matter remained largely unpublicized until 1990, when a *resistoleros* shelter program was established to combat the addiction problem. Along the way, Fuller scientists had labored to develop a substitute product sans toluene, to no avail. Another problem was that a lot of the small shoe factories worked under specifications that called for Resistol by name. Without a viable substitute, many of Fuller's manufacturing customers would be unable to ply their trade.

Still, there were things Fuller could do, and ultimately did. The company had been selling Resistol in two ways: in industrial-sized, 55-gallon drums, and in smaller, "over-the-counter" quart- and pint-sized containers. It was the latter version, commonly sold in hardware stores, that was the principal source for abusers. In 1991, Fuller announced that it would stop selling Resistol in small containers. It also tried to tighten its control of industrial-sized containers. "We sat down with the management of those companies and said, 'We will continue to supply you only if you can convince us that you have control in your shop and that there is going to be no leakage of the product out of the factory into the street,' " says Andersen. "Then we would go through what control devices they have, who has access, how they have access, and other matters. We wanted to go the extra mile to assure ourselves that if we sold that product over there, it wasn't going to find its way into the street." At the same time, Fuller initiated a social program that aims to educate kids about the danger of addiction and urges them to stay in school so that they can escape the grinding poverty that is at the root of the social problems. Fuller still spends an estimated $100,000 a year on these education efforts.

Such efforts didn't stop Fuller's critics, who became progressively more vocal. The Resistol debate dominated the company's 1993 annual shareholders' meeting, which was picketed by a group of protesters calling themselves the Coalition on Resistoleros. They accused the company of failing to keep its pledge to stop Resistol production in problem areas and said Fuller products continued to damage children's health. They called for the company to add a noxious substance—mustard oil—to Resistol to discourage sniffing. Andersen countered, explaining that the additive wouldn't attack the social and economic reasons that sent Latin American kids onto the streets and into addiction. Andersen also noted that organizations such as Street Kids International, the World Health Organization, and Childhope, a United Nations group, supported the company's approach of funding social and education programs as the most effective means of dealing with inhalant abuse.

In the fall of 1993, the company became yet another target of "Dateline: NBC," which aired a segment alleging that Resistol continued to be abused by Latin American street kids. Four days after the broadcast, Fuller announced that it would take all Resistol products out of Honduras and end all but industrial supplies to Guatemala. But the *resistoleros* activists remained suspicious of the firm's intentions—primarily because Fuller did not recall all the Resistol on the market and because the product continued to be available in neighboring countries where it was smuggled across borders and onto the streets of Guatemala and Honduras. Finally, in the spring of 1994,

Fuller announced that together with an unnamed partner it would develop new polymers for use in water-based adhesives that could replace Resistol.

The entire episode has been a trial by fire for Andersen, whose company has a generally good reputation on workplace, community, and environmental issues. Fuller is a member of Minnesota's Five Percent Club, the group of corporations that contribute 5 percent of their pre-tax profits to the community. It was only the second *Fortune* 500 company to endorse the CERES Principles, the environmental code of ethics detailed in chapter 6. And yet Fuller's name is linked with a horrific addiction affecting thousands of poverty-stricken children.

For Fuller—and, potentially, other companies caught in similar quagmires—the Resistol affair has provided some difficult, albeit valuable, lessons about how to respond to such situations. "If we learned one thing, it's that when you discover you've got a problem like that, the best thing to do is to not just get on your knees and hope and pray that the lab comes up with a solution, but make the move of getting the product out of the marketplace where it's doing harm," says Andersen. "Then, if you come up with a product that's less harmful or not harmful at all, you can always come back into the market. In hindsight, I guess we saw that, but did not take the action at the time.

"As we were beginning to recognize this was a problem," he continues, "we could see that this was a classic case of a socially responsible company caught up in a very complex subject. The conundrum of it is, how much responsibility does a manufacturer have for the illegitimate use of a product that was designed to do something and when used legitimately really isn't a problem? My sense is that you cannot draw a hard-and-fast line. I believe that there is some responsibility no matter how benign. It's a very gray area. But there has to be some sensitivity of the degree to which the product could be harmful or hurtful."

Andersen asked the University of Minnesota business school to do a case study on the subject. Two professors (one of whom held the Elmer L. Andersen Chair in Corporate Social Responsibility, endowed in the name of Tony Andersen's father, a former Fuller CEO) visited Latin America and later wrote a case study; it is now used at Columbia University's business school, among other places. Fuller is still learning, too, because the problems continue. Despite Fuller's efforts to develop a substitute, Resistol is still being sold to industrial users

Dealing with Ethical Dilemmas

Often, a company's operation runs up against local customs and cultures. It is during those tough times that the true nature of a company's philosophy and ethics shines through. Many companies have well-established policies holding their overseas employees to the same ethical standards as when doing business at home.

Executives at Cargill, Inc., a large, privately held grain-trading company, deal with both small and big business issues in the same way. For example, they have wrestled with whether a company employee should slip the phone company clerk a few extra dollars to get an office telephone installed in a certain West African city. Or whether to pay a "management fee" to an intermediary in order to secure a long-term contract in East Africa for tea. The answer to both questions is no. Cargill's foremost business principle states, "We will be involved only in businesses or markets where ethical, legal, and responsible business conduct is possible." Local customs notwithstanding, said the company's leaders, Cargill employees worldwide must operate under a single set of ethical standards.

in Central America. And dozens of other companies have stepped in to fill the market for smaller "over-the-counter" quantities of toluene-based glue abandoned by Fuller.

"We as a single company are not going to be able to solve by ourselves the problems that create the need or the want of inhalant abuse," Andersen acknowledges. "Against that challenge, we are a very small voice. But society is slowly beginning to understand that they've got some real problems and they're going to have to deal with them. Inhalant abuse goes on in Washington, D.C. It goes on in St. Paul, Minnesota. It goes on everywhere."

Andersen agrees that this fact does not absolve Fuller or any other company from the responsibility it has over the fate of the products it makes. Nor does it establish whether the company adequately addressed its responsibility in trying to keep its product on the market while attacking what it perceived to be the root of the problem by funding the education and rehabilitation of addicted children.

Whatever the verdict, the Resistol case shows that even companies with laudable mission statements and track records are not immune from external factors that may undermine their best intentions. That's a simple reality of doing business. The challenge is for socially responsible companies to confront head-on what problems do arise, addressing them openly and honestly, in a spirit of putting people before profits. In the long run, that approach inevitably yields the greatest returns for everyone.

CREATING ECONOMIC OPPORTUNITY

Much as William Norris, the driving force behind Control Data Corporation, recognized the potential benefits in "addressing unmet societal needs as profitable business opportunities" (see chapter 2), some companies have sought out such opportunities among the citizens of Third World nations. Tabra Tunoa, the entrepreneur we met in chapter 7, whose jewelry designs and materials come from her travels to Asia, Africa, Latin America, and elsewhere, is one example. Among her joys and satisfactions is identifying groups of indigenous women in remote parts of these countries and contracting with them to provide beads or artifacts for her work. In so doing, she helps provide income to some of the world's poorest citizens without disrupting their cultures.

A number of companies have tapped the resources of the tropical rain forests in a manner aimed at ensuring their ecological sustainability, as well as the economic sustainability of those living there. For example, Shaman Pharmaceuticals, a startup founded in 1990, is discovering and developing new low-cost, plant-based pharmaceutical products, isolating active compounds from tropical plants that have a history of medicinal use. So far, it has created two products. The first, Provir, is a substance taken orally that has demonstrated efficacy against a broad spectrum of respiratory viruses. The second, Virend, is a topical antiviral product for the treatment of herpes simplex virus. Both are undergoing clinical trials. Also in development is a compound potentially useful to treat fungal infections associated with AIDS.

Another company, the Aveda Corporation, which manufactures a line of cosmetics, skin care, and hair care products, operates a 25,000-

square-foot research-and-development center at its headquarters out-side Minneapolis, where it develops products made from plants collected from around the world. Horst Rechelbacher, Aveda's chair-man and founder, has integrated into the company's operating phi-losophy the importance of working with indigenous cultures in nearly fifty countries to obtain the plants used for his company's products. "By working with organic growers, indigenous tribes, and sustainable sources of agriculture, we are enabling small local cul-tures to help their people preserve their wisdom," says Rechelbacher.

In 1994, for example, Rechelbacher signed an agreement with the chief of the Yawanawa tribe from the Brazilian rain forest, in which the tribe will grow bixa—a traditional red coloring used for tribal ceremonies—for use in Aveda's cosmetics. "In Brazil, white profi-teers interested in establishing cattle farms and wood mills are ag-gressively pursuing the last vast rain forest in the world," explains Rechelbacher. "As a result of protecting their land, the indigenous tribes throughout Brazil are facing economic dependence, bondage, and terrorist attacks. The tribes can only survive by establishing technological and commercial alliances to justify their stand against cattle ranchers and wood millers." Aveda's efforts have attracted the attention of Brazilian government agencies, which have stepped in to offer the tribes technical support.

On another scale altogether is Merck & Co., the pharmaceutical company, which in 1991 signed an agreement with the Instituto Nacional de Biodiversidad (Inbio), a nonprofit, private organization in Costa Rica, in which Merck paid $1 million over two years to support Inbio's research on rain forest plants. Costa Rica, a country only the size of West Virginia, is thought to possess 5 to 7 percent of the world's biodiversity. Merck and others believe that many of these species of plants and microorganisms have medicinal value and can help create a sort of natural pharmacy of healing ingredients. Already, roughly half of the prescription drugs and over-the-counter medi-cines available today contain active ingredients derived directly from flowering plants, bacteria, and fungi. The kind of "biodiversity pros-pecting" in which Merck and other pharmaceutical companies are engaged has the potential to provide jobs and steady income to local residents, who can harvest and process this lode of natural ingredi-ents in a manner consistent with their culture and values. The trop-ical rain forest regions are teeming with entrepreneurial companies seeking to build similar types of business relationships with indige-nous populations.

A World of Opportunity

Companies that implement employee programs overseas enjoy many of the same benefits that accrue to community involvement programs on home turf. The initiatives often foster new skills, teamwork, and self-confidence in participants. Beyond that is the sheer satisfaction that comes from building bridges across cultures. "They come back so proud about what they've done themselves," says Anita Roddick of the employees who volunteer for Body Shop programs in Mexico and other countries. "They become heroes in their communities. When any résumé comes my way, nothing impresses me less than scholastic education, because it is just no longer relevant. What impresses me is, what have they done on their holidays? If they hitched around the world, I'd be in awe of them."

Roddick certainly doesn't represent your typical personnel director, and one may question the need to send employees off to volunteer in foreign lands, but her larger point is valid: In addition to the benefits such company efforts may bring to people in other countries, they return benefits to the companies themselves in the form of better-skilled, more self-assured employees who are able to work well in teams. It also generates pride and enthusiasm among employees. As Roddick says of another company project in which employees and customers successfully pressed for the release of political prisoners: "There was a euphoria there that could never be matched by my introducing a new moisture cream."

Such efforts are part of a new view of developing nations, which recognizes that short-term, large-scale public works projects aren't always the best method of assisting local economic activity. It's a philosophy that Anita Roddick calls "trade, not aid," the slogan that has become a call to action on posters and pamphlets in The Body Shop's retail stores. Roddick will be the first admit that there's nothing inherently wrong with foreign aid. But she is among those critical of many large-scale international development programs, saying that they strive for large, one-time projects that don't always relieve poverty, create sustainable jobs, or enhance environments for local residents. Her criticism is backed up by studies from such organizations as the World Bank, showing that many antipoverty projects fail because they promoted technologies and development schemes unsuitable for local social and economic conditions.

The kinds of projects Anita Roddick and others support are smaller ones focusing on low-impact technologies—culturally sensitive projects that add value to existing resources and environmental conditions. As an example, Roddick points to an effort in a region on the west coast of Mexico, where local Indians fished for turtles until the practice was banned. An environmental group has been teaching the Indians how to sustain an alternative, community-based economy by growing organic crops. They are also setting up eco-tour groups, where outsiders can come to live and work with the Indians. Companies trying to do good things in foreign countries often bemoan the difficulty they have instilling in their country managers the need to become involved with the local community, and to do so in a culturally and environmentally sensitive manner. Often, operating goals focus on short-term business interests, with few incentives to managers to step outside that box. That creates a dichotomy between a company's vision and its practices that may require a formal statement of policy and measurable goals if it is to be overcome.

TIMBERLAND TAKES ON RACISM

Some social issues confronted by multinational companies may not affect profitability directly, but they can still have a profound impact on a company's leaders, as well as the rest of the work force. When someone at the top of a company is moved to take on a social issue of personal concern, there's no telling where it can go.

No one knows that better than Jeff Swartz, Timberland's chief operating officer. The issue that moved him to act was racism—or, to be more precise, the need to counter racism with increased tolerance and respect for diversity.

The story begins with a Timberland comptroller, an Ethiopian, who works in the company's office in Munich, Germany. A few years earlier, he had arrived in Germany to work for Motorola, then came to Timberland. "He is a wonderful guy," says Swartz. "You'd better not ask him how he's doing, or you'd better be interested in the answer, because he's going to tell you. One day I asked him, 'How you doing?' He said, 'Not so good.' " It turned out his six-year-old son had come home from school one day and asked his father, "Why are the kids calling me nigger?"

Swartz, who is Jewish, was well aware of the rise in racism and neo-Nazism in Germany—as well as growing signs of racism, anti-Semitism, and white supremacy in many American cities. He wanted to help. "History has shown that people cannot, and must not, be silent when they see injustice and oppression," says Swartz. "As members of the international business community and as human beings, we can't simply sit back and conduct business as usual." He recalled a Robert Kennedy quote he once heard: "Each time a man stands up for an ideal, or acts to improve the lot of others, or strikes out against injustice, he sends forth a tiny ripple of hope, and crossing each other from a million different centers of energy and daring, builds a current which can sweep down the mightiest walls of repression and resistance." Swartz called Timberland's advertising agency and asked them to create an ad addressing this new wave of hatred, to run in the German media. The ad chosen featured a quote attributed to a Nazi Holocaust survivor:

> In Germany they came first for the Communists, and I didn't speak up because I wasn't a Communist. Then they came for the Jews, and I didn't speak up because I wasn't a Jew. Then they came for the trade unionists, and I didn't speak up because I wasn't a trade unionist. Then they came for the Catholics, and I didn't speak up because I was a Protestant. Then they came for me, and by that time no one was left to speak up.

The headline read, STAMP OUT HATRED, which had a double meaning, since it also displayed the sole of a Timberland boot. The ad copy announced that Timberland would make a contribution to an anti-racism organization for every pair of its boots sold in Germany—an irony, given that many of the boot buyers were skinheads and others attempting to foment racist sentiment.

Swartz's ad ran in *Der Stern* magazine in 1992 and caused an immediate sensation. Timberland received a flood of responses, nearly all positive. "The chairman of Mercedes-Benz called us up and said, 'How can we participate?' " recalls Swartz. "We got a letter from the people at Lufthansa saying, 'We were inspired to act.' " Lufthansa subsequently ran its own antihate ad campaign. More ads followed from other companies. Meanwhile, versions of the Timberland ad ran in England, France, and Switzerland.

When Timberland's U.S. employees caught wind of this, "I got slammed," as Swartz puts it. "They said, 'Why aren't you running these ads in the States? Are you waiting for right-wing violence before you speak out? And the other thing you did wrong, Jeff, is that there's no call to action. This is like editorializing. It's self-indulgent.'" So Swartz ordered up U.S. versions of the ad. They ran with two different headlines: GIVE RACISM THE BOOT and THIS BOOT PERFORMS BEST WHEN MARCHING AGAINST HATRED. The U.S. ads also featured a somewhat different message: "This message is from Timberland, but when it comes to racism and hatred it doesn't matter who makes your boots. Just pull them on, join hands with City Year, and stand up to racial intolerance." The ad gave a phone number to contact City Year, the urban youth work corps that Timberland supports, and offered sweatshirts and T-shirts saying: GIVE RACISM THE BOOT. All proceeds from shirt sales went to City Year.

Swartz's ad campaign garnered worldwide press attention and has come to be considered an advertising classic. It is far from the first ad to deliver a social message rather than promote its sponsor's product, but it stands as a worthy symbol of the tremendous power of business to communicate to the world. For the past few decades, the principal messages of business have centered on promoting consumption and growth, sex and glamour, fitting in and standing out. In asking the world to "Give Racism the Boot," Timberland used the company's communication power to send a message of tolerance and understanding, healing and hope.

Bobby Kennedy's words may ring as true for businesses as for people: When a company stands up, it sends forth a ripple of hope. And there's no telling where it might stop.

EPILOGUE:

The Road from Here

"One day we will wake up and there won't be anything very exciting about social responsibility. It will just be the norm. Executives will think about employees as something other than throwaway objects because they understand that's a fundamental rule of business. Businesses will try to leave the world a little bit better than they found it."

—GARY HIRSHBERG,
President, Stonyfield Farm

As the state of the art of socially responsible business grows and flourishes—as more business leaders recognize the financial and societal benefits that accrue from adopting the philosophies, policies, and programs we've described in this book—one thing will be certain: Much of what now seems cutting edge will become mainstream. And some of the more enlightened ideas about how business can and should operate will be improved upon and replaced by new and better ideas. That is the way of the world in a dynamic, competitive, market-driven society.

In just a few short years, we've already witnessed this. Family-friendly workplace policies are now commonplace, for example, where they were rarely seen five years ago. Corporate environmental

It is the year 2000. The most admired company in America is the healthy, quality-committed, family-friendly, socially responsible, learning enterprise. Its leaders are healthy, the organization high-performing, and its success is measured by a broad team of stakeholders: the shareholders, customers, employee-partners, and the community at large.

—ROBERT H. ROSEN,
president, Healthy Companies

policies have soared in sophistication since the late 1980s, with the most enlightened companies leapfrogging one another in their ability to engage in cleaner, less wasteful, more resource-efficient ways of doing business. Business partnerships with community development groups have evolved from a handful of initiatives nationwide to several in nearly every major city.

The continuous improvement model well known in the arena of total quality management (TQM) applies nicely to socially responsible business practices. One of the key concepts behind TQM is that nothing in business is ever so good that it can't be improved upon, and that even the best-performing companies must constantly fine-tune their products and policies to keep up with or ahead of changing conditions, new thinking, innovative technologies, customer demands, and, of course, the competition. Continuous improvement is certainly a reality when it comes to integrating socially responsible vision and values into your company's operation. Stonyfield Farm president Gary Hirshberg puts it this way: "Even the most successful practitioners among us have more questions than answers about how to put these concepts into practice."

Clearly, Hirshberg's search for answers has paid off. His company has managed to create a synergy of yogurt culture and corporate culture that has put it among the fastest-growing companies of its kind, experiencing between 45 percent and 60 percent annual growth since the late 1980s—"more growth than we can handle," Hirshberg says. Stonyfield's gross and net margins are at the top of the industry, even after a generous 10 percent-of-pretax-profits allocation to environmental causes, and a 20 percent profit-sharing plan. The company has been visited by Bill and Hillary Clinton and Al

Gore, who have come to discuss Hirshberg's social vision and business practices. And along the way, Hirshberg and Stonyfield have received a wallful of honors and awards from local and national organizations and publications.

Despite his personal and professional successes, Hirshberg is cautious in his optimism about the current ascendance of corporate social responsibility. As he witnesses the increased scrutiny being given to socially responsible companies, particularly those that have actively promoted their vision and practices, Hirshberg recognizes that not every company will stand up to the scrutiny. "We've moved from a phase of being media darlings to being forced to eat a lot of our own words," he says. "The tide has turned." The scrutiny is putting increased pressure on companies to "walk their talk"—to make sure their actions match their words—perhaps even to tone down the public rhetoric. "We try to be extremely up front about the places where we have not yet succeeded," says Hirshberg. "I think that whatever your definition is of social responsibility, if the message is, 'Look how great we are,' then you're missing the boat."

Hirshberg envisions the day when the term "socially responsible business" will become a redundancy—when such practices will have become the rule rather than the exception. "One day we will wake up and there won't be anything very exciting about social responsibility," he predicts. "It will just be the norm. Executives will think about employees as something other than throwaway objects because they understand that's a fundamental rule of business. Businesses will try to leave the world a little bit better than they found it."

Perhaps. But others already envision the next step in the evolution: As socially responsible values become commonplace, some business leaders will be asking themselves ever larger questions. "As we enter the next century, I think we must question many of our old assumptions," says Eliott Hoffman of Just Desserts. "Why are we here? Is it merely to amass huge quantities of money and material possessions? When is enough enough?" And finally: "What is really important in life?"

Hoffman finds these fundamental philosophical questions lacking in most discussions about socially responsible business. And yet he believes they must be raised if companies are to make the necessary shifts in values and vision. "The fact is that we are fast approaching, if not already arrived at, major decision points for society and the planet," says Hoffman. "What is business's role and responsibility?

> Businesses that master and embrace change can accomplish great things for themselves, their people, and the communities in which they do business. As leaders, they have the power to bring about complete paradigm shifts in the way they conduct business—which, in turn, enables them to thrive, to become known as an employer of choice for thousands of people, and to be a valued and respected member of society at large.
>
> —JOHN MARTIN,
> *president and CEO, Taco Bell*

When we talk about making a fair return on investment, in the strict business and financial sense, who ever said that the return must be measured by the quarter, or even the year? Don't we have a responsibility to measure our impact, our 'success,' in the longer term—in years, decades, and generations?"

Many companies won't likely address such heady questions for some time, if ever. For them, implementing incremental change will be challenge enough. For these leaders, the many daily pressures of business life—from customers, competitors, regulators, suppliers, lenders, and the like—mean that "saving the world" often takes a back seat to "saving the day." Says The Gap's Bob Fisher: "I don't think we've come to the realization that our corporate mission is to change society. That's not to say we're not going to eventually get there. In the same way that as a company our job is to interpret the future tastes of the consumer, our job as management is to interpret the future social concerns of both our employees and the population at large. We're probably a little bit ahead of the wave, but not a lot."

And so the debates over the role of business in society are destined to continue, much as they have for decades. But unlike the debates of a quarter century ago, today's are far less theoretical. As the number of companies embracing socially responsible visions and values continues to grow, and the links between their social performance, their impact on stakeholders, and financial performance become more firmly established, the overriding question will not be whether companies should adopt these policies and practices, but rather when, and how quickly, they should do so.

When Ben & Jerry's first started, I used to be a hot ticket on the Rotary Club speaker circuit. The assignment was to drone on a bit after lunch in order to help people digest their meals. Ben & Jerry's was a real small company at the time—we were a homemade ice cream parlor—and we used to do things for the community, like show free movies during the summer on the wall outside our gas station, and sponsor community celebrations, and give away free ice cream on our anniversary.

I'd be talking to the Rotary Club about these things and at the end of the talk somebody would kind of lift up his head and say, "Well, you know, those things you're doing for the community—you're just doing them because it's good for business, right?" And I responded, "Well, I don't know, but our reason is that we genuinely believe that business has a responsibility to give back to the community, and we're doing it out of altruism."

That was my old answer. My new answer is, "Yeah, it is good for business. And if you're smart, you'll jump on the bandwagon."

—BEN COHEN,
chairperson, Ben & Jerry's Homemade

THE NEXT GENERATION

In case you had any thoughts that the idea of socially responsible business practices will eventually fade away as yet another fleeting management trend, spend a few minutes with Heather Corcoran, Jim Shelton, Jean-Paul Valensi, or any of a number of today's business school students or recent graduates. More and more of these future business leaders are launching their careers with a firm grasp of the importance for companies to integrate socially responsible thinking throughout their operations in order to remain competitive. And many of these graduates are seeking out employers that share their beliefs in these areas, or in some cases starting their own companies rooted in a philosophy that blends bottom-line accountability with a desire to play a positive role in the world.

Business schools haven't yet integrated socially responsible thinking into their core curricula in any substantive way—it often surfaces in a course on business ethics or in case studies—but increasingly business school professors are recognizing the need to do so. Several have zeroed in on one or more socially responsible companies as case studies. One common focus is The Body Shop. "The friends that I never expected to find are in the business schools," says Anita Roddick, who in 1994 spent a month as a guest lecturer at Stanford's business school. "We've had dissertations written about our leadership role, our values, and our social auditing. I think there's a legitimate educational role in taking our so-called bizarre and eccentric practices and bringing them to be studied by these academic groups." As we saw in chapter 7, other business schools have studied the socially responsible practices of such companies as Fel-Pro, Johnson & Johnson, and H. B. Fuller.

As continued research and corporate experience help students link business success to respect for employees, communities, and the environment, they will inevitably bring these values to their future employers. "All executives know that in order to promote a new creativity, you're going to have to change the culture," says Reebok CEO Paul Fireman. "And in the process of changing it by bringing in younger people with less rigid approaches, you're automatically bringing in people who have a different way of looking at life, who feel more committed to the ecology, the way the world works, and the way people operate."

Whether through formal curricula or not, some students are managing to find others of their generation who share their interest in the role of business in society. In 1993, a few dozen business school graduate students formed Students for Responsible Business (SRB).

> I believe we're on the verge of what might be a genuine shift in our nation's priorities—an official end to the "me" and "greed" decade. We now know that the conditions of our businesses cannot be separated from the conditions of the society in which we operate, and that we must advocate, promote, and even fight for responsible business.
>
> —PAUL FIREMAN,
> *CEO, Reebok International Ltd.*

"We are a community of graduate business students and alumni committed to conducting business responsibly and honestly by integrating our values into our business decisions," reads the SRB mission statement. "As a new generation of business leaders, we will achieve financial success while contributing to the creation of a more human, just, and sustainable world." In its first six months, with little formal recruitment effort, SRB attracted more than 500 students at 40 U.S. college and universities.

"It caught us a little bit by surprise," says Heather Corcoran, a 1994 Yale University graduate and a founding co-chair of SRB. "We didn't realize how much this would catch on." What surprises Corcoran most are the number of undergraduates considering entering business school who have expressed interest in joining SRB. "It's sort of tapped into something for people who are seeking a career that's a little bit bigger than just themselves."

Corcoran is typical of the generation of students whose job search extends beyond considerations of financial and career advancement. While in graduate school she spent a summer working at Odwalla, a California company with a strong record of forward-thinking environmental and social policies. "They were creating jobs, creating value, and at the same time creating wealth, some of which they funneled back into their local communities," she says. After graduation, Corcoran began working at Quartermaine Coffee Roasters in Rockville, Maryland, as the company's first management trainee. "They have what I'm looking for in a company: enlightened management, tremendous integrity, an excellent product. They treat their employees very well." As an example, she points to a policy in which part-time employees can receive full-time benefits.

Corcoran is not solely an idealist. She wants to succeed in the business world. But she is driven by a desire, as she puts it, "to do things differently." For her, business as usual just won't cut it.

For Jim Shelton, a 1993 Stanford MBA now working as a consultant at McKinsey & Company in Atlanta, being in business is a means to help turn tattered inner-city neighborhoods into viable communities. Shelton grew up in Washington, D.C.'s impoverished Anacostia neighborhood. "We just always had an ethic that working in the community was the right thing to do," he says. "It was what you were supposed to do."

At age twenty-six, Shelton already has an impressive history of turning that ethic into deeds. He attended Morehouse College in Atlanta, which prides itself on a student body that makes outstanding contributions to their communities. He became director of community service at Morehouse, part of the student body government. After graduation, he spent two years working as a computer systems developer for Exxon Corporation in Houston. While at Exxon, Shelton helped organize his department's diversity program, as well as a program in which Exxon adopted disadvantaged schools throughout Houston.

Next came Stanford University's Graduate School of Business, where Shelton worked with youth in East Palo Alto, while working on his MBA. There he also helped found Students Offering Alternative Realities (SOAR), a program that provides tutoring, mentoring, and summer job placement for disadvantaged teens. The summer after the 1992 Los Angeles riots, he worked for McKinsey & Company in Los Angeles, providing assistance to Rebuild L.A., the public-private partnership focusing on revitalizing that city's deteriorating neighborhoods. After graduation, he traveled to South Africa to assist with voter education in anticipation of the country's 1994 elections. Finally, he returned to McKinsey in Atlanta.

For Shelton, McKinsey's commitment to volunteerism was key to his decision to work there." A lot of corporations have taken the attitude that if they give money and will let their people go out and do some volunteer work, that's enough," says Shelton. "But they don't recognize that their success is dependent on the success of the community in which they operate, if only because they won't be able to attract the best people to their headquarters if they're in a place that is not a desirable city. They need to recognize that they have fundamental resources and skills that most communities lack. Through the management skills and resources they have, companies can make contributions beyond giving a few token dollars here and there to special projects, or letting their employees who so desire go out and do a little volunteer work." For example, he says, companies can help nonprofits or government agencies structure community projects or provide jobs for disadvantaged teens.

Says Shelton: "I could go on all day about the opportunities that companies can offer—but don't unfortunately—which would exponentially facilitate the process of community development and urban revitalization."

Like Shelton, Jean-Paul Valensi hopes to be among those who help change corporate attitudes toward giving back to their employees, their community, and the environment. Valensi, a grad student at New York University's Stern School of Business, intends to combine

his interests in business and science in the field of biotechnology—
indeed, to start his own biotech firm some day, mining the microbi-
ology of the oceans for potential drugs, vaccines, and foods.

Says Valensi, "I think a lot of big businesses out there are realizing
today that in order to survive—and not just to survive, but to surpass
other businesses—they have to make changes to benefit their customers, their employees, and the environment."

Valensi, who heads his school's SRB chapter, acknowledges that
the majority of his classmates don't share his perspective, though a
growing number seem to be catching on. "I think people get a dose
of social responsibility in their classes," he says, "but most people
don't have the courage to do anything about it. They don't want to be
the iconoclast. They don't want to stick out. They don't want to go
into a big business and tell people what they really feel. I wish more
people would go out there and say, 'Hey, this is not right.' "

But Valensi is encouraged by the generation of business students
coming after his. "It's definitely going to change over time," he predicts. "You're going to have students follow in our footsteps who
have been taught a lot more about these issues as children, from
grade one and up. They have computers in school. They have more

---

One of the great strengths and simultaneously great weak-
nesses of this network is that there's sort of a heady campaign
aspect of it. In ten or twenty years, this campaign will be a
historical footnote. The only way we'll be successful is when
it ceases to be a campaign, when it just becomes incredibly
obvious that these practices are fundamental to being a successful business person. I'm not sure that some of the folk
heroes of our network really do want that day to come. I
think there will be a little bit of sadness when there isn't a
funky Ben Cohen and a zany Anita Roddick up there. When
it's actually the vice president of finance for Time Warner
saying things we never dreamed would come out of the
mouth of a big business executive. It's going to be a sad day,
but it's also going to be the day that we've arrived.

—GARY HIRSHBERG,
president, Stonyfield Farm

awareness about the environment. By the time they get to where I am right now, there will be such a heightened awareness that socially responsible business will be the rule rather than the exception to the rule."

Exactly how many Heather Corcorans, Jim Sheltons, and Jean-Paul Valensis will soon be entering the business world is unclear, as is the number that will end up working for big companies, where they could potentially have the largest impact. What is clear is that these three young people, along with the hundreds or thousands of peers who share their enlightened views about business, will play a central role in ensuring the future growth of socially responsible thinking in business.

Collectively they will fuel the undeniable new spirit of business that is emerging: Business as an engine for profits and principle. Business as a force for economic and personal growth. Business as an empowerer of employees. Business as a steward of the environment. Business as a rekindler of community spirit.

That will be good for business, and good for us all.

Corporate Reputation/ Responsibility Assessment Tool

This assessment tool—developed at Levi Strauss & Company—is intended to provide a framework for identifying and evaluating corporate policies and practices that collectively influence a company's reputation.

There are rating criteria that may not apply to some companies, some industries, or in some countries or cultures.

There are other criteria that need to be added to reflect issues of importance for particular companies, industries or countries.

The criteria key business stakeholders use to assess reputation also change over time, and this tool may need to be updated.

Despite these limitations, the tool has been designed to help corporate managers and others think comprehensively about the factors that most directly affect company reputation.

CORPORATE PRACTICES AND STANDARDS	SECTOR	SIZE	ALL
A. Compliance with all legal requirements	___	___	___
B. Adherence to a comprehensive code of ethics	___	___	___
C. Global application of values and standards	___	___	___
D. Quality, diversity, and independence of board of directors	___	___	___
E. Protection of shareholder interests	___	___	___
F. Supplier relations	___	___	___
G. Competitor relations	___	___	___
H. Company purchasing policies, e.g., minority contracting	___	___	___
I. Socially responsible investment of company funds	___	___	___
J. Respect for human rights	___	___	___
K. _____	___	___	___
L. _____	___	___	___
OVERALL RATING:	___	___	___

FINANCIAL PERFORMANCE	SECTOR	SIZE	ALL
A. Consistency in meeting shareholder expectations	___	___	___
B. Financial soundness	___	___	___
C. Profitability (sustained earnings growth over a 5-year period)	___	___	___

FINANCIAL PERFORMANCE (Continued)	SECTOR	SIZE	ALL
D. Average earnings per share (5-year)	___	___	___
E. Average return on assets (5-year)	___	___	___
F. Timely and accurate disclosure of financial performance	___	___	___
G. _____	___	___	___
H. _____	___	___	___
OVERALL RATING:	___	___	___

PRODUCTS AND SERVICES	SECTOR	SIZE	ALL
A. Consistency in meeting customer product expectations/commitments	___	___	___
B. Consistency in meeting customer service expectations/commitments	___	___	___
C. Quality of products	___	___	___
D. Quality of customer service	___	___	___
E. Product safety record	___	___	___
F. Responsible management of defective or harmful products	___	___	___
G. Avoidance of inherently harmful products	___	___	___
H. Pricing policies and practices	___	___	___
I. Honest, accurate, and responsible advertising and product labeling	___	___	___
J. Avoidance of animal testing	___	___	___
K. _____	___	___	___
L. _____	___	___	___
OVERALL RATING:	___	___	___

MANAGEMENT	SECTOR	SIZE	ALL
A. Quality of management	___	___	___
B. Diversity of management	___	___	___
C. Innovative business practices	___	___	___

MANAGEMENT (continued)	SECTOR	SIZE	ALL
D. Responsible use of corporate assets	___	___	___
E. Open and honest communications with internal audiences	___	___	___
F. Open and honest communications with external audiences	___	___	___
G. Consideration of all stakeholder interests in decision-making process	___	___	___
H. Business and civic leadership	___	___	___
I. Respect for the intellectual property of others	___	___	___
J. Advocacy of responsible business practices	___	___	___
K. _____	___	___	___
L. _____	___	___	___
OVERALL RATING:	___	___	___

WORKPLACE POLICIES	SECTOR	SIZE	ALL

EMPLOYMENT PRACTICES

	SECTOR	SIZE	ALL
A. Merit-based hiring and promotion (non-discrimination)	___	___	___
B. Diversity of workforce	___	___	___
C. Labor relations	___	___	___
D. Layoff policies and practices	___	___	___
E. _____	___	___	___
F. _____	___	___	___
OVERALL RATING:	___	___	___

WORKPLACE POLICIES	SECTOR	SIZE	ALL

WAGES AND BENEFITS

	SECTOR	SIZE	ALL
A. Wage and salary levels (including executive compensation)	___	___	___
B. Equitable distribution of wages, salaries, and benefits	___	___	___

Workplace Policies (continued)	Sector	Size	All
C. Health care benefits	——	——	——
D. Work/family policies and benefits, e.g., flextime, child care, elder care	——	——	——
E. Availability of training and development programs for all employees	——	——	——
F. Other benefits, e.g., employee assistance programs, scholarships, product discounts, domestic partner benefits, health and wellness programs, etc.	——	——	——
G. Retirement benefits (including level of retirement plan funding)	——	——	——
H. _____	——	——	——
I. _____	——	——	——
OVERALL RATING:	——	——	——

WORKPLACE ENVIRONMENT

	Sector	Size	All
A. Safe and healthy workplace for all employees	——	——	——
B. Respect for employee privacy	——	——	——
C. Workplace "culture," i.e., a fair, respectful, and trusting work environment	——	——	——
D. _____	——	——	——
E. _____	——	——	——
OVERALL RATING:	——	——	——

Corporate Citizenship	Sector	Size	All

ENVIRONMENTAL STEWARDSHIP

	Sector	Size	All
A. Compliance with environmental laws	——	——	——
B. Energy reduction efforts	——	——	——
C. Waste management procedures	——	——	——

CORPORATE CITIZENSHIP (continued)	SECTOR	SIZE	ALL
D. Environmental sensitivity in packaging and product design	——	——	——
E. Recycling efforts and use of recycled materials	——	——	——
F. Pollution prevention efforts	——	——	——
G. Authority of environmental officer or committee	——	——	——
H. Goals to reduce production and/or use of toxins	——	——	——
I. Commitment to periodic environmental auditing	——	——	——
J. Public disclosure of environmental record	——	——	——
K. Global application of environmental standards	——	——	——
K. Environmental practices of suppliers	——	——	——
M. _____	——	——	——
N. _____	——	——	——
OVERALL RATING:	——	——	——

COMMUNITY INVOLVEMENT

	SECTOR	SIZE	ALL
A. Percentage of profits designated for cash contributions	——	——	——
B. Innovation and creativity in philanthropic efforts	——	——	——
C. Philanthropic efforts wherever company has employees	——	——	——
D. Product donations	——	——	——
E. Availability of company facilities and other assets for community use	——	——	——
F. Support for employee community involvement and volunteer efforts (including management recognition, community service leaves, matching gifts programs, etc.)	——	——	——

CORPORATE CITIZENSHIP (continued)	SECTOR	SIZE	ALL
G. "Good Neighbor" policies, i.e., consideration of community and neighborhood needs in policy making and business practices	___	___	___
H. Responsible advocacy of public policy	___	___	___
I. _____	___	___	___
J. _____	___	___	___
OVERALL RATING:	___	___	___

SUMMARY	SECTOR	SIZE	ALL
Corporate Practices and Standards	___	___	___
Financial Performance	___	___	___
Products and Services	___	___	___
Management	___	___	___
Employment Practices	___	___	___
Wages and Benefits	___	___	___
Workplace Environment	___	___	___
Environmental Stewardship	___	___	___
Community Involvement	___	___	___

Business for Social Responsibility

Business for Social Responsibility was created in 1992 to develop, support, advocate, and disseminate business strategies and practices that aim for high performance, innovation, and corporate prosperity. It focuses on policies that are responsible for the well-being of the bottom line as well as the work force, the environment, and our communities. Recognizing the impact of business on society, the BSR alliance of companies brings the unique perspective of the business community to address the many problems and opportunities that confront our businesses and our society today.

BSR has a diverse membership of large, medium, and small companies in manufacturing, retailing, and service from across the United States. The organization welcomes companies that already have implemented socially responsible corporate programs as well as those that want to build their futures through strategies that respond to both the need for and the benefits from socially responsible policies.

BSR provides access to successful corporate strategies and practices through member education and information programs and materials. The organization has created regional learning and action networks for business leaders that deliver programs and opportunities to help members integrate and benefit from a full range of responsible practices. BSR also offers a strong national voice that introduces the policies and goals of the organization as well as the winning practices of individual members to the national and local media and the public.

The BSR Education Fund, which supported the development of this book, is an independent nonprofit organization that gathers and develops socially responsible policies and practices, while serving as a resource for and disseminator to the public, the academic community, and other businesses.

For more information, contact Business for Social Responsibility, 1030 Fifteenth Street N.W., Suite 1010, Washington, DC 20005. Phone: 202-842-5400. Fax: 202-842-3135.

Business for Social Responsibility Membership

A Steno Service, New York, NY
A Success Resume, Smithtown, NY
A Thousand Cranes, New York, NY
The Acacia Group/Calvert, Phoenix, AZ
Acadia Consulting Group, Providence, RI
ACCION International, Cambridge, MA
ACE Financial Services, Boulder, CO
Adolescent Employment Readiness Center, Washington, DC
The A.D.S. Group, Andover, MA
Aegir Systems, Oxnard, CA
AIDS, Medicine and Miracles, Boulder, CO
Akasaka, Ortiz & Varela, Orange, CA
Alaska Animal Eye Clinic, Anchorage, AK
Albion Financial Associates, Berkeley, CA
All That Glitters, San Francisco, CA
The Alliance Network, Mesa, AZ
Ally Capital Corp., Sausalito, CA
Aloe & Ash Ltd. dba The Body Shop, Scottsdale, AZ
Alpha Partners, Chapel Hill, NC
Alphawave Designs, Beltsville, MD
Alternative Garden Supply, Streamwood, IL

AM Consulting, Mill Valley, CA
Amalgamated Life Insurance Co., New York, NY
American Data Management, Mt. View, CA
American Income Life Insurance Co., Waco, TX
Eva Anderson Design, Providence, RI
Hanna Andersson, Portland, OR
Applied Waste Minimization, Sebastopol, CA
Arch Drafting Supply, San Francisco, CA
Ariel Capital Management, Chicago, IL
Armstrong Creative, Boulder, CO
Eric Arnow, CLU, Mill Valley, CA
Asheville Fund, Asheville, NC
ASI International, Levcadia, CA
Association for Portland Progress, Portland, OR
Au Bon Pain Co., Boston, MA
Auchan U.S.A., Houston, TX
Aurora Press Inc., Santa Fe, NM
Austin Sculpture, Holbrook, NY
Avalon Consulting Group, Harvard, MA
Avant Garden Vermicomposting System, Ross, CA
Aveda Corp., Minneapolis, MN

Babylon Burning Screen Printing, San Francisco, CA

Babyworks, Portland, OR

Baccharis Capital, Menlo Park, CA

Bagel Works, Keene, NH

The Bagelry, Durham, NH

Susan Baldomar Public Relations, Wellesley, MA

The Bank of Boston/First Community, Boston, MA

The Bank of Newport, Lake Oswego, OR

Bank of Newport, Newport, RI

Banquet Sound/Media Sonics, Santa Rosa, CA

Patricia Bario Associates, Washington, DC

Barrett Sportswear, Bloomington, MN

Bart's Homemade, Northampton, MA

Bass and Howes, Inc., Washington, DC

Bay Area Ethics Consortium—CSEP, Berkeley, CA

Beans and Grains and Things, Little Rock, AR

Bearsdley's Natural Foods, Ashland, OR

Beauty Service, Carlsbad, CA

Beethoven's, Ridgewood, NJ

Beliard Gordon & Partners, Chicago, IL

Ben & Jerry's Homemade, Waterbury, VT

Ben & Jerry's, Old Town, Alexandria, VA

Ben & Jerry's San Francisco, San Francisco, CA

Benson Woodworking Co., Alstead, NH

Bernstein-Albano Associates, San Francisco, CA

Bertucci's, Woburn, MA

Bewley Irish Imports, West Chester, PA

Beyond Boundaries, Oakland, CA

Beyond Words Publishing, Portland, OR

Susie Biehler & Associates, San Francisco, CA

BioBottoms, Petaluma, CA

Blaising St. Claire Associates, Carmel, IN

J. A. Blauner & Co., Mattapoisett, MA

Marvin Blitz Real Estate, Santa Barbara, CA

Maurice F. Blouin, Rollinsford, NH

Blue Fish Clothing, Frenchtown, NJ

Blue Moon Industries, Barrington, RI

Blue Muse, Novato, CA

BlueSky, Unlimited, Berkeley, CA

BlueSky, Unlimited, Los Angeles, CA

N. Susanna Bluestein, D.C., Ross, CA

The Body Shop International PLC, West Sussex, England

The Body Shop-Stanford, San Carlos, CA

The Body Shop USA, Wake Forest, NC

Boulder Barter Network, Boulder, CO

Braddock Group, Alexandria, VA

Breadsmith, Narberth, PA

Brenneke School of Massage, Seattle, WA

The Brewford Group, Denver, CO

The Brightside, Brattleboro, VT

Broadside Bookshop, Northampton, MA

Brookwood Cos. Inc., New York, NY

Brown Glass & Aluminum, Melrose, MA

Buck Consultants, Washington, DC

The Buffalo Exchange, Tucson, AZ

Bullivant, Houser, Bailey, Pendergrass & Hoffman, Portland, OR

Burness Communications, Bethesda, MD

Burrito Brothers, Washington, DC

Business Against Drunk Drivers, Springfield, VA

Business Ethics Magazine, Minneapolis, MN

Business Resource Institute, Tiburon, CA

C3 Strategies, Portland, OR

Cabbages and Kings, Weston, CT

Cable Science Network, Inc., Wilton, CT

Cafe De La Paz, Berkeley, CA

Cafe Via Teatro, San Francisco, CA

Caltan East Distributors, Syracuse, NY

The Calvert Group, Bethesda, MD

Cambridge Translation Resources, Boston, MA

Camel's Hump Christmas Trees, Huntington, VT

Castle Dental Group, Glendale, AZ

The Castle Group, Lake Oswego, OR

Center for Children's Environmental Literature, Washington, DC

Center for Economic Organizing, Washington, DC

Center for Ethics and Social Policy, Berkeley, CA

Center for International Leadership, Washington, DC

Center for Responsible Investing, Boulder, CO

Centsible Ideas, Nederland, CO

CFS BenSalem, Naturally!, Bensalem, PA

Change for Planet Earth, Phoenix, AZ

Charlotte's Webb Children's Bookstore, San Francisco, CA

H. K. Chatham & Co., Harwich, MA

Chicago Focus, Chicago, IL

Childreach, Warwick, RI

Chlopak, Leonard, Schechter & Associates, Washington, DC

Choice Sales & Marketing, Chicago, IL

Christopher's Restaurant, Cambridge, MA

Kelley Chunn Consulting, Boston, MA

Church & Dwight Co., Princeton, NJ

Cid's Food Market, El Prado, NM

The Cin-Made Corp., Cincinnati, OH

Cities Management, Minneapolis, MN

The John A. Clark Co., Washington, DC

Clivus Multrum, Cambridge, MA

C.L.L. Properties, South Dartmouth, MA

CMHS, East Greenwich, RI

Coastal International, San Francisco, CA

Cohn & Wolfe, New York, NY

CoHousing Co., Berkeley, CA

C. M. Collins & Associates, San Francisco, CA

Community Products, Montpelier, VT

Compas, Brooklyn, NY

Conant Custom Brass, Burlington, VT

The Concept Organization, San Francisco, CA

Concord-Assabet Adolescent Services, Concord, MA

Cone/Coughlin Communications, Boston, MA

Conover & Company Communications, Washington, DC

Conrad & Associates, McLean, VA

The Conscientious Investor, South Hadley, MA

The Continuum Center, Minneapolis, MN

Convention Newspapers, Villanova, PA

Co-op America, Washington, DC

Coopers & Lybrand, Boston, MA

Corporation for Enterprise Development, San Francisco, CA

Coyote Found Candles, Port Townsend, WA

Coyuchi Inc, Point Reyes Station, CA

The Crafts Center, Washington, DC

Creative Associates International, Washington, DC

Creative Solutions, Boulder, CO

Creatrix, Rumford, RI

Crib Diaper Service, Crystal, MN

Crystal Blue Beading Co., Watertown, MA

Crystal Point, Inc., Bothell, WA

Cummings Consulting, Concord, MA

The Curator, Walpole, NH

Cyberlore Studios Inc., Northampton, MA

Dairy Concepts, Marietta, NY

Dancing Tree Recycled Paper, Berkeley, CA

Daniels and Associates, San Rafael, CA

D'Artefax, Fairfax, CA

Carol Davis Reporting, Houston, TX

The Delahaye Group, Portsmouth, NH

Delstar Group, Phoenix, AZ
Delta Dental Plan of MA, Medford, MA
Design Matters, Sarasota, FL
Diaperaps Ltd., Chatsworth, CA
Diarchy Development, Gloucester, MA
DMA Group, Hampton, NH
Double Rainbow Gourmet Ice Cream, San Francisco, CA
The Dreyfus Corporation, New York, NY
Ducktrap River Fish Farm, Belfast, ME
Lucy Dunaway & Associates, Falls Church, VA
Dunbar, Hunter and Associates, Boston, MA
The DXTR'S, Los Angeles, CA
Dynamic PC Systems, Needham, MA

E Magazine, Norwalk, CT
Earth Communications, Mogadore, OH
Earth Share, Washington, DC
The Earth Shop, Latham, NY
Earthbath, San Francisco, CA
Earthrise Co., Petaluma, CA
EarthWrite Environmental/Business Communications, Minneapolis, MN
East Bluff Cleaning Systems, Tustin, CA
East End Food Co-op, Pittsburgh, PA
Eastern Computer Systems, New York, NY
Eco Clean, Scottsdale, AZ
Eco-Cycle, Boulder, CO
Eco Expo, Sherman Oaks, CA
Ecofranchising, New York, NY
Econatural Solutions, Boulder, CO
Economic Innovation Center of Rhode Island, Middletown, RI
Economy Linen and Towel Service, Dayton, OH
Ecoprint, Silver Spring, MD
Eden Rising, Bar Harbor, ME
A.G. Edwards & Sons, Inc., Portsmouth, NH

Effective Communities International, Tiburon, CA
Eileen Fisher Inc., Irvington, NY
Emerald Consulting, Hayward, CA
eMerchants, Oakland, CA
Emily's Toy Box, Altamount, NY
Encore Press Works, Nashville, TN
Energia Global Inc., Washington, DC
Energy Unlimited, Villanova, PA
Enersave, New York, NY
Enterprise Social Investment Corporation, Columbia, MD
Enviro Monde Inc., New York, NY
Environmental Effects, San Francisco, CA
Environmental Federation of New England, Boston, MA
Environmental Futures, Boston, MA
Envirotire Technologies, Amagansett, NY
Erickson's Diversified Corp., Hudson, WI
Drs. Escalante & Morphopoulos, D.D.S., Kensington, CA
Esprit de Corp, San Francisco, CA
Essex Conference & Retreat Center, Essex, MA
Estate Conservation Associates, San Rafael, CA
Estates of America, Brooklyn, NY
Everything Earthly, Tempe, AZ
Executive Citizen, Cambridge, MA
Exline Environmental Evaluation, Chandler, AZ
Exploration Inventories, Eden Prairie, MN

Faces Typography, Providence, RI
Falcon Trading, Santa Cruz, CA
Family Care Necessities, Summit, NJ
Fanlight Productions, Boston, MA
Fasolino Consulting, Portland, OR
Feeling Mind Institute, Lexington, MA
Ronald Feldman Fine Arts, New York, NY
Fel-Pro, Skokie, IL
Fenton Communications, Washington, DC

Fetzer Vineyards, Redwood Valley, CA

Financial Architects, Lexington, MA

Fingerhut Companies, Minnetonka, MN

Fitness Food, Dallas, TX

Flagship Bank & Trust, Worcester, MA

T. Wilson Flanders, Attorney, Northampton, MA

Flocksholm Design, Cambridge, MA

Fly By Night Rubber Stamps Co., Ithaca, NY

Tom Flynn, Inc., Larkspur, CA

Follow Your Heart, Canoga Park, CA

Forum Travel, Pittsburgh, PA

Fossil Rim Wildlife Center, Glen Rose, TX

Four Winds, Tucson, AZ

Foxboro Stadium Associates, Boston, MA

Frameworks, Cambridge, MA

Franklin Research & Development, Boston, MA

Franzen & Associates, Woodland Hills, CA

Freddie Mac, McLean, VA

Friday Harbor Snack Foods, Vancouver, WA

Fried & Sher, Herndon, VA

Gil Friend and Associates, Berkeley, CA

Fudgecycle Bike Shop, Key West, FL

Funny Times, Cleveland Heights, OH

The Future Group Sportswear Co., Bellingham, WA

G & A Recycling, Wilmington, MA

Gaia Bookstore, Berkeley, CA

Gordon Gamm, Boulder, CO

The Gap, San Francisco, CA

Gardeners Supply Co., Burlington, VT

GCS Services, Danbury, CT

General Management Solutions, St. Paul, MN

General Parts & Supply Co., Minneapolis, MN

Gentle Strength Co-operative, Tempe, AZ

J. Gibson & Co., Washington, DC

Gifts From Madagascar, San Francisco, CA

Give Something Back, Oakland, CA

Global Gourmet, Cambridge, MA

Global Insights, Berkeley, CA

Global Resource Consultants, Manassas, VA

Goldman Associates, Oakland, CA

Good Harvest Financial Group, Huntington, NY

Goodman Group, San Rafael, CA

Goodwill Industries of ME, Portland, ME

Gozdz & Associates, Menlo Park, CA

Graffik Natwicks, Pacifica, CA

Graham Contracting Inc., Wayland, MA

Graham Photography, San Anselmo, CA

Bill Graham Presents, San Francisco, CA

Grand Circle Travel, Boston, MA

Graphics Unlimited, San Rafael, CA

Green Communications, Topanga, CA

Green Goods, Takoma Park, MD

The Green Money Journal, Spokane, WA

The Greenworld Project, Kingston, NY

Greyston Corp., Yonkers, NY

Gryphon Stringed Instruments, Palo Alto, CA

Harrington Investments, Napa, CA

Jay Harris, Berwyn, PA

Hary Dary International, South Burlington, VT

Hasbro, Pawtucket, RI

Hasenfuss Management Associates, Concord, NH

Hasten Design, Washington, DC

HCC Group, Goshen, CT

Healthy Companies, Washington, DC

Heartwood Creations, Rockford, IL

Heidi Wise, Mill Valley, CA

Hemmings Motor News, Bennington, VT

Herman Stoller Coliver Architects, San Francisco, CA

Hermanson's Employment Services, San Francisco, CA
Hertlein Consulting, San Francisco, CA
Hexacomb Corp., Lincolnshire, IL
HFG Expansion Fund 1. L.P., Wellesley, MA
Higher Octave Music, Los Angeles, CA
Highpoint Graphics, Claremont, CA
Hill International, Tucson, AZ
HMS Associates, San Francisco, CA
Hoka-Hai Associates, Philadelphia, PA
Holman Cooking Equipment, Saco, ME
Homeopathic Educational Services, Berkeley, CA
Homestone Financial, Wayland, MA
Honeywell Inc., Minneapolis, MN
Hope Unlimited, Vancouver, BC
HRG, San Diego, CA
Hudson Dental Care, Hudson, MA
Human Investment Program, New York, NY
Human Works, South Orange, NJ
Human-I-Tees, Pleasantville, NY
Hunter Industries, San Marcos, CA
Hyde Street Studios, San Francisco, CA

IdeaScope Associates, Cambridge, MA
IKEA U.S.-Washington, Woodbridge, VA
Imagine, San Rafael, CA
IMF Financial Corp., San Rafael, CA
Phillys Imonti, Consultant, Dana Point, CA
Innovative Management Systems, Arlington, MA
Innovative Moves, Jamaica Plain, MA
Input Culture, Trumansburg, NY
Insights in Action, Washington, DC
Integral Results, Inc., San Francisco, CA
Integrated Financial Services, Boulder, CO
Internews, Arcata, CA
Interval Research Corp., Palo Alto, CA

Investments in Nature, San Jose, CA
Isaacson, Miller, Boston, MA
Issue Network Group, Grand Rapids, MI

J & P Consulting, Boulder, CO
Robert William James & Associates, Portland, OR
Jennings, Chicago, IL
Robert B. Johnson, DMD, FAGD, Herndon, VA
Edward D. Jones & Co., Cranston, RI
Joule Paintings, Eugene, OR
JourneyWare Media, Moraga, CA
JTM Reports, New York, NY
Jubilee Jobs, Washington, DC
Jumpstart, Del Mar, CA
Just 'Cause Marketing, Phoenix, AZ
Just Desserts, San Francisco, CA

Kahn-Sults, Ltd., Boulder, CO
Katzinger's Delicatessen, Columbus, OH
Neil Kelly Designers/Remodelers, Portland, OR
Kent Homeopathic Associates, Fairfax, CA
Kepler's Books & Magazine, Menlo Park, CA
Keystone Coffee Co., San Jose, CA
Kids' Stuff, South Portland, ME
Kinder, Lydenberg, Domini & Co., Cambridge, MA
Kinderworks Corp., Portsmouth, NH
King Avenue Coffeehouse, Colombus, OH
Kirkpatrick & Associates, Corte Madera, CA
Klara Simpla Store, Wilmington, VT
K-Medic, Leonia, NJ
Mel Knox Barrel and Bottle Broker, San Fransico, CA
Katherine Krefft, Ph.D., Plymouth, MA
Kripalu By Mail, Lenox, MA

La Flecha Amarilla, San Francisco, CA
La Paloma Clothing & Jewelry, Portland, OR
Lampein, Sacramento, CA
Landmark Publishing Co., York, ME

Scott Larson Construction, Portland, OR

Laufer Associates, Los Angeles, CA

Laughing Horse Inn, Taos, NM

Ann L. Laughlin & Daughters, Phoenixville, PA

Law Office of Bruce D. Todesco, Providence, RI

Law Office of Douglas K. Mertz, Juneau, AK

Law Office of Patricia J. Cummings, San Rafael, CA

Sam Lawson, Consulting, San Francisco, CA

The Leadership Corp., Boulder, CO

Learn PC, Minneapolis, MN

Lenore Vanderkooi Pottery, Nashville, TN

Les Amis De La Terre, New Orleans, LA

Levi Strauss & Co., San Francisco, CA

Life Tools Adventure Outfitters, Green Bay, WI

Light Work for Body, Mind and Spirit, Syracuse, NY

Lighten, Berkeley, CA

Lightlife Foods, Greenfield, MA

Little Oak, Portland, ME

Alan Littman & Associates, Boulder, CO

L.M.S. Associates, Maitland, FL

Longfellow Clubs, Wayland, MA

Lotus Development Corp., Cambridge, MA

Lotus Publishing Corporation, Cambridge, MA

Dr. Frank H. Lucido, M.D., Berkeley, CA

Lynch Jarvis Jones, Minneapolis, MN

Lynx Systems, Winooski, VT

The Madison Co., Kentfield, CA

Madison Publishing Corp., Boston, MA

Josh Mailman, New York, NY

Maineshare, Augusta, ME

Terry Mandel Communications, San Fransico, CA

Marketing Communications, Albuquerque, NM

Marketing Magnetics, Boulder, CO

Marketing Partners, Burlington, VT

Marketing Works, Phoenix, AZ

Marlene's Market & Deli, Federal Way, WA

Massachusetts Credit Union Association, Southborough, MA

Larry Maurer, C.P.A., Huntington Beach, CA

MBL Group, Portland, OR

McCarthy Medical Marketing, Vancouver, WA

McCoffee, Half Moon Bay, CA

McCrillis & Eldredge Insurance, Newport, NH

C. E. Macdonald, Colchester, VT

McGovern Communications, Arlington, VA

Medical Lease Management, San Francisco, CA

Merix Corporation, Forest Grove, OR

Merlin Metalworks, Cambridge, MA

Message! Check Corp., Seattle, WA

MGMT Consultant, Portsmouth, NH

Millenium Communications Group, Washington, DC

Miller Communications, Kentfield, CA

The Mills Group, Fairfax, VA

Milwaukee Recycling Services, Milwaukee, WI

Minnesota Environmental Initiative, Minneapolis, MN

Minutemen Press of Providence, Providence, RI

Mirror Image, Cambridge, MA

Missabe Group, Minneapolis, MN

Miyako Hotel-Japan Center, San Francisco, CA

Michael Moore, Consultant, Boulder, CO

Morgan Memorial Goodwill Industry, Boston, MA

Morgin Press, Wayne, PA

S. W. Morris & Co., Bethesda, MD

Robert K. Morrison, Cambridge, MA

The Morrison Co., San Francisco, CA

Mother Jones, San Francisco, CA

Motherwear, Northampton, VA

Moving Comfort, Springfield, VA

Multi Media Associates, Northport, NY

Multi-Fax Services, Santa Rosa, CA

Munro & Company, Hot Springs, AR

Music for Little People, Redway, CA

Musical Energi, Wilkes-Barre, PA

Nataraj Publishing, Novato, CA

Nature's Acres, New Freedom, WI

Nature's Food Patch, Clearwater, FL

Net Worth Consulting, Washington, DC

New Leaders Press, San Francisco, CA

Newsweek, New York, NY

Miwot Chiropractic Center, Niwot, CO

Nobody's Girl, Fredericksburg, TX

Noel Hosiery, Old Bridge, NJ

North Loop Chiropractic, Chicago, IL

Northwest Strategies, Portland, OR

Odwalla, Davenport, CA

Odyssey House, Hampton, NH

Office Information Systems, Oakland, CA

Olde Sturbridge Country Farms, Sturbridge, MA

Open Communications, Costa Mesa, CA

Organix Ag Advisors, Colfax, CA

Organizational Futures, Providence, RI

Outback, Berkeley, CA

Pacific Partners, New York, NY

Lincoln Pain, Consultant, Berkeley, CA

Pan Vera Corp., Madison, WI

Pandora Systems, San Francisco, CA

The Parker Group, Del Mar, CA

Patagonia, Ventura, CA

Pathways Through Career Transition, Portland, OR

Ron Paul, Portland, OR

Peaceable Kingdom Press, Berkeley, CA

Peak Dynamics, Brookline, MA

Penn's Village Natural Foods, Doylestown, PA

Penret Services, Holliston, MA

The Perennial Tea Room, Seattle, WA

Philadelphia Coca-Cola Bottling, New York, NY

Phoenix Rising, Providence, RI

Pilgrim New Media, Cambridge, MA

Pioneer Nutritional Formulas, Shelburne Falls, MA

Planet Central TV, Los Angeles, CA

Plastic Bottle Corp., Libertyville, IL

Platinum Technology, Oakbrook Terrace, IL

Pleca Communcacion, S.A. de D.V., Mexico City, Mexico

Point of View Productions, San Francisco, CA

Pollution Prevention Consulting, Hartford, CT

Precision Motorcars, Cincinnati, OH

PreDent, Ltd., Hudson, MA

Prince Communications, Portsmouth, NH

Princeton Entrepreneurial Resources, Princeton, NJ

Principle Profits Asset Management, Amherst, MA

Printers Inc. Bookstore, Palo Alto, CA

Prism Associates, Boulder, CO

Pro Tem Professional Staffing Service, Portland, OR

The Professional Movers, Los Altos, CA

Progressive Asset Management, Oakland, CA

The Progressive Group, Hadley, MA

The Proscenium Group, San Rafael, CA

Puna Orchards, Pahoa, HI

Putumayo, New York, NY

Quad/Graphics, Pewaukee, WI

Quality Media Resources, Bellevue, WA

Quantum Construction Corp., Bayonne, NJ

Quorum Communications, Oakland, CA

Radical Food, Mill Valley, CA
Rainbow Bridge Trading Co., San Francisco, CA
Rainbow Programming Holdings, Woodbury, NY
Rainforest Products, Berkeley, CA
Real Goods Trading Corp., Ukiah, CA
Red Rose Collection, Burlingame, CA
Red Victorian Bed & Breakfast, San Francisco, CA
Redkey Associates, Easthampton, MA
Reebok International, Ltd., Stoughton, MA
RE Festival, Portola Valley, CA
Rejuvenation Inc., Portland, OR
The Relaxation Station, Augusta, GA
The Renaissance Group, Durham, NC
Renewable Energy Development Corp., Villanova, PA
Resource Decision Consultants, San Francisco, CA
Resource Management, San Francisco, CA
Response Management Technologies, Berkeley, CA
Rex Art Co., Miami, FL
Rhino Records, Santa Monica, CA
Richardson & Co., Boulder, CO
Rio!, Ithaca, NY
Riverside Industries, Easthampton, MA
John Rizzo Photography, Portland, OR
The Roanoke Co., Menlo Park, CA
Roberta's Bed & Breakfast, Seattle, WA
Robertson Stephens & Co., San Francisco, CA
Robinson & Associates, Washington, DC
Rodale Press, Emmaus, PA
Rosemary's Bakery, Point Richmond, CA
Rosemary's Garden, Sebastopol, CA
Rosewood Stone Group, Sausalito, CA
Round River Records, Seekonk, MA
The Rumpp Company dba The Body Shop, Portland, OR
Ryka, Norwood, MA

Sage Co., Minnetonka, MN
St. Albans Cooperative Creamery, St. Albans, VT
St. Moritz Eyewear, Chatsworth, CA
SAIRA Corp., King of Prussia, PA
Salt River Project, Phoenix, AZ
Santana Management, San Francisco, CA
Satori Fine Herbals, Santa Cruz, CA
Save A Tree Bag Company, Berkeley, CA
Save the Bay, Providence, RI
John Scherer & Associates, Spokane, WA
Sea Change, Sausalito, CA
2nd Street Photography, Encinitas, CA
Seeds of Change, Santa Fe, NM
Sequoia Realty Corporation, Mentor, OH
Sgro Promo Associates, Emeryville, CA
Shaman Pharmaceuticals, South San Francisco, CA
Share Systems, Somerville, MA
Shearer & Connelly, Auburn, NH
J. L. Sherwin & Associates, Denville, NJ
Shingle Belting, Plymouth Meeting, PA
Shirt Stains, Chicago, IL
Shorebank Corp., Chicago, IL
Signature Coffee, Redway, CA
Simply Natural, Incline Village, NV
Siteworks, Hinesburg, VT
Slide Center, Boston, MA
Smart Choices, Raleigh, NC
Robert Smith, Personal Consultant, Sausalito, CA
Soap by the Yard dba The Body Shop, Newtown, MA
Soapbox Trading Co., Fairfax, VA
Sokol Blosser Winery, Dundee, OR
Solar Light Co., Philadelphia, PA
Soloflex, Hillsboro, OR
Joel Solomon Co., Nashville, TN
Jay Sordean, O.M.D., L.A.C., Berkeley, CA
Sorensen's Resort, Hope Valley, CA

Sound Rx Cassettes and CDs, San Anselmo, CA

Soundings of the Planet, Tucson, AZ

South Mountain Co., Chilmark, MA

Spanky's, Fairfax, CA

Spic and Span, Milwaukee, WI

Springfield ReManufacturing Corp., Springfield, MO

Squash Blossom Market, Memphis, TN

Starbucks Coffee Co., Seattle, WA

Starlane Farms, Lansing, NY

Stein No-Load Mutual Fund Service, Venice, CA

Stonyfield Farm, Londonderry, NH

Strategic Foundation, Washington, DC

Strategic Resource Management Associates, San Francisco, CA

Stauber & Associates, Madison, WI

Stride Rite Foundation, Boston, MA

Subway Guitars, Berkeley, CA

Success By Design, Mill Valley, CA

Sufficient Systems, St. Paul, MN

Summa Associates, Tempe, AZ

The Summit Group, Minneapolis, MN

Sundance Natural Foods, Eugene, OR

Sunfeather Herbal Soap Co., Potsdam, NY

Sunrise Retirement Homes & Communities, Fairfax, VA

Supermarket Communications Systems, Norwalk, CT

Surplus Agents of America, St. Petersburg, FL

Surya, San Diego, CA

Synchromic Studios International, Kihei, HI

The Synchronicity Group, Vienna, VA

Tabra Inc., Novato, CA

Tackett Barbaria Designs, Sacramento, CA

Taco Bell Corp., Irvine, CA

Take the Lead, Fort Lee, NJ

Tangent Corp., Washington, DC

TAOC Marketing & Communications, Riverdale, NY

Target Stores, Minneapolis, MN

Queenie Taylor, San Francisco, CA

Taylor, Keene, Blanchard, Lyon, Watson, Portsmouth, NH

Teamwork Promotions, Topanga, CA

TeamWorks Training Corp., Boulder, CO

Technical Risks, Houston, TX

Telegroup/The ICA Group, Cambridge, MA

Telesis, Washington, DC

Tempxpress Temporaries Inc., Boston, MA

Tender Loving Things, Oakland, CA

Tenth Planet, San Francisco, CA

Thanksgiving Coffee Co., Fort Bragg, CA

Theoria Association for Health, Mansfield Center, CT

Sue Thomas & Associates, Cameron Park, CA

Eric Thompson Consulting, Oakland, CA

Thumb & Thimble, Willits, CA

Tierra Pacifica Corp., Irvine, CA

Tilden Press Inc., Washington, DC

Timberland Co., Hampton, NH

Time Warner Inc., New York, NY

Times Change Press, Ojai, CA

Times Square Scoop Shop Corp., New York, NY

TKR Associates, Mill Valley, CA

Tom's of Maine, Kennebunk, ME

TouchStone Consulting, Acton, MA

Tower Records/Video, West Sacramento, CA

Trade Routes Alternative Market, Boulder, CO

Traditional Medicinals, Sebastopol, CA

Training & Development Corp., Bucksport, ME

Transitions Collaborative, Providence, RI

Travel Inc., Washington, DC

Trees for Tomorrow, Mahopac, NY

Trust for Public Land, Boston, MA

Turning Point Consultants, Newton, MA

Tweezerman Corp., Glen Cove, NY

Twin Cities Public Television, St. Paul, MN

Ultradian Institute, Falls Church, VA

Uma Jewelry/Music, San Rafael, CA

United Special Events, Mt. View, CA

United Way of Southeastern NE, Providence, RI

University of New England, Biddeford, ME

UNUM Corp., Portland, ME

US Assist, Washington, DC

U.S. Electric Car Inc., Sebastopol, CA

USTeleCenters, Boston, MA

Utne Reader, Minneapolis, MN

Vagabond Imports, Quintam Roo, Mexico

Valley Plastics Manufacturing, Santa Rosa, CA

Venture Designs Network, Baldwin, NY

The Venture Group Ltd., Washington, DC

Venture Point Consulting, Boston, MA

Vermont National Bank, Socially Responsible Banking, Brattleboro, VT

Veryfine Products, Westford, MA

Vesper Society Institutional Development, Oakland, CA

Viable Systems International, Princeton, NJ

Jacqueline L. Viau, Harvard, MA

Amy Vickers & Associates, Boston, MA

Victorian on Main Street Antiques, Washington, DC

Video Update, San Francisco, CA

Violet Crown Instruments, Austin, TX

Vision III Architects, Providence, RI

Vista Productions, Phoenix, AZ

The Vital Voice, Boulder, CO

Vizion Corp., Red Bank, NJ

Vogt & Associates, Upper Montclair, NJ

V.T.R. Associates, Berkeley, CA

Walden 1120, Concord, MA

Walker Research & Analysis, Indianapolis, IN

Wallack Management Co., New York, NY

Mal Warwick & Associates, Berkeley, CA

Waste Management Co., Cranston, RI

WDHB, Walnut Creek, CA

Wet Light, Cambridge, MA

White Dog Cafe, Philadelphia, PA

Wieder Enterprises, San Francisco, CA

Wild Horse Records & Tapes, Garberville, CA

Wild Oats Market, Boulder, CO

Wild Planet, Minneapolis, MN

Wild Planet Toys, San Francisco, CA

Willow Bay Co., Cincinnati, OH

Willpower Productions, Portsmouth, NH

Nancy Wilson Consulting, Scottsdale, AZ

WLNE-TV 6, Providence, RI

Women's Opportunities Resource Center, Philadelphia, PA

Woodstock Percussion, West Hurley, NY

Work/Family Directions, Boston, MA

Working Assets Common Holdings, Portsmouth, NH

Working Assets, San Francisco, CA

Workways, Cambridge, MA

World Environment Technology System, Wayland, MA

Worldware, San Francisco, CA

Worldwide Events & Environmental Programs, Sausalito, CA

Wyoming Wildcrafters, Wilson, WY

Youth Project, Framingham, MA

R. W. Ziegler Enterprises, Lexington, MA

Acknowledgments

This book would not have been possible without the generous efforts of many individuals who deserve recognition and thanks.

Michael Levett, the founding president of Business for Social Responsibility, played a major role in shaping the book, both conceptually and editorially. His original vision of a defining work on socially responsible business, the considerable insights he contributed, and his dedication throughout the editorial process are reflected on every page.

Bob Dunn, Arnold Hiatt, and Helen Mills played an especially enthusiastic and supportive role, including reading and commenting on early drafts. Their unwavering commitment and generous availability were vital to this project every step of the way. Thanks also for the valuable support and feedback of Debbie Aguirre, Chuck Blitz, Ben Cohen, Sharon Cohen, Michael Durney, Ron Grzywinski, Alan Hassenfeld, Tom Higgins, Gary Hirshberg, Elliot Hoffman, Peter Kinder, Ashley Korenblat, Dominic Kulik, Harry Quadracci, David Robinson, Mitch Rofsky, Laura Scher, Gail Snowden, Nan Upin, and Ella Williams.

The staff and interns of BSR, the BSR Education Fund, and the Eco-Efficiency Project were important to this book, providing both research and logistical support. Special thanks to Kathy Grimes, who worked tirelessly behind the scenes in support of this project, and to Rebecca Calahan Klein, for her contributions to the environmental chapter. Grateful appreciation is due Catina Carter, Sidney Friedman, Teresa Harris, Holly Henning, Debbie Miller, Mariann Payne, Laurie Sneiderman, and Rick White.

Gail Ross played a key role in shepherding this book from its earliest incarnation on through to final publication. As always, Becky Saletan of Simon & Schuster provided her keen editing, abundant energy, and warm spirit. Thanks also to Denise Roy for her dogged support, and Christina Young for her ongoing enthusiasm.

Finally, thanks to others who contributed time and resources to this effort, among them Tony Andersen, Judy Babbitts, Liz Bankowski, Ann Beaudry, Bill Belknap, Betty Bothereau, Doug Cahn, Tom Chappel, Wayne Charness, Susan Cohn, Bob Frey, Tom Gladwin, Alisa Gravitz, Kirk Hanson, Paul Hawken, Lisa Herling, Paul Herman, Patricia Hoven, Shirley Hughes-English, John Imes, Nancy Katz, Elise Klysa, Frances Kwan, Robert Leaver, Elliot Lehman, Steve Lydenberg, Bob MacGregor, Stephanie Maddoff, Josh Mailman, Marty Manley, Alice Tepper Marlin, John May, Kathy Meyer, Mary Ann Mills, Larry Mitchell, Richard Morgan, Craig Neal, Jamie Queoff, Richard Reiben, Anita Roddick, Fran Rodgers, Bob Rosen, Randy Rosenberg, Shayna P. Rosenberg, Dave Samson, Steve Schueth, Elissa Sheridan, Rena Shulsky, Mark Sissman, Jack Stack, Tina Sullivan, Jeffrey Swartz, Felicia Tiller, and Donna Wood.

Index